Cognitive Science and
Folk Psychology

Cognitive Science and Folk Psychology

The Right Frame of Mind

W.F.G. Haselager

SAGE Publications
London • Thousand Oaks • New Delhi

SAGE Publications Ltd
6 Bonhill Street
London EC2A 4PU

SAGE Publications Inc.
2455 Teller Road
Thousand Oaks, California 91320

SAGE Publications India Pvt Ltd
32, M-Block Market
Greater Kailash – I
New Delhi 110 048

British Library Cataloguing in Publication data

A catalogue record for this book is available from the British Library

ISBN 0 7619 5425 2
ISBN 0 7619 5426 0 (pbk)

Library of Congress catalog card number 97–067389

Typeset by Mayhew Typesetting, Rhayader, Powys
Printed in Great Britain by Redwood Books, Trowbridge, Wiltshire

To my parents

Contents

Foreword

William Bechtel

In this book Haselager takes us to a hilltop to watch the pitched battle for the soul of cognitive science. Beneath us is the Valley of the Frame Problem, the problem of explaining how we humans are so good at drawing upon relevant information and using it to change our beliefs appropriately in the face of new information or action. But we soon see that both camps are bedeviled from within. To the east, the champions of symbolic models of cognitive are confused. General Jerry Fodor proclaims that symbolic models offer the only hope of salvaging our ability to explain and predict each other's behaviour in terms of belief and desires, but frets that symbolic models are not up to the frame problem. The troops are confused as he announces his first law of the non-existence of Cognitive Science, thereby seemingly surrendering both the battle and the war. But, as Haselager shows, not all of the troops are listening. At least one captain, Paul Thagard and his program, PI, offers some promise of succeeding against the frame problem (albeit by employing associationist weapons that Fodor disavows). Meanwhile, to the west, General Paul Churchland exudes great confidence. Representing human knowledge as vectors in connectionist networks, he proclaims the battle over the frame problem already won. Haselager, however, punctures Churchland's bravado by pointing out that while the nets are formidable in toy simulations, they may not be up to winning the main battle. Haselager leaves the two forces at an impasse, each struggling mightily to conceive a strategy grand enough to insure a decisive victory in the battle of the frame problem. Through Haselager's very clear presentation and analysis, readers will acquire an exceptionally clear understanding of what is at stake and the prospects for victory by either side in this great conflict in current cognitive science.

Acknowledgements

This book has been written in the context of a research project at the unit for theoretical psychology at the Vrije Universiteit, Amsterdam. It has also profited from my teaching activities at the cognitive science department at the Katholieke Universiteit Nijmegen. Over the years I received support from many people. In particular, I would like to thank Xandra Pennings, Hans van Rappard, Huib Looren de Jong, René Jorna, Monica Meijsing, Eduard Hoenkamp and Bill Bechtel.

Introduction

A computer program capable of acting intelligently in the world must have a general representation of the world in terms of which its inputs are interpreted. Designing such a program requires commitments about what knowledge is and how it is obtained. Thus, some of the major traditional problems of philosophy arise in artificial intelligence.

(McCarthy & Hayes, 1969, p. 463)

Essential to cognitive science is the idea that cognition is the transformation of information. Animals and human beings possess information concerning their environment and their (history of) interactions with it. They use this information[1] while interacting with their surroundings in order to pursue their goals, recording and storing the results of each interaction. In a very general sense, cognitive science is the study of how information is acquired, stored and utilized.

Human beings are different from (at least most) animals in that they not only have and use this knowledge but also explicitly talk about it. A large part of our daily communication is devoted to the exchange of information concerning the way we view the world, how we would like it to be, and how this influences our behavior. In these exchanges we use an age-old, standard, traditional way of describing our inner states and processes, generally referred to as *folk psychology*. By delineating our thoughts, beliefs, hopes, desires, fears, etc., we not only explain our behavior to others, but also enable them to predict it. If I tell my friend that I am in bad shape and that I want to lose some weight, she will not only understand why I refuse the offered crisps, but also be quite confident that I will accept a challenge to a tennis match. By informing her of my beliefs (I am in bad shape) and my desires (I want to lose weight) I have indicated some prominent determinants of my behavior and have thereby made it understandable and predictable. At first sight, it seems that we normally take our internal states and processes to be adequately described by the above outlined vocabulary of beliefs and desires, and that we consider these mental states to be causally relevant to our behavior. I will investigate this (what I will call) *literal* interpretation of folk psychology more deeply, and address some serious questions about its appropriateness in Chapter 1.

The main question of this book, stated in its most general form, is whether folk psychology provides the right frame of mind. More specifically, I will investigate the work of J.A. Fodor and P.M. Churchland,[2] as they have both addressed the acceptability of folk psychology while coming to

Fodor → intentional realism
Churchland → eliminative materialism
2   *Cognitive Science and Folk Psychology*

completely opposite conclusions based on fundamentally different kinds of computational models. Fodor defends an intentional realism according to which the essential elements of cognition are satisfactorily identified by folk psychological notions like beliefs and desires. That is, our ordinary way of individuating mental states basically provides the right framework for a scientific understanding of cognition. Churchland, however, vigorously rejects the traditional view of the mental. According to his eliminative materialism, the common-sense taxonomy of mental states does not provide an adequate account of cognition and should be completely discarded in favor of an entirely new conception of our internal states and processes based on a neurocomputational theory of cognition. Some general arguments for intentional realism and eliminative materialism are discussed in Chapter 1.

Although Fodor and Churchland are both philosophers, their theoretical musings are connected to empirical investigations of cognition. One might best view their work as principled (not to say extreme) developments of the philosophical implications of two main empirical approaches in cognitive science. Fodor's approach can be related to classical cognitive science, GOFAI (good old fashioned artificial intelligence) or symbolic AI, which takes cognition to consist of the structure-sensitive processing of symbolic representations.[3] Fodor provides a further specification of the nature of the symbolic representational system by attributing to it certain semi-linguistic characteristics. His 'language of thought' thesis is a specific proposal to substantiate intentional realism. I will investigate the nature of this proposal in Chapter 2. Churchland's work can be connected to an approach in connectionism or PDP (parallel distributed processing), where cognition is seen as the transformation of distributed representations. His particular version of this approach, to be explicated in Chapters 2 and 5, is known as neurocomputationalism. Churchland claims that a thoroughly neuro-computational understanding of cognition would show the untenability of folk psychology. For the purposes of the current investigation, I propose that classical cognitive science and neurocomputationalism may be considered as empirical counterparts of Fodor's intentional realism and Churchland's eliminative materialism respectively.[4]

The contrast between the two approaches centers around the nature of representations. According to Fodor's views, classical cognitive science is committed to a representational system that has a compositional syntax and semantics, made possible by its constituent structure. Fodor's suggestion of a language of thought provides for a literal understanding of folk psychological descriptions and explanations. When we describe our beliefs and desires we give a description of our informational states that is closely matched by internal representational structures that are causally relevant to our behavior. Churchland's neurocomputational theory utilizes distributed representations that make it effectively impossible to take folk psychology literally. The internal informational structures and processing mechanisms postulated by this theory as the true causes of our behavior are, Churchland claims, radically different from our folk psychological descriptions of our inner events. In Chapter 2, I will focus on the suggestion that, on the basis of connectionist models with distributed representations, the question as to *which* mental states play a crucial role in the determination of behavior is unanswerable. Nevertheless, the practice of folk psychology essentially consists in identifying the relevant beliefs and desires for descriptive, explanatory and predictive purposes. A model of cognition that precludes a functionally discrete identification of behaviorally relevant mental states may well be considered to be incompatible with folk psychology.

The background of this inquiry should now be clear. The discussion about the value of folk psychology as an adequate model of the mind leads, in the case of Fodor and Churchland, to the requirement that it be sustained by a scientific theory of cognition. At present, there are two competing[5] classes of theories and models in cognitive science which, again according to Fodor and Churchland, offer entirely different prospects. Classical cognitive science seems to be capable of merging smoothly with folk psychology, whereas a neurocomputational theory seems to be incompatible with it. Broadly speaking, this book focuses on the consequences the two main kinds of models have for our common-sense view of the nature of mental states and processes. The issue ultimately comes down to the question of which of the two computational models provides a better, more scientifically acceptable, theory of cognition.

A problem for evaluation is that at this stage both models are not even close to being completed, but are rather in a phase where some of their important characteristics as well as their advantages and disadvantages are beginning to become clear. Final verdicts about which theory is better are therefore not to be expected soon. A straightforward comparison between the two approaches is also not immediately possible, since classical cognitive science and neurocomputationalism tend to concentrate on different areas of cognition in their modeling attempts.[6]

It seems, however, that any theory that claims to provide a good model of cognition is bound to explain how our cognitive processes can be (by and large) rational. Normally, the connections between mental states and processes are not entirely random or 'unreasonable'. Instead, they are related to one another in a way that is semantically coherent or rational. That is, there is some *sense* in the way internal states are combined. Since the 1960s, cognitive science has been extensively involved in finding a mechanical, materialistic explanation of how this semantic coherence of causally relevant internal states is possible. Unfortunately, the problem of mechanical rationality is still very broad, and in many cases computational models are developed for domains that are not easy to connect to folk psychology. There is, however, a central and important phenomenon to be observed in everyday life that, I propose, may serve as a useful focal point for an examination of computational models in relation to folk psychology.

Human beings have an amazing ability to keep track of relevant changes in their environment. They easily see what is going on in their surroundings, *frame* [handwritten margin note]

as is evident from their capacity to rapidly predict, react or adjust to the important consequences of a certain event. Somehow humans can quickly make sense of the situation they are in or of the event they are confronted with, and the ease and speed of common-sense reasoning and understanding have proven to be unexpectedly difficult to model. This source of uneasiness for cognitive science has become known as *the frame problem*, despite certain claims that this label had been reserved for another, more restricted but related, issue in logic. I will analyze the frame problem in Chapter 3. The fundamental difficulty, in my view, is that *everything* we know is potentially relevant for our interpretation of what is happening around us. Since we know a great deal, the knowledge we possess must be stored and utilized in such a way that the relevant parts of it are immediately brought to bear on the formation of our beliefs. This imposes heavy demands on both the structuring and the processing of information.

If classical cognitive science is potentially able to answer the frame problem in a way that is compatible with at least the most central characteristics of folk psychology then, I think, it is fair to say that folk psychology has a fair chance of being vindicated by recent work in cognitive science. If the rival neurocomputational attempt turns out to be more attractive, however, then folk psychology is likely to take a heavy blow, and the question as to what the alternative will look like becomes all the more urgent and intriguing. In all then, I investigate the frame problem as a means to engage in a systematic inquiry of cognitive science, its study of common-sense reasoning and its relation to folk psychology.

I will connect my analysis of the frame problem to the difference between classical and neurocomputational models. According to (what I will call) the *representational* approach, the frame problem is the result of some unfortunate characteristics of the symbolic representational format. From this perspective, the frame problem can be seen as a major embarrassment for classical cognitive science. Symbolic structures might not be very well suited to represent large amounts of knowledge in a way that allows speedy application. Classical cognitive science is therefore likely to falter on the paradoxical task of not only having to make a system that knows a lot, but also enabling it to ignore most of what it knows, most of the time. This stands in great contrast with the seemingly effortless way in which neuro-computational models can cope with this issue. Given the basic representational and computational abilities of neural networks, it is argued, the frame problem cannot even arise. In Chapter 5, I will therefore examine connectionist investigations of distributed representations and relate them to the frame problem.

Alternatively, one can refrain from doubting the value of symbolic representations and view the frame problem as intimately related to the more general problem of non-demonstrative inference. This (what I will call) *inferential* approach to the frame problem leads to an examination of how human beings generally tend to arrive at beliefs that are likely, but not guaranteed, to be true. Remarkably, although Fodor views the frame problem as essentially the problem of non-demonstrative inference, he has spoken very pessimistically about the prospects of solving it. If this view is correct, the frame problem would, in my opinion, constitute a major embarrassment not just for classical cognitive science, but also for Fodor's intentional realism. Obviously, any approach that attempts to vindicate folk psychology should be able to give at least an indication of how to model common-sense reasoning. Fodor's pessimism is all the more surprising since those working in symbolic AI seem, in general, not to share it. Indeed, one of the main motives for writing this book is to examine the different lines of reasoning involved in the evaluation of the severity of the frame problem.

Therefore, in Chapter 4 I will investigate an illustrative attempt to understand and model the psychological processes involved in non-demonstrative inferences in classical computational terms. The main kind of non-demonstrative inference that I will be investigating is hypothetical induction (sometimes called 'abduction' in AI and 'inference to the best explanation' in philosophy), which from a psychological perspective can be seen as the process of generation and evaluation of explanatory hypotheses in order to account for encountered phenomena.

Interestingly, scientific progress is also substantially dependent on non-demonstrative inference. Scientists too are continuously faced with the task of deciding what to think about the world, though their approach is, of course, much more methodical and intersubjective. But in essence, a scientist on completion of an experiment and a person faced with an everyday event are both confronted by a similar challenge: given all that I know, what am I to think of the information that I have just received? Indeed, a conviction shared by Fodor and Churchland is that issues in cognitive science are in many ways similar to issues in the philosophy of science. It is therefore not surprising that attempts to model individual cognitive processes have tried to derive information from theories about the discovery, development and evaluation of scientific theories. Conversely, computational investigations in the philosophy of science have tried to utilize basic insights of cognitive science regarding mental processes.

Investigations in the philosophy of science have tried to develop computational models of the process of hypothesis generation and evaluation, and there are claims that historical examples of scientific non-demonstrative inference have been simulated realistically. For my purposes the work of Paul Thagard is especially interesting because he has explicitly, and in the context of a long term research project, investigated the cognitive processes involved in hypothetical induction from both a theoretical and a computational point of view. The parts of his work that I will concentrate upon can be viewed as representative of classical AI. It is also significant that Thagard has expressed optimism at precisely the point where Fodor is pessimistic. A large part of Chapter 4 will be devoted to an investigation of the difficulties involved in developing computational models for non-demonstrative reasoning and Thagard's suggestions to remedy them. It will be found that associative mechanisms play an important role in Thagard's models. Although I will indicate some (in my view) strengths and weaknesses of Thagard's approach, my main purpose in this chapter is to use his work as an illustration of a pragmatic and psychological, rather than a strictly logical, approach to cognition and hypothetical induction. In the final part of Chapter 4, I will argue that investigations of the way human beings reason non-demonstratively should not be identified with attempts to justify the beliefs arrived at through these means. Whether one accepts or rejects the use of associative mechanisms in computational models is closely connected to this issue. I will suggest that a clear distinction between descriptive and normative issues may help to alleviate Fodor's pessimism about solving the frame problem. A better understanding of the proper place of associative mechanisms in classical cognitive science is one of the requirements for a classical solution to the frame problem.

In Chapter 5, I will investigate the nature of Churchland's neurocomputational perspective on cognition as an extension of the representational approach to the frame problem. Churchland suggests that the frame problem can be prevented from arising if a radically different, connectionist view of cognition is accepted. Basically, because the knowledge a system possesses is represented in a distributed fashion over its set of weights, its instantaneous application to the processing of incoming information is no problem. In neurocomputational models there is no need for the cumbersome search for and selection of relevant knowledge that plagues classical models. The computationally simple processes of prototype vector activation and pattern transformation can, it is claimed, provide an account of higher cognitive processes and common-sense reasoning. However, a consideration of some connectionist models and proposals will reveal some fundamental problems. Though a speedy application of knowledge to the generation of an explanatory hypothesis with respect to incoming information does seem possible in connectionist models, the complexity of the knowledge that can be represented seems severely limited. Churchland's own suggestions concerning the representation and use of structured information provide, in my view, an instance of simple associationism and should be rejected. I will consider more complex proposals by Van Gelder and Chalmers, which, in my view, are more promising, though still unsatisfactory. Finally, I will consider the consequences of Churchland's eliminativist program with respect to the evaluation of explanatory hypotheses. As Churchland's new view of cognition results in a completely different interpretation of the nature of information bearing states, it implies a basic revision of the way we think about knowledge and epistemic virtue. I will argue that Churchland's proposals in this respect are both less revolutionary and less attractive than they may seem at first sight. Ultimately, then, I do not think that a neurocomputational solution to the frame problem is as simple and effective as initially proclaimed.

This book, in short, concentrates on the bearing of scientific and philosophical investigations of common-sense reasoning on folk psychology.

How are the informational states of a cognitive system to be understood? Are they adequately described by common-sense mental notions like beliefs and desires or is a radically new view of 'the mental' required? The focusing point will be the frame problem. I will indicate that the misgivings surrounding the ability of classical cognitive science to solve the frame problem are not entirely warranted. Furthermore I will argue that the solution suggested by neurocomputationalism is not as effortless as it is claimed. The upshot of my investigations, then, is that the frame problem provides no principled reason to refrain from taking folk psychology literally. Furthermore, a clear understanding of the issues involved indicates that the proper role of associative mechanisms in both classical and connectionist computational models of common-sense reasoning should be thoroughly investigated.

Notes

1 Sometimes the information a system possesses about its environment is referred to as the knowledge of the system. Although it is common in philosophy to distinguish between information, belief and knowledge (see, for instance, the suggestion that a sign carries information about its cause, and the discussion about whether knowledge can be seen as justified true belief), in cognitive science (especially cognitive psychology and artificial intelligence) it is not uncommon to use these concepts interchangeably (e.g. Newell, 1992, p. 426).

2 I will sometimes refer to the work of Patricia Smith Churchland in order to further illustrate and clarify Paul Churchland's ideas. Paul M. Churchland and Patricia Smith Churchland both defend and develop eliminative materialism. They regularly publish together (Churchland & Churchland, 1990; 1994), and sometimes claim to be speaking for one another (Churchland, 1987, p. 545). If there are some subtle differences between their views (see, for instance, Braaten, 1988, p. 251; Preston, 1989, pp. 293–294), these are in my estimation more a matter of emphasis than a divergence of opinion. One could perhaps say that whereas Patricia Churchland focuses more on the importance of neuroscience for the study of cognition, Paul Churchland focuses more on the philosophical (especially epistemological) consequences of the resulting neurocomputational theory of the mind/brain. They share a particular dislike of folk psychology and they both reject classical cognitive science as an insufficient model of cognition.

3 Fodor is one of the most important philosophers involved in classical cognitive science. He has been called 'the complete cognitivist' (Gardner, 1985, p. 81), 'a leading ideologue of cognitive science' (Dennett, 1987b, p. 214), and 'the most important philosopher of psychology of his generation' (Loewer & Rey, 1991, p. xi). Yet it would be a mistake to take everything Fodor says as the received view of classical cognitive science. Several of his views, for instance with respect to the innateness of all concepts, are quite extreme and are not accepted by other important classical cognitive scientists such as, for instance, Newell and Simon. However, I think that Fodor's analysis of the theme that will figure most prominently in this work (the importance of symbolic representations and structure-sensitive processing for explaining rationality) can be taken as representative for classical cognitive science.

4 This is of course not to imply any priority of philosophy over cognitive science. It merely indicates that for the purposes of this work the main interests lie with the theories of Fodor and Churchland, and that the empirical theories and actual computational models of cognitive science will only serve as illustrations of their theories.

5 It should be acknowledged that, strictly speaking, the portrayal of classical cognitive science and neurocomputationalism as outright competitors may be neither necessary nor

universally endorsed. Much work, for instance, is being done on the construction of so-called hybrid models that attempt to combine the best of both worlds. Yet I think that the differences between symbolic and distributed representational formats are genuine and of enough relevance to the study of cognition to justify a competitive comparison of their respective strengths and weaknesses.

6 Indeed, there have been discussions about 'the gap' between the two approaches that has to be closed (Dinsmore, 1992).

1

Folk Psychology and Cognitive Science

There are many names to refer to the way we normally speak and reason about mental states; everyday psychology, common-sense psychology, folk psychology, naive psychology, belief–desire psychology, and even grandmother psychology. In the literature the phrase 'folk psychology' is most often used (though not without opposition; see Wilkes, 1991b, p. 16), and I will conform to this practice. At a minimum, folk psychology is characterized by the use of a vocabulary in which mentalistic concepts like 'belief', 'desire', 'fear', 'hope', etc., play a major part. As such, folk psychology plays an important role in scientific psychology (Hewson, 1993).

A more substantial analysis of folk psychology is not easy to give, despite its ubiquity in daily life (Dennett, 1987b, p. 46; Fodor, 1987b, p. 3). This is largely because in our normal practice folk psychology is used, but not reflected upon. A closer analysis of folk psychology will illuminate some of its normally invisible aspects. This leaves considerable room for discussion whether the analysis does justice to folk psychology as it 'really' is. As Dennett puts it:

> We are virtuoso exploiters of not so much a theory as a craft. That is, we might better call it a folk craft rather than a folk theory. The *theory* of folk psychology is the ideology about the craft, and there is lots of room, as anthropologists will remind us, for false ideology. (Dennett, 1991c, p. 135)

The safest strategy, therefore, is to treat every characterization of folk psychology that goes beyond noticing the centrality of a mentalistic vocabulary as a 'reconstruction' or an 'interpretation'.

In this book I will focus on an interpretation of folk psychology that is shared by J.A. Fodor and P.M. Churchland, as well as by several, but not all, cognitive scientists. They construe folk psychology as a theory which posits mental phenomena or entities like beliefs and desires that play a crucial role in its descriptive, explanatory and predictive functions. This interpretation, which I will discuss in more detail in Section 1.2, can best be characterized as a 'strict', 'serious' or 'literal' rendering of folk psychology. Fodor and Churchland represent opposite stances with respect to the veracity of folk psychology, literally construed. Whereas Fodor holds that folk psychology is basically correct and indispensable for both practical purposes and scientific psychology, Churchland claims that it is radically wrong and impedes a proper understanding of cognition. I will examine their positions in greater detail later in this chapter.

An important question is how one goes about showing that folk psychology in its literal version is 'right' or 'wrong'. An answer to this question is far from straightforward. Any attempt at giving a response consists of many intermediate and hotly debated steps and at many points different options are available. Below I will give a short outline of the path that I will follow in order to determine the acceptability of the literal interpretation of folk psychology, and indicate in general terms why I think it is a useful path. Furthermore, I will examine the literal interpretation more closely and contrast it with two alternatives.

1.1 Folk psychology as a theory

A *first* step towards evaluating the status of folk psychology consists of characterizing it as precisely and accurately as possible. A standard way of doing this is by construing folk psychology as a theory, treating beliefs and desires as theoretical constructs we use for descriptive, explanatory and predictive purposes in daily life.

Questions have been raised about whether it is justified to interpret folk psychology as a theory.[1] To some it seems that mental states and processes are not theoretical posits at all, but rather observationally (especially introspectively) 'given'.[2] Against this suggestion it can be argued that one should make a distinction between our internal states and our conceptual responses to them. This distinction seems to me to be perfectly legitimate and, once it is made, I can find no good reason not to call this conceptual framework a theory. Folk psychology provides us with the conceptual resources we use in noticing and describing our inner events (Churchland, 1979, pp. 38–41). The mentalistic concepts and their systematic relations to one another collectively constitute a complex taxonomy of internal states that makes it possible to distinguish explanatory and predictively relevant phenomena. The most important categories of phenomena are placed in an encompassing structure, and the global laws or regularities operative in the domain of the mental can be formulated within the theory (Churchland, 1989, p. 120; Fodor, 1987b, pp. 14–16; Stich & Ravenscroft, 1994, p. 458). Folk psychology can furthermore be called a theory because it functions as such in fulfilling a descriptive, explanatory and predictive role (Churchland, 1986, p. 303; Fodor, 1987b, pp. 3–7; Stich & Ravenscroft, 1994, pp. 456–457). As Churchland says:

> we share a command or tacit understanding of a framework of abstract laws or principles concerning the dynamic relations holding between causal circumstances, psychological states, and overt behaviour. Bluntly, we share a moderately detailed understanding or *theory* of what makes people tick. (1979, p. 92)

The fact that we currently use folk psychology so effortlessly and with so much faith is in itself not an argument against it being a theory, as Sellars has indicated. Sellars engages in a (as he calls it) 'piece of anthropological science fiction' by describing how our current mentalistic theory might have developed by first being applied to others and only later to oneself (1963, pp. 178–196; see also Churchland, 1979, pp. 5, 38; Stich & Ravenscroft, 1994, pp. 450–453). The point of this suggestion (which, to be sure, he himself called a myth) is that, if it were true, it would make *no* difference to our self-observation. As Stich and Ravenscroft put it:

> If the Sellarsian myth were true, then we would talk *just as we now do* about inner mental states. But this talk would be both theoretical and fallible. (1994, p. 452)

In other words, our current use of folk psychology does not imply that mental states and processes are observationally given, for the same practice could arise from the development of a theory as described by Sellars.

Furthermore, several developmental studies suggest that children between the age of 3 and 4 years do engage, albeit implicitly, in theory construction about the mind by postulating unobserved entities like beliefs and desires and by noticing the regularities in their interconnections. Gopnik has reviewed some salient findings and concludes:

> The developmental evidence suggests that children construct a coherent, abstract account of the mind which enables them to explain and predict psychological phenomena. (1993, p. 10)

This strengthens the claim that our common-sense ideas and suppositions concerning our mental states and processes are not based on given facts. The theory can be further systematized in order to characterize our common-sense practice as precisely as possible. This can be achieved, for instance, by accepting the commonly found folk psychological descriptions and explanations of behavior at face value, while systematizing them as much as possible, and possibly rendering them in the form of law-like generalizations.[3]

So, it seems, interpreting folk psychology along the lines of a theory does not mutate it beyond recognition. Folk psychology can be seen as an organized conceptual scheme that we use as a tool in our common-sense practice. As such, it is not beyond critical evaluation. Indeed, it is an advantage of the 'theory theory of folk psychology' that it prevents us from uncritically accepting this conceptual scheme as given. And even though it might be the case that folk psychology in ordinary circumstances is looked upon not as an explicit theory (and most certainly not as a scientific theory) but rather as a largely implicit body of knowledge, it seems undeniable that it functions like a theory in its descriptive, explanatory, and predictive applications. Finally, much clarity can be gained by interpreting it as a theory, outlining its central characteristics in the most conspicuous way possible. Fodor and Churchland have, in my view, good reasons to accept the theory interpretation of folk psychology.[4]

1.2   The literal interpretation of folk psychology

If we accept that the nature of folk psychology is elucidated rather than obscured by construing it as a theory, we can take the *second* step: precisely what are the central characteristics of the basic posits of folk psychology? On the literal reading of folk psychology, mental states have four essential characteristics.

First, mental states have *content*. My belief that it is raining has 'it is raining' as its content. This content says something about how I take the world to be and makes my belief semantically evaluable with respect to that world: beliefs can be true or false (Fodor, 1987b, pp. 10–11). The content of a belief is generally thought to be characterizable by a proposition. A proposition is an abstract, language-independent entity that has a truth value (see Section 2.2). Content bearing mental states have what is called 'intentionality', they are *about* something (Dennett & Haugeland, 1987, p. 383). To be sure, there are many problems about how anything can have the content that it has. This topic has been extensively discussed within the context of cognitive science, and is likely to remain an important issue for quite some time. Following Cummins (1989, pp. 1–20), I distinguish between problems of representation and problems of representations. The problem of representation is how to explain (mental) content. The problem of representations is how they should be characterized, for instance whether mental representations should be thought of as symbolic or as distributed structures. I will concentrate on the role the problem of representations plays in the discussion concerning the status of folk psychology.

It should furthermore be noted that not all mental states have propositional content. Feelings (being angry or happy) and sensations (seeing the color red) have no 'aboutness', so to speak. Mental states that are essentially characterized by their accompanying experience, the way they 'feel', are called qualia. Although the qualitative character of this kind of mental state presents specific difficulties for a materialistic approach to the mind, these can be conveniently ignored here. As my major concern is to examine accounts of rationality (i.e. coherence *qua* content), qualia fall outside the scope of this book.

Second, it is possible to take several different *attitudes* towards the content: I can believe a proposition, but also doubt it, hope it or fear it. The kind of attitude (its being a belief or desire or fear, etc.) and the content together individuate the mental state. A standard, though not unopposed, way of expressing this is that mental states can be interpreted as propositional attitudes (Russell, 1940, pp. 65, 167–168).

Third, mental states play an *explanatory role* in folk psychology.[5] The literal reading proposes to take this seriously: folk psychology takes mental states (now interpreted as propositional attitudes) to be relevant to the explanation of behavior because these mental states actually *cause* the behavior (Fodor, 1987b, pp. 12–14). Suppose someone asks me why I am going to the bookshop, and I answer that I believe that the latest work by

Fodor is out and that I want to have it. In such a case I have explained my behavior by indicating the mental states that, on the literal interpretation, effectively cause my behavior. The underlying folk psychological law is: if someone wants *p* and believes that by doing *q* he will get *p*, he will, *ceteris paribus*, do *q* (Churchland, 1989, pp. 113–122; Fodor, 1991b, p. 19; Stich & Ravenscroft, 1994, p. 458). In the same vein, mental states can cause other mental states, as for instance the thought about buying a book causes me to think about my financial situation.

A fourth important characteristic of mental states is that they are *functionally discrete*, as indicated by Stich (Ramsey, Stich & Garon, 1991, pp. 97–98; Stich, 1983, pp. 237–238).[6] Mental states are separate or separable entities: they can be distinguished from each other. It is possible (indeed essential to folk psychological descriptions, explanations and predictions) to indicate *which* beliefs and desires play the crucial role in the production of behavior. Of course it is often the case that several beliefs and desires together cause behavior or a resulting mental state. Generally not all of them are specified in an explanation of behavior but many are taken as common background knowledge. Some have taken this as an indication that folk psychology is not committed to functional discreteness at all, but to a good deal of holism (O'Brien, 1991, p. 174). Stich has warned against reading too much into the meaning of functional discreteness. All that is required is that a certain belief can be causally active in specific cognitive processes while being causally inert in others (Stich, 1991, p. 179). In this modest sense of functional discreteness folk psychology is clearly incompatible with the kind of informational holism where everything one knows is causally involved in the production of behavior or other mental states. As a further indication that folk psychology is committed to functional discreteness it is to be noted that it is entirely reasonable from a folk psychological perspective for someone to acquire or lose one specific belief. Similarly, in reasoning, specific beliefs play a role:

> On the commonsense view, it may sometimes happen that a person has a number of belief clusters, any one of which might lead him or her to infer some further belief. When that person actually does draw the inference, folk psychology assumes that what he or she inferred it from is an empirical question, and that this question typically has a *determinate* answer. (Ramsey et al., 1991, p. 99, my emphasis)

On the literal interpretation, then, folk psychology is a largely implicit theory containing law-like generalizations[7] over mental phenomena that have the above-mentioned characteristics. Propositional attitudes play a traceable, functionally discrete, causal role in the production of behavior and mental states.

An, in my view, attractive feature of the literal interpretation is that it takes folk psychology as seriously as possible. It provides the most straightforward way of understanding why folk psychology is as successful as it is (see also Fodor, 1981b, p. 121). In other words, if one really values the descriptive, explanatory and predictive power of a theory, then why not take it, and the phenomena it postulates, literally? Furthermore it seems to me that in everyday life we do take our mental states seriously. Someone who has sincerely told me about his beliefs and desires has not just handed me a useful tool to explain and predict his behavior but has given me, almost literally, 'a piece of his mind'. This is, I would maintain, a strong common-sense sentiment concerning mental states which deserves to be taken seriously in discussions concerning the status of folk psychology.

Most discussions about the status of folk psychology are dominated by the question of how to square the individuation of mental states based on their content with the individuation of mental states based on their computational role. Instead of following this well-trodden path, I intend to concentrate on the fourth characteristic (functional discreteness). My motive for this choice is that this characteristic is directly related to actual modeling approaches in cognitive science instead of being a primarily philosophical issue. It is therefore that functional discreteness is, at the present stage of cognitive science, of greater empirical significance than the issue of content.

Intentional realism and eliminative materialism

For those who agree that the literal rendering is an acceptable interpretation of folk psychology as such, a parting of ways is possible. Fodor defends a version of intentional realism according to which the essential character-istics of mental states will turn out to be scientifically respectable. According to intentional realists folk psychology is basically right. The concepts used by folk psychology are taken as literally referring to genuinely existing, individually contentful and causally operating mental states and processes. An important reason for Fodor to advocate intentional realism is that he thinks that it is impossible to do without folk psychology (1987b, pp. xii, 8–10, 131–132).[8] Indeed, it can even be argued that it was part of the original agenda of cognitive science to take folk psychology seriously again, after its downplaying by behaviorism. G. Miller, arguably one of the 'founding fathers' of cognitive science (Gardner, 1985, p. 23), describes the general feeling of that time as follows:

> If there was anything 'common', it was the old 'common-sense' about the way people are, how the mind works, that there *is* a mind; that memory, expectations, beliefs, emotions, all those words refer to something real, and that it's our job as psychologists to find out what it is. (Miller in Baars, 1986, p. 210; see also Loewer & Rey, 1991, p. xiv)

Contrary to Fodor, Churchland suggests that folk psychology, literally construed, is fundamentally wrong and should be eliminated.[9] Churchland has argued for this negative judgment in a very straightforward way. It is useful to briefly investigate his arguments, as this throws more light on the nature of folk psychology as well as on Churchland's attitude towards it.

Churchland suggests evaluating folk psychology on the basis of three criteria that are regularly applied to scientific theories in general (1989, pp. 6–9). First of all, when looked at from an objective point of view, how successful are the explanations of folk psychology? Second, is there anything like explanatory progress? And third, is it possible to integrate folk psychology with successful scientific theories operative in neighboring domains?

According to Churchland, there is much that remains inexplicable for folk psychology. Creativity, mental illnesses, the origin of differences in intelligence between people, all these issues fall outside the scope of folk psychology. Worse, even common-sense phenomena like sleep or the functioning of our memory are complete riddles from the perspective of folk psychology. Concerning the second criterion, Churchland posits that folk psychology has remained the same since at least the time of the ancient Greeks. Though any scientific theory is expected to grow in explanatory power, folk psychology has failed to make any progress in this respect. Third, folk psychology is far from integrated with the rest of modern science, though these sciences themselves continuously form an increasingly consistent whole. Intentional mental states remain outside the scientific image.

Nevertheless, I would like to argue that the criteria of explanatory power, explanatory progress and integration with other sciences are not well suited to judge the value of folk psychology. The end result of an evaluation on the basis of these criteria shows not so much that folk psychology is radically wrong but rather that folk psychology, though a theory, is not a *scientific* theory. It consists of a largely implicit organized structure of mentalistic concepts, and it is not as rigorously tested against empirical evidence, or as thoroughly checked on its internal consistency, as is a scientific theory. It has to be realized that folk psychology is primarily a descriptive, explanatory and predictive scheme for interpersonal behavior.[10] Folk psychology is for *daily use*, and in that respect it serves quite well.[11] From this perspective, the criteria used by Churchland in his evaluation seem rather awkward. After all, why *should* folk psychology give an explanation of the kind of phenomena listed by Churchland as an illustration of his first criterion?[12] In the same vein, explanatory progress also seems an irrelevant criterion. Since folk psychology had functions to fulfill other than scientific ones, and since it accomplished these tasks satisfactorily, there has never been enough incentive to transform folk psychology into a 'better' theory.[13] With respect to Churchland's third criterion of integration with other sciences it should be noted that folk psychology is fully integrated with, if not indispensable to, sciences like economics, political science, sociology and anthropology.[14] Taking all the above into account, a straightforward rejection of folk psychology has to be dismissed as too direct and simplistic. My position is comparable to Preston's, who argues that folk psychology has the status of 'an empirical pre-scientific theory' (Haselager, 1993b, pp. 9–11; Preston, 1989, p. 300). Criteria with respect to the scientific value of folk psychology should be directed not at folk psychology itself, but at the scientific theories based on it, i.e. classical cognitive science.

It is important not to misunderstand the consequences of an elimination of folk psychology. To be sure, if folk psychology goes, there will be no more beliefs and desires. As Heil puts it:

> The demise of a theory makes for the demise of its ontology. Theoretical posits survive theories only to the extent that they find a home in a successor theory. (1991, p. 125)

However, Churchland is not asserting that once folk psychology is eliminated we will no longer experience sensations or be in specific information bearing states concerning the world. He is asserting that the way we will *conceptualize* these experiences and informational states will be completely dissimilar to our current practices (1979, pp. 89–99, 116–120; 1988, pp. 165, 178–180). This should not be taken to imply that for instance the phenomenon we now call 'pain' is no longer unpleasant because it has been shown scientifically that the concept 'pain' does not succeed in singling out a cognitively important kind of mental state. Nor will (what we now call) 'a burning desire' no longer involve a yearning feeling. Eliminativism is simply the thesis that a neurocomputationally inspired taxonomy of cognitive states and processes will be radically different from our current folk psychological one. The new neurocomputational theory of cognition will lead, Churchland expects, to a better understanding of the true nature of our internal states and processes.

1.3 Folk psychology's relation to science

After taking the first two steps, namely that folk psychology can be viewed as a theory that postulates contentful states that cause behavior and other mental states in a functionally discrete way, the *third* step consists of establishing how well folk psychology comports with modern science. That is, in a sense science is taken to be the ultimate arbiter on what is real or taken for real. As Sellars has put it:

> in the dimension of describing and explaining the world, science is the measure of all things, of what is that it is, and of what is not that it is not. (1963, p. 173)

There are many questions here with respect to what we mean by 'real', and to how we can be sure that science has anything authoritative to say about 'reality' in whatever way we might understand it. I intend to ignore these questions and will proceed on the basis that in order to be acceptable, folk psychology must comport with science.[15] Indeed, this much is accepted without much argument by both Fodor and Churchland.

What cannot be ignored, however, is the issue of exactly which part of science folk psychology should comport to. It is, after all, doubtful that there is much gain in investigating how folk psychology comports with astronomy or geology, while for instance physics is at least a debatable option. Yet it seems obvious that theories in cognitive science are the foremost candidates for inspection. However, as cognitive science is an interdisciplinary study, there can be considerable argument as to the exact level of theories with which folk psychology should be compared. The relevance of neuroscience in particular, as distinct from computational science, is a significant topic.

On many occasions, both Paul and Patricia Churchland have suggested that in order to be scientifically respectable, psychological concepts and theories should at least in principle be reducible to neurobiological and neurocomputational concepts and theories (Churchland, 1989, p. 1; Churchland & Churchland, 1994, p. 48). However, this suggestion should not be taken to mean that the fate of folk psychology depends directly on its correspondence with neuroscientific theories. It is fallacious to argue that since neurocomputational theories make no use of beliefs and desires, folk psychology has therefore to be rejected. After all, the two theories operate on different levels of analysis.[16]

With respect to intertheoretic reduction, the Churchlands envisage a continuum ranging from a smooth reduction of one theory to the other, through a significant modification of the theory to be reduced, to a complete elimination of the theory to be reduced (1994, pp. 46–47). They believe that the relationship between folk psychology and neuroscientific theories lies at the eliminative end of the continuum.

However, as McCauley (1986; 1996) has noted, this way of looking at intertheoretic reduction fails to make a distinction between *intra*level and *inter*level relations between theories. Intralevel contexts involve the relationships between two successive theories at the same level of analysis in a certain domain. It is in this context that the elimination of the old theory can be expected. For instance, Lavoisier's oxygen theory, which he developed from 1772 to 1783, explained at a chemical level the phenomena of combustion, calcination and respiration as the results of the absorption of oxygen. Stahl's phlogiston theory, presented in 1730, had explained the same phenomena, also at the chemical level, as the result of the extraction of phlogiston from matter. Lavoisier's theory proved to be better and as a result it eliminated and supplanted Stahl's phlogiston theory. Phlogiston, as it turned out, did not exist (Thagard, 1992, pp. 39–47, 105–107).

In contrast, interlevel contexts involve the relationships between concurrent theories at different levels of analysis. Both theories address the same phenomena but use different concepts and principles, appropriate for the level on which they operate. In the case of interlevel relations, McCauley (1986, p. 194; 1996, pp. 33–34) argues, elimination of one of the theories is no option. On the contrary, a higher-level theory can guide research at a lower level by specifying the kinds of phenomena that are the result of the interactions of phenomena at the lower level. Theories influence each other by indicating promising directions of research which, ultimately, should lead to the establishment of identities between higher-level phenomena and collections of phenomena at the lower level.[17]

This point of McCauley's is well taken but, as he himself notes, it does not constitute a rebuttal of Churchland's eliminativism concerning folk psychology. It merely makes clear that the only way in which the development of theories at lower levels can result in the elimination of a theory at a higher level is if the lower-level theory gives rise to a new view of the phenomena at the higher level that is incompatible with the old higher-level theory (McCauley, 1986, p. 197). In other words: interlevel developments in science can result in an intralevel competitor of folk psychology. The eliminativist suggestions of the Churchlands could be described as follows: if neurocomputational theories generate a new understanding of cognitive phenomena at the psychological level (for instance by resulting in a radically new taxonomy of cognitive states and processes) this new psychological theory might eliminate the old folk psychological one.[18] Such reasoning can indeed be found in the work of Patricia Churchland:

> the psychological generalizations that are eventually considered ripe for reduction may be both richer and substantially revised relative to current generalizations in folk psychology. If that is the direction taken by the co-evolution of psychology and neuroscience, future historians of science will see folk psychology as having been largely displaced rather than smoothly reduced to neurobiology. (1986, p. 312)

That is, Churchland expects neuroscience and psychology to develop as a result of their interaction into an integrated view of cognition that will be incompatible with folk psychology at the psychological level. Ultimately, then, the question will be which direction psychology will take under the influence of the developments in other disciplines of cognitive science, especially neuroscience, AI and philosophy. With respect to this last question, the Churchlands (1996, pp. 225, 230) claim that connectionism has already provided a fundamentally different psychological intralevel competitor for folk psychology.

1.4   Vindicating folk psychology

The requirement that folk psychology should comport with modern science if it is to be vindicated leads to a *fourth* question: what exactly is meant by 'comports'? Precisely when do we eliminate the entities posited by a theory instead of merely claiming that we have changed or improved our understanding of them?[19] Unfortunately, there is no generally agreed 'point of no return' and no determinate method for deciding when a mere change in a theory amounts to an elimination of it. Yet there are some converging intuitions with respect to a minimal construal of 'comports' that I will adhere to in the following.

I think an acceptable interpretation of 'comports' in this case comes down to the requirement that the theoretical posits of the current best theories in cognitive psychology should have, to a substantial degree, the properties attributed by folk psychology to mental states. This much is accepted by Fodor, Churchland and several others. For instance, Ramsey et al. write:

> In the absence of a principled way of deciding when ontological elimination is in order, the best we can do is to look at the posits of the old theory – the ones that are at risk of elimination – and ask whether there is anything in the new theory that they might be identified with or reduced to. If the posits of the new theory strike us as deeply and fundamentally different from those of the old theory . . . then it will be plausible to conclude that the theory change has been a radical one, and that an eliminativist conclusion is in order. (1991, p. 96; see also Loewer & Rey, 1991, p. xiv; Stich, 1992, p. 254)

This strategy is also defended by Dennett when it comes to establishing what someone is really talking about while giving a mentalistic self-description (gathered and systematized in a heterophenomenological rapport). As he says:

> if we were to find real goings-on in people's brains that had *enough* of the 'defining' properties of the items that populate their heterophenomenological worlds, we could reasonably propose that we had discovered what they were *really* talking about – even if they initially resisted the identifications. And if we discovered that the real goings-on bore only a minor resemblance to the heterophenomenological items, we could reasonably declare that people were just mistaken in the beliefs they expressed, in spite of their sincerity. (1992, p. 85)

This means in the case at hand that the four essential characteristics of mental states according to the literal interpretation of folk psychology should be recognizable in the constructs of the best higher-level theory available in cognitive science, otherwise beliefs and desires will be discredited and folk psychology with them. If the new scientific understanding of the essential cognitive states and processes was fundamentally different in its 'categorial profile' (Churchland, 1986, p. 312), i.e. by not being based on these four characteristics, then folk psychology would be incompatible with its intralevel competitor.

1.5 Alternative views on folk psychology and its relation to cognitive science

The approach to the relation between cognitive science and folk psychology outlined above is not uniformly accepted. The most interesting alternative proposals attempt to avoid Churchland's eliminativist conclusions while steering clear of Fodor's specific version of intentional realism. I will investigate two suggestions that reject the literal interpretation of folk psychology, combined with an alternative view of the relationship between folk psychology and cognitive science. Though the two proposals are interrelated, I will discuss them separately. My main goal in this section is to indicate that the alternatives do not show the general approach outlined in this chapter to be wrong, superfluous or otherwise uninteresting. Moreover, the alternatives offer no cast-iron safeguard against the possibility of an elimination of folk psychology.

The instrumentalist interpretation of folk psychology

The main alternative to the literal interpretation is to take an instrumentalist or 'mild realist' stance towards folk psychology (which is sometimes also called a 'neo-Wittgensteinian' perspective: Greenwood, 1991a, pp. 1, 5). From this point of view, most vigorously defended by Dennett (1978; 1987b; 1991a; see also Clark, 1989), the concepts of folk psychology are seen as useful in describing certain real patterns observable in behavior but not as literally referring to the internal causes of these patterns.[20] As we have seen, in the approach shared by Fodor and Churchland it is necessary that the four characteristics of mental states and processes as outlined by folk psychology will have identifiable counterparts in the theories of modern cognitive science, or elimination will follow. According to instrumentalism, however, cognitive science need not result in theories that recognize these four characteristics. Folk psychology can live without them being preserved as long as it is predictively successful.

Though Dennett claims that there must be information-representing elements in the brain he strongly doubts that these elements will be identifiable with 'beliefs' as individuated by folk psychology:

> I expect that the actual internal states that cause behavior will not be functionally individuated, even to an approximation, the way belief/desire psychology carves things up. (1987b, p. 71)

This is no problem, according to Dennett, for it is not part and parcel of folk psychology that its mentalistic terms refer to actually existing, causally vigorous, internal states and processes. Folk psychology is in no danger of elimination because the mental states it postulates are useful abstracta, *qua* ontological status comparable to centers of gravity (1991b, pp. 27–29). Talk about belief has enough predictive power to license the practice of calling beliefs real (1991b, pp. 45–46). Therefore, attributions of beliefs, though not literally true, can be taken as true. They are true, as Dennett (1987b, pp. 70–73) puts it, if taken 'with a grain of salt'.

First of all, I would like to point out that indicating how we could take folk psychology to be more or less true even if the literal interpretation were shown to be mistaken is not the same as showing that the literal interpretation *is* mistaken. And though Dennett (1991c, p. 138) is certainly right in claiming that it would be premature[21] to reject folk psychology if Fodor's defense of it turns out to be untenable, this is not the same as showing Fodor's defense to have failed. That is, the question of the veracity of the literal interpretation stands, even granted the possibility of Dennett's alternative.

Second, a possible reason why instrumentalism seems such an attractive interpretation of folk psychology is that it can readily be turned into a defence of folk psychology.[22] According to the instrumentalist position, we can keep folk psychology as long as it is useful, no matter how different the portrait of cognition as painted by cognitive science becomes.

Yet it seems that if cognitive science produces a fundamentally different view of the nature of our cognitive states and processes and if it furnishes a better and deeper understanding of human cognition, it will mean that a novel and more useful tool for the prediction and explanation of behavior has come along. So why still use the old and comparatively clumsy one? It should be stressed that this is precisely what Churchland claims and uses as an argument for his eliminativism. Dennett offers no clear arguments against this line of reasoning, other than the assertion that folk psychology, properly idealized, currently lacks serious rivals, and is predictively successful enough to retain (1987b, p. 234; 1991a, p. 46). He does, however, allow for the possibility that alternative 'objective' patterns might be discernible in human behavior and that there will be hard facts concerning their respective predictive adequacy (1987b, p. 29).

I think instrumentalism is no guarantee of folk psychology's continuing existence, and a careful reading of Dennett's work will reveal many conclusions that go entirely against common-sense views, for instance with respect to pain (1978, p. 228), consciousness (1992), and many other 'ordinary mental-entity terms'.[23] In the quotation given above Dennett expresses his expectation that beliefs and desires will turn out to be literally non-existent, and elsewhere he expresses his doubts about the viability of several principles underlying folk psychology:

> Certain deeply intuitive principles of folk psychology, perhaps never before articulated, may have to be given up. (1991c, p. 136)

Indeed, Dennett's position could well be likened to that of the tailor in the fable of the emperor's new clothes. Dennett continuously strips believers in folk psychology of many of their fundamental views about the mind, while assuring them that everything will continue to look the same. Ultimately, however, they might find themselves stripped to the bone.

It therefore seems to me that an instrumentalist interpretation of folk psychology, though possible, does not show the literal interpretation to be wrong or misguided. Moreover, an instrumentalist construal of folk psychology does not constitute a safeguard against Churchland's eliminativist arguments. The defense it offers should, I suspect, be taken with 'a grain of salt'.

Folk psychology as a job specification for cognitive science

Closely related to Dennett's instrumentalism is the interpretation of folk psychology as a job specification. Bechtel and Abrahamsen (1993, pp. 342,

355) reject the (what I call) literal interpretation of folk psychology as being merely a philosophical construction or even 'invention'. Two characteristics (functional discreteness and causal efficacy) are seen as strong commitments (1993, pp. 344–345). They claim that seeing folk psychology as a way of characterizing systems in terms of their relations to their environment is closer to the truth (1993, p. 360). It is, however, entirely unclear to me why the latter would not constitute as much of a philosophical construction as the literal interpretation. Bechtel and Abrahamsen provide the following interpretation of a folk psychological description:

> When we say that 'a person knew that the brakes on the car were bad', we are saying that the person was so situated as to acquire that information about the world. (1993, p. 360)

This does not strike me as substantially less far-fetched than interpreting 'he believed that his brakes were bad, so he went to the garage' as the statement that it was this belief that was the main cause of the ensuing behavior. *Both* the literal and the alternative interpretation attempt to obtain a philosophically and scientifically acceptable analysis of ordinary folk psychological practices. Both should therefore be seen as philosophical constructions.

In agreement with Dennett,[24] Bechtel and Abrahamsen point out that folk psychology is to be construed not as an account of internal states and processes but rather as a characterization of a cognitive system that makes it possible to indicate what the system will do in a specific environment. They argue that folk psychology is not a causal explanatory theory at all (though it is still theoretical: 1993, p. 342), but a specification of what has to be explained. In this sense, folk psychology provides an important constraint for cognitive science by giving it a 'job description'. An account of internal processes as developed by cognitive science should be in accordance with folk psychological characterizations of behavior (e.g. by explaining how these kinds of behavior can arise) but it need not posit internal states corresponding to the folk psychological concepts (1993, p. 363). Folk psychology indicates certain abilities we have and these can subsequently be investigated, but not eliminated, by neuroscientists. From this perspective the value of folk psychology lies in its providing 'a first observational inventory' of mental phenomena (Sleutels, 1989, p. 274; 1994, p. 74). On the basis of this interpretation, folk psychological descriptions of a cognitive system do not have to be literally true in order to remain acceptable. Folk psychology provides a description of the behavior of a system at a high level[25] of analysis, indicating the competence of the system that has to be explained at lower levels.

Underlying this suggestion is a view of the nature of explanation different from the traditional deductive-nomological (D-N) model of logical positivism. Contrary to the traditional model, the states and processes recognized at the lower level do not have to be identifiable with the states and processes individuated at the higher level. By way of a functional analysis, one can explain phenomena at one level of analysis by pointing out which mechanisms at lower levels produce them (Bechtel, 1988b; Cummins, 1983; Looren de Jong, 1992; Schwartz, 1991). The internal structures and processes that cognitive science is likely to find will be quite different from beliefs and desires as posited by folk psychology. Still, since these internal structures and processes do give rise to the behaviors or propensities to behave which folk psychology describes as the result of having specific beliefs and desires, there is no need for a rejection of folk psychology.

However, this kind of attempt to salvage folk psychology from elimination seems to miss the point of Churchland's eliminativism. Churchland's claim is that folk psychology is inadequate not only as a specification of our internal cognitive states and processes but also as a high-level characterization. Churchland (1989, p. 282; see also Churchland & Churchland, 1996, pp. 222, 225) first of all strongly objects to the suggestion that a common-sense taxonomy should be taken as a given by science. Secondly, Churchland contests the adequacy of the job specification itself by suggesting that there might be better ones. That is, even though it might be possible to describe systems in a folk psychological way this does not imply that a better, predictively more accurate high-level description (on the basis of a better understanding of the underlying mechanisms) is impossible.

In this context it is interesting that Dennett (1987b, p. 75) has noted that the point of Marr's ideas on levels was that a seriously mistaken description of the behavior of the system at the highest level has profoundly negative consequences for ensuing research at the lower levels. Taking this into account, it seems that even on the job specification interpretation, an elimination of folk psychology is possible (though, surely, it remains an empirical issue).

In short, Churchland argues that the identification of faculties to be explained (the job specification) could be wrong or inaccurate. Some have argued that there is no reason to think that folk psychology is wrong as a task analysis or job specification since it has proven its worth in many centuries of daily use. Yet Churchland has indicated that even false theories (for instance Ptolemy's system of earth-centered epicycles in astronomy, or the theory of essences in alchemy) can have impressive predictive and explanatory power. This in itself is no reason to preserve their ontology at all costs (1989, p. 126). The fact that we have identified cognitive states in a folk psychological way for many centuries is no guarantee of the correctness of the resulting view. Indeed, difficulties encountered by scientific investigations of the entities and abilities specified by folk psychology could be taken as indications of the incorrectness of the view folk psychology provides. It is important to realize that folk psychology, though it functions adequately in daily life, could obstruct a *better* understanding of our mental processes. The first observational stock-taking could eventually turn out to be inadequate in comparison to a substantially different and more adequate inventory based on a deeper understanding of the true nature of cognition.

Once a fundamentally better and radically different theory comes along the false theory goes, along with its concepts and ontological claims.

Finally, even if one would accept the instrumentalist or job specification point of view, Fodor's and Churchland's discussion about the viability of the literal interpretation would still remain an important issue. For instrumentalists the question would be how folk psychological descriptions and explanations could be as useful as they are. For those preferring the job specification interpretation, the question is which mechanisms do the job. An eventually mature and correct theory answering these questions could perfectly well turn out to be one that shows folk psychology to be literally true. Though some philosophers and cognitive scientists do not *expect* this to be the case, there is no good *a priori* reason to rule out this possibility. In this sense, then, the debate between Fodor and Churchland concerning the adequacy of the literal interpretation would remain important as an investigation of the mechanisms underlying cognitive processes.[26]

1.6   Conclusion

In this chapter I have examined the interpretation of folk psychology that forms the basis of both Fodor's intentional realism and Churchland's eliminative materialism. Folk psychology can be seen as a pre-scientific theory, that is not beyond critical evaluation. I have argued that a literal interpretation of our everyday descriptive, explanatory and predictive practice with respect to behavior and its cognitive causes is plausible and useful. According to this interpretation, mental states such as beliefs and desires are essential elements of folk psychology, which can be analyzed as attitudes with respect to a determinate, propositionally specifiable, content, and which play a functionally discrete and causal role in the determination of behavior. The adequacy of folk psychology, literally interpreted, is an empirical issue, to be decided by developments in cognitive science. The acceptability of folk psychology depends on whether its central concepts find, in a recognizable form, a place in the best high-level scientific theories of cognition. Finally, alternative interpretations of folk psychology and its relation to cognitive science do not show the literal interpretation to be mistaken, nor do they preclude the possibility of folk psychology being eliminated.

Notes

1 The 'theory theory' of folk psychology has been most forcefully doubted by proponents of the so-called 'simulation theory' (Goldman, 1989; 1992; Gordon, 1986; 1992b). Details aside (but see Gordon, 1992a, pp. 87–88; 1992b, pp. 11–16), it is suggested that one imagines someone else's beliefs and desires (i.e. by pretending to have them oneself) and decides what one would do given these mental states (by using one's 'decision making mechanism' or 'practical reasoning system'). This imagined decision can then be used to predict the behavior of the person simulated. To explain behavior, one tries to find beliefs and desires that, when

fed into the decision mechanism, would result in behavioral specifications of the kind observed (Stich & Nichols, 1992, pp. 38–45). Discussions about the adequacy of the simulation theory typically focus on developmental studies, in which the child's growing capacity to describe, explain and predict behavior is investigated. The results, however, are far from unequivocal and there is considerable room for different interpretations of the empirical material. In the introduction to a recent collection of essays on the simulation theory, Stone and Davies (1995, pp. 8, 14) point to some interesting examples of this.

In my view, it is a serious weakness of the simulation theory that it does not provide an account of *how* the practical reasoning system transforms input (i.e. beliefs and desires) into output (i.e. specifications of behavior). If this system turns out to be exploiting a tacit folk psychological theory as, indeed, Fodor has suggested (see Stich & Nichols, 1992, p. 47, n. 7), then the simulation theory would no longer constitute a genuine *alternative* to the theory theory of folk psychology. Instead it would merely provide a suggestion as to how the folk psychological theory is applied.

2 Searle has argued that mental states are not postulated but experienced phenomena and hence cannot be eliminated (1992, pp. 59, 61). Similarly, Double asserts that we have direct experience of the explananda (Double, 1986, p. 213). Churchland (1986, p. 219) has replied to Double along the lines indicated in the text and has pointed to the fact that Double is arguing on the basis of (what Sellars called) the myth of the given.

3 This way of creating an interpretation of folk psychology has interesting similarities with what Dennett calls 'heterophenomenology', a neutral method of collecting data concerning reportedly mental phenomena, without directly addressing the question of whether these phenomena really exist (1992, pp. 66–98).

4 They are not the only ones. Although they do not share the literal interpretation of folk psychology, as outlined in section 1.2, Bechtel and Abrahamsen state: 'Adopting a Quinean notion of a theory, it seems unproblematic to regard folk psychology as a theory' (1993, p. 342). Quine saw theories as a fabric of sentences, structurally related to one another and to sensory stimulations (1960, pp. 9–13).

5 Actual folk psychological explanations can (but need not) be understood as instances of the deductive-nomological model of explanation (Fodor, 1987b, pp. 12–13; 1991b, p. 19; 1994b, pp. 3–4). From this perspective, the folk psychological explanation of behavior is an instance of the subsumption of an event under a law. Noting that the event conforms to these laws provides the explanation for the event. See Bechtel (1988b) for more information on the covering law model of explanations and the problems surrounding it.

6 A note on terminology: Stich (1983, pp. 237–238) speaks not of functional discreteness but of 'modularity' of beliefs. He means exactly the same as functional discreteness: a belief is an isolatable part of a system that plays the central role in the causation of behavior or of other mental states. Ramsey et al. (1991, pp. 97–99) use the phrase 'propositional modularity' to refer in a general way to propositional attitudes that are functionally discrete and semantically interpretable and that play a causal role in the production of behavior and other mental states. In order to avoid confusion with Fodor's modularity thesis, I will not use the phrase 'propositional modularity' in the remainder of this book, but instead use 'functional discreteness' to refer to the fourth characteristic of folk psychology according to the literal interpretation.

7 Cognitive science tries to describe and explain human behavior. To that end it searches for the conceptual frame that is most suited to reveal patterns of interest (Pylyshyn, 1984, p. 2). And, as Pylyshyn has said: 'Whatever the shortcomings of folk psychology . . . the level of abstractness of its concepts . . . and particularly its appeal to the way situations are *represented* in the mind (i.e. its appeal to what human agents think, believe, infer, want, and so on, as opposed to the way they actually are), seems precisely suited to capturing just the kinds of generalizations that concern cognitive psychology' (1980, p. 112).

8 Fodor's position is not completely clear as to how strongly he wants to cling to the original belief–desire taxonomy of folk psychology. Although he does claim that it is part of his project to preserve the generalizations of common-sense belief–desire psychology (1987b,

pp. 10, 14–16), he sometimes seems to be prepared to settle for a preservation of intentional realism while accepting a revision of the old belief–desire taxonomy (1990, pp. 174–175).

9 The classical statement of his eliminative materialism is the following: 'Eliminative materialism is the thesis that our commonsense conception of psychological phenomena constitutes a radically false theory, a theory so fundamentally defective that both the principles and the ontology of that theory will eventually be displaced, rather than smoothly reduced, by completed neuroscience' (Churchland, 1989, p. 1). Patricia Smith Churchland has also stated the main point of eliminative materialism quite succinctly: 'Once folk psychology is held at arm's length and evaluated for theoretical strength in the way that any theory is evaluated, the more folkishly inept, soft, and narrow it seems to be' (1986, p. 395). Feyerabend's 'Materialism and the mind–body problem' (1963/1970) counts as one of the earliest papers in the tradition of eliminative materialism.

10 Greenwood notes that, when compared to several domains of psychology, folk psychology comes closest to social psychology (1991a, p. 17; 1991b, p. 88).

11 Indeed, even Paul Churchland acknowledges that folk psychology has a 'remarkable' utility in the daily practical interaction between ordinary human beings (1989, p. 2). This acknowledgment of the importance of folk psychology for daily use, by the way, is not incompatible with the interpretation of folk psychology as a theory. As Churchland says: 'The fact that folk psychology serves a wealth of practical purposes is no evidence of its being non-theoretical. Quite the reverse . . . there is no inconsistency in saying that a theoretical framework should also serve a great many nontheoretical purposes' (1989, p. 117). Yet it does make the treatment of folk psychology as a *scientific* theory rather debatable, and I follow Wilkes (1984; 1991a) in rejecting this interpretation.

12 Thus, Horgan and Woodward argue: 'There is no good reason, *a priori*, to expect that a theory like FP, designed primarily to explain common human actions in terms of beliefs, desires, and the like, should also account for phenomena having to do with visual perception, sleep, or complicated muscular coordination. The truth about the latter phenomena may simply be very different from the truth about the former' (1985, p. 201; see also Wilkes, 1986, p. 170). Although it should be agreed with Churchland that folk psychology, for instance, has relatively little to say about many important mental phenomena, this does not imply that scientific theories based on folk psychology cannot successfully investigate them. There are several cognitive psychological theories about, for instance, memory and learning that connect to and utilize folk psychological concepts like 'belief' and 'desire' (1985, p. 200; see also Hewson, 1993).

13 For instance, Horgan and Woodward state: 'The typical user of FP is interested in applying a pre-existing theory to make particular causal judgments about particular instances of human behavior, not in formulating new causal generalizations' (1985, p. 202). Similarily Haldane (1988, pp. 251–252) notes that judgments concerning empirical progress are interest relative. In this sense it is not justified to call folk psychological explanations stagnant or infertile since they suffice for ordinary human concerns. A different reaction can be found in the work of Stich (1983, p. 213), who claims that progress can only be expected when investigations are carried out in a scientific way and that in this respect psychology is a young science. Expecting progress, then, is premature.

14 This illustrates how enormous the consequences of an elimination of folk psychology would be. And although Churchland is obviously not afraid to make radical changes, for others the idea that these sciences should go together with folk psychology is somewhat difficult to swallow. See, for instance, Stich (1983, pp. 213–214) and Campbell (1986, p. 151).

15 In fact, a strong dissonance between science and folk psychology is bound to have significant consequences for at least one of the two. As Stich has put it: 'If our science is inconsistent with the folk precepts that define who and what we are, then we are in for rough times. One or the other will have to go' (1983, p. 10; see also pp. 221–222). For a recent attack on the received view, as expressed by Sellars, see Baker (1995).

16 This point has been made repeatedly by Searle (1992, pp. 46–47, 60–61).

17 Indeed, McCauley (1996, p. 38) argues that a high-level science offers not just guidance but also a 'body of evidence' that can be used by low-level science to evaluate competing

models. Because the high-level science is sufficiently distant from the debates going on within the low-level science it ensures an 'honest check' on the theories proposed. Against this point, the Churchlands (1996, pp. 220–224) have replied that it is question-begging to suppose that folk psychology is sufficiently trustworthy and distant to provide this kind of control. They point out that many theories or domains that were once thought to be of different scientific levels finally turned out to belong to one and the same level.

18 Searle (1992) does not provide a counterargument to this more complex line of eliminativist reasoning.

19 This is one of the questions ignored by Searle in his attack on eliminativism. Although he explicitly acknowledges that many folk psychological beliefs about mental phenomena are and will turn out to be false (1992, p. 63), he simply assumes that this will never lead to a fundamental revision in our conceptual understanding of cognition. Yet it is exactly this point that is put into question by eliminativists.

20 Because of the reality of the patterns Dennett (1991b) prefers to call his position 'mild realism' instead of instrumentalism.

21 The word he uses is 'curious', but it is clear from the ensuing paragraph that he means that if Fodor's defense turned out to be wrong, that would in itself mean the end not of folk psychology but only of the literal interpretation of it. See also Heil (1991, p. 129).

22 See, for instance, Dennett (1991c, p. 138) where he explicitly connects a rejection of Fodor's (literal) interpretation of folk psychology with its increasing chances of survival.

23 The following quotation is illustrative of Dennett's eliminative tendencies: 'Not only are beliefs and pains not good theoretical things (like electrons or neurons), but the state-of-believing-that-*p* is not a well-defined or definable theoretical state, and the attribute, being-in-pain, is not a well-behaved theoretical attribute. Some ordinary mental-entity terms (but not these) may perspicuously isolate features of people that deserve mention in a mature psychology; about such features I am a straightforward type-intentionalist or "homuncular functionalist" . . . About other putative mental entities I am an eliminative materialist' (1978, p. xx).

24 Bechtel and Abrahamsen (1993, p. 360) note that their position is close to what Dennett calls taking the intentional stance, though they specifically claim that they do not endorse Dennett's instrumentalism or his specific proposals concerning homuncular functionalism (see also Bechtel, 1985b). It is not clear, however, if the difference with Dennett's 'selective' and in a sense realistic view (1987b, pp. 71–72; 1991a) amounts to much. Bechtel (1985b, pp. 478–479) claims that Dennett's instrumentalism is based on the idea that the environment of a system figures extensively in the determination of the truthfulness of an intentional description of the system. Bechtel (1985b, pp. 490–491) agrees with this but adds that on the design level too, the environment of the organism needs to be taken into account. I am not sure, however, if Dennett would (or needs to) object to this suggestion. But I will not investigate this issue further, as it would lead us too far astray.

25 Marr (1982) has given an influential account of the role that levels of description play in cognitive science. He used the term 'computational level' to refer to the highest level, where Dennett prefers the label 'intentional' (coupled with an interpretation of a level as a stance taken by an observer), Pylyshyn 'semantical', and Newell 'knowledge'. Marr's term is generally thought to be a misnomer, as genuine computational processes are investigated at a lower level which Marr called the algorithmic level, but which is also named the design (Dennett), syntactical (Pylyshyn), or symbol (Newell, although he actually makes a more fine-grained distinction between several levels) level. Below this, there is a third, physical (Dennett, Pylyshyn, Newell) or implementational (Marr) level. (See Dennett, 1978; Haselager, 1990; Jorna, 1990; Newell, 1982; Pylyshyn, 1984.)

26 Although the debate would have less direct consequences for folk psychology (since on the alternative accounts the veracity of the literal interpretation is not necessary for the acceptability of folk psychology), these consequences should not be underestimated. Even if we keep folk psychology as a manner of speech, the knowledge that this is all there is to it might have unsettling consequences comparable to those following the wisdom that the sun does not rotate around the earth, but that this solid earth we walk upon itself rotates. Although this

insight has not changed our way of speaking about the sun coming up or going down, it has with good reason been called a revolutionary change in our world view. Another example is the disturbing effect of the insight that at the level of physical microstructure, ordinary solid objects (like tables and chairs) surrounding us consist almost entirely of empty space. Though Schwartz, who discusses this example in detail, concludes: 'no one's worldview will be too shaken if we have to give up the idea that tables are not solid in that, for example, they exclude empty space all the way down' (1991, p. 217), I think this seriously underestimates the effect of the new view. The realization that the chairs we sit on consist mostly of empty space *is* disturbing. One may further note discussions about the 'alienating' effects of these and other modern scientific findings. Likewise, it would seem that knowing that our current way of describing our inner events has very little to do with what is actually going on inside us will have great impact.

2

Representations and Cognition

In *The language of thought* Fodor (1975) presents an example of 'speculative psychology', describing what the then current research was leading to, in order to guide future research. He observes that even the remotely plausible theories in psychology model cognition as a computational process. A computational model of cognition leads by necessity to a representational theory of mind:

No representations, no computations. No computations, no model. (1975, p. 31)

A cognitive agent has to possess a representational system that allows him or her to think about the world. The idea of representations can be found throughout the history of philosophy and psychology.[1] More importantly, Fodor (1981b, p. 27) claims, there is almost no theory in cognitive psychology without postulating representations.

One of Fodor's main projects has been to investigate the nature of this representational system. On both philosophical and psychological grounds, he suggests that the representational system of organisms capable of cognitive behavior (to be contrasted with pure reflex-like behavior) must share certain characteristics with natural languages. In the first part of this chapter (Sections 2.2 and 2.3) I will discuss the essential characteristics of the language of thought as far as they are relevant to the current context. That is, I will examine how, on the basis of a semi-linguistic representational system and a computational theory of thought, classical cognitive science is able to give, at least in principle, an answer to the question of how rationality can be mechanically possible in a way that is compatible with folk psychology. To understand the answer properly, it is useful to see how classical cognitive science developed out of and in reaction to behaviorism and the central state identity theory, which can, in turn, themselves be considered as reactions to Cartesian dualism. As this development is well known and has been described many times before (Bechtel, 1988a; Churchland, 1988; Fodor, 1975; 1981b; Meijsing, 1986), I will merely review some basic insights and arguments in Section 2.1. In the second part of this chapter I will examine the nature of distributed representations and investigate how they differ from symbolic representations (Section 2.4). I will then discuss the relationship between connectionist models and folk psychology (Section 2.5). It will be seen that distributed representations do not allow for the functional discreteness of mental states, which, as shown in Section 1.2, is an important characteristic of folk psychology according to the literal interpretation.

2.1   How is rationality mechanically possible?

The basic problem of explaining rationality in a purely mechanical and material way is that rationality is a form of semantic coherence. A rational thought sequence seems to require the understanding of the contents of the thoughts involved, thus presupposing understanding and intelligence, thereby defying any mechanistic explanatory attempts at the outset.

> In a word, if a process or system is mechanical, it can't reason; if it reasons, it can't be mechanical. That's the paradox of mechanical reason. (Haugeland, 1985, pp. 39–40)

Cartesian dualism can be taken as a vivid illustration of the difficulty of this paradox. Unable to explain or even imagine how semantic coherence could be mechanically produced, Descartes resorted to assuming a thinking substance that is responsible for the rationality of cognitive processes. The postulation of a homunculus is, of course, the opposite of providing a mechanical explanation of rationality. Furthermore, the non-material nature of the thinking substance makes it hard to explain how mental states can causally influence behavior. For a long time the question has been, therefore, whether there is a scientifically acceptable mentalistic alternative to Cartesian dualism or whether reference to the mental has to be omitted altogether.

Behaviorism in psychology and philosophy

Behaviorism dominated psychology for a long period during the twentieth century. Watson started off with an ardent rejection of mental states as commonly conceived. He claimed that it would be strongly misleading to say that a behaviorist is 'merely' ignoring mental states, since behaviorists ignore mental states in a very strong sense:

> He 'ignores' them in the same sense that chemistry ignores alchemy, astronomy horoscopy, and psychology telepathy and psychic manifestations. The behaviorist does not concern himself with them because as the stream of his science broadens and deepens such older concepts are sucked under, never to reappear. (1920, p. 94; see also Sanders, 1972, p. 53; and Sanders, Eisenga, & van Rappard, 1976, p. 287)[2]

Although this extreme version of behaviorism never gained great popularity, it has always been a central characteristic of behaviorism (most clearly in Skinner's radical behaviorism, but also in Hull's and Tolman's more theoretical versions of behaviorism) to avoid reference to mental states, as they were not thought to be scientifically respectable phenomena.[3] Psychology should stick to the objectively observable phenomena of stimulus and response and study the causal relations between environment and behavior, at best allowing intervening variables[4] in between. Skinner (1953, p. 35) has proposed a 'causal or functional' analysis of behavior according to which the causes of behavior are the external conditions of which the behavior is a function. These external conditions, like the behavior itself, are intersubjectively observable and describable in physicalist terms.

> The objection to inner states is not that they do not exist, but that they are not relevant in a functional analysis. (1953, p. 35; see also p. 31)

According to Skinner (1986, p. 83), we only use mental concepts when the real environmental causes of behavior are obscure.

The behavioristic approach in psychology had a parallel in philosophy. Logical behaviorists proposed a semantic theory concerning the meaning of mental predicates. According to the main proponent of logical behaviorism, Ryle, it is a mistake to take the ascription of a mental state to someone as a reference to some causally efficacious internal state of that person (1949, p. 300).[5] Instead, by making a correct ascription, one is conforming to common practice with respect to the use of mental predicates. It means that the person to whom one is ascribing a mental state is likely to behave in a specific way in specific situations. Mental terms refer, if to anything, to behavioral dispositions (1949, p. 112).[6]

According to this view, then, the project of cognitive science is based on a category mistake (1949, pp. 17–25), a misunderstanding of the meaning of mental predicates. There is no causal relation between behavior and what mentalistic terms supposedly denote but rather a conceptual relationship between behavior and mentalistic terms. Mental concepts are explanatory fictions as they do not refer to true causes of behavior.

Fodor has noted, however, that even if the conceptual account of the meaning of mental predicates were correct, this does not imply that a causal story in which mental states actually cause behavior must be wrong or misguided. That is, the conceptual and the causal interpretations of mentalistic terms do not exclude each other (1975, pp. 6–8). It is perfectly legitimate to investigate the causes of behavior separately from analyzing the conditions for correct use of mentalistic concepts. Cognitive science, therefore, does not rest on a version of the category mistake.

Moreover, the proposed reduction of mental states to behavioral dispositions provides an unsatisfactory account of the etiology of behavior. One reason is that it seems impossible to do completely without reference to mental states in the analysis of behavioral dispositions. Especially in reasoning, there are complex mental processes and chains of mental states, presenting major difficulties for a behavioristic analysis.

> Mental causes typically have their overt effects *in virtue of their interactions with one another*, and behaviorism provides no satisfactory analysis of statements that articulate such interactions. (Fodor, 1981b, p. 5)

Behaviorism is no longer predominant in psychology (Dennett, 1978, pp. 53–70; Flanagan, 1984, pp. 116–117), which may be seen as a clear sign that internal or mental causes of behavior are taken seriously.

The central state identity theory

According to the central state identity theory (also called 'the type identity theory'), mental states are identical with neurophysiological states instead of merely correlating with them. Neurophysiological and mentalistic terms, though different in sense, have exactly the same reference. This can explain how causal sequences of mental states are possible because, since mental states *are* brain states, there can be no problem as to their causal efficacy.

The central state identity theory is also called 'type physicalism', since it claims the existence of an identity between psychological and neurophysiological *types* or properties. Every kind of mental event is thought to be identical with a specific kind of neurophysiological event. An interesting consequence of type physicalism seems to be that only beings with a neurophysiological constitution can have mental states. Since mental properties are thought to be identical with neurophysiological properties, nothing can have the former without the latter (Fodor, 1981b, p. 7). This has sometimes been thought to be needlessly restrictive. However, identity theorists have denied the necessity of this conclusion by arguing that there is only a contingent identity relationship between mind and brain states. That is, identity theorists hold that, as far as we *now* know, mental states are identical with brain states, though we might very well discover some day that mental states can be identical to states realized in, say, silicon (Bechtel, 1988a, p. 97).

A more serious problem for the type identity theory is that it seems possible to have psychological laws that do not correspond to neurophysiological laws in any straightforward sense. That is, the kinds of properties that neuroscience takes as natural kinds[7] may turn out to be quite different from the natural kinds identified by psychology.

The token identity theory

The main reason for proposing a type identity theory is the perceived need for a reduction of psychology to neuroscience in order to stay within the bounds of materialistic monism as opposed to Cartesian dualism. However, as Fodor has shown, there is no need to revert to reductionism (and therefore to embrace the type identity theory) in order to avert ontological dualism, since accepting a mere *token* identity theory is sufficient for this purpose (1975, pp. 9–26; 1981b, pp. 127–145).

The token identity theory holds that all mental states and processes are physical states and processes but, importantly, denies that a psychological natural kind must be identical to a (neuro)physiological kind. Instead, a psychological property can be identical with a large disjunctive set of neurophysiological properties, which makes it impossible to seamlessly translate psychological laws into neurophysiological ones. In other words: there are no bridge laws connecting psychological and neurophysiological natural kinds, though there are bridge statements (1975, p. 20). The token identity theory acknowledges the fact that different disciplines or 'special sciences' try to formulate generalizations about interesting and important phenomena without necessarily being reducible to physical generalizations. Put differently, psychological properties are multiply realized (1994b, p. 11). The token identity theory, then, holds that psychological properties are ultimately physically instantiated (thereby avoiding dualism) without being committed to the view that all psychological laws should be reducible to (neuro)physiological ones.

Functionalism

As Fodor (1981b, p. 9) puts it, in the first decade of cognitive science the dilemma was that both behaviorism and the central state identity theory seemed only half right. Behaviorism rightly stressed the relational character of internal states (as, at best, intervening variables between environmental conditions and behavior), though it had a too impoverished view of what phenomena were allowed to participate in these relations. The central state identity theory indicated how mental states could causally interact with one another, thereby making them ontologically respectable, yet imposed too strict conditions on the set of acceptable mental states by requiring a type identity with neurophysiological states. Functionalism seemed to combine the best of both worlds.

An important aspect of functionalism is that it ensures a specific, irreducible level of analysis for psychology without rejecting (token) physicalism. The main intuition behind functionalism is that the causal role played by a mental state determines what *kind* of state it is. The causal relations a mental state has with input, output and other mental states determine whether it is a belief that *p*, a desire that *q*, a fear of *r*, etc. Functionally equivalent states are, from a mentalistic perspective, identical despite possible differences 'in kind' on an implementational level (and this is where functionalism conflicts with the type identity theory). In this way, functionalism provides cognitive science with the natural kind predicates with which to formulate its generalizations, which, in the case of 'mere' token identity theory, would consist of large disjuncts (1981b, p. 25). It provides psychology with a 'canonical notation' of the relevant states and processes (1981b, p. 13).

However, functionalism should not be mistaken for an *explanation* of mental states or processes. Functionalism does no more than individuate something on the basis of its causal relations. Functionalism says what something is on the basis of what it does, but it does not explain *how* that something does it. In other words, functionalism gives, from a causal explanatory perspective, only question-begging answers.[8] Though it uses the causal relations of a mental state for its individuation, functionalism does not explain how the mental state acquires these specific causal abilities, or how (or even if) the content of mental states can play a role in the determination of their causal role. This explanation must be given, however, because otherwise the behavioristic criticisms concerning the explanatory fictitiousness of mental states would be valid.

Clearly then, classical cognitive science consists of a combination of the token identity theory and functionalism. The token identity theory can be seen as a way of escaping the limiting constraint that a type identity between the implementation and the implemented should be preserved. Functionalism provides the right predicates to formulate interesting psychological generalizations, but only becomes interesting when it is accompanied by a specification of how the functionally individuated theoretical constructs can be implemented materially and processed mechanically in a way that respects the logical relations between their contents (1981b, pp. 24–26).

At this point, a crucial connection has been made with computers or, to be more precise, with Turing machines.[9] Putnam (1960/1975) has suggested that only mental states whose functional definition can be expressed in terms of the machine table states of a Turing machine are acceptable to cognitive science. A machine table of a Turing machine specifies what kinds of transitions between input, output and internal (machine) states govern the behavior of the machine. There are, however, several problems concerning Putnam's specific 'machine table' version of Turing machine functionalism (Bechtel, 1988a, pp. 112–140; Fodor, 1981b, pp. 79–99; Meijsing, 1986, pp. 100–105; Putnam, 1975, p. 298) that make it unattractive from a psychological point of view.[10] Nevertheless, the basic idea has remained a central tenet of classical cognitive science. Instead of viewing a mental state as a logical state specified in a machine table, it is equated with a computational state of the machine, identical to the operation the machine is performing.

The interesting aspect of universal Turing machines, i.e. computers, is their computational promise. Church ventured the thesis that every procedure that is effectively computable can be performed by a recursive procedure. Turing proved that a universal Turing machine could compute all recursive functions (Bechtel, 1988a, pp. 116–117; Haugeland, 1985, pp. 133–140). Put together, the Church-Turing thesis says in essence that every process that can be formally specified by way of an effective procedure is mechanically performable.

The suggestion that a psychological state should be understood in terms of computational states of a machine constitutes a methodological constraint on the mental phenomena acceptable to cognitive science. As long as the mental states and processes referred to in a psychological theory can be formally specified, we can be sure that they are mechanically implementable in a universal Turing machine. This assures us that the mental states and processes that figure in an explanation are not fictions with unexplained causal powers.

2.2   Mental processes and syntactical symbol processing

The operation of computers as utilized in classical cognitive science consists of the processing of symbols.[11] In effect, *the* basic idea of the classical computational theory of mind is that the mind is a symbol processing system (Fodor, 1975; Haugeland, 1985, p. 106; Jorna, 1990; Newell, 1981; Newell & Simon, 1981; Pylyshyn, 1984). As an automated formal system, a computer can perform all formally specified symbol manipulations (Fodor, 1981a, p. 130; 1981b, p. 16; Haugeland, 1981, p. 12).

The importance of symbols can easily be seen when one considers two of their aspects. First of all, symbols are representational structures, they can be *about* things (as, for instance, the word 'books' refers to books). Second, symbols are physically instantiated or tokened.[12] Because of this physical instantiation, it is no mystery that symbols can have causal consequences. Both aspects of symbols lead in a straightforward way to the suggestion that mental states can be conceived of as relations between an organism and tokenings of mental symbols.

Propositional attitudes as relations to symbols

Let us look again, at this point, at one of the characteristics of folk psychology, i.e. that mental states have content. As indicated in Chapter 1, a standard way of speaking about content is in terms of propositions. Mental states are considered to be propositional attitudes, i.e. they involve a relationship of the organism with a proposition that specifies the content of the mental state. A clear definition of a proposition is given by Schiffer:

> Propositions are abstract, objective, language-independent entities that have essentially the truth conditions they have. (1986, pp. 83–84)[13]

The most important characteristic of propositions in the current context is that it belongs to the essence of a proposition to have truth conditions. They are, as Fodor (1987b, pp. 10–11) puts it, semantically evaluable. It is for this reason that logical relationships between propositions can exist and that questions concerning the semantic coherence of propositional attitudes can be addressed (Fodor, 1981b, p. 182).[14]

However, the nature of the relationship between an organism and a proposition is obscure. A proposition is something to be grasped or apprehended, but exactly how this 'grasping' should be interpreted is unclear. Fodor holds that propositions are of no help in explaining how someone can 'grasp' the content of a thought or utterance due to their abstractness. Mental states cannot, therefore, be direct relationships between organisms and propositions. Furthermore, propositions are useless as objects of mental acts since they are causally inert, as they have no specific form. Something else must play the role of being the object of mental states, i.e. something that can have both content and causal effects.

Symbols are the obvious candidates: they are physically instantiated, which makes them causally efficacious, and they can have propositional content. As Fodor says:

> I don't see how an organism can stand in an (interesting epistemic) relation to a proposition except by standing in a (causal/functional) relation to some token of a formula that expresses the proposition. (1981b, p. 201)

That is, in Fodor's account, propositional attitudes are three-place relations between an organism, a representational structure and a proposition (1981b, pp. 177–203; 1994b, p. 47; see also Loewer & Rey, 1991, p. xvi). The suggestion that there are tokenings of symbolic types that function as intermediaries between the organism and propositional content forms the basis for the representational theory of thought (RTT).[15]

Semantical coherence and syntactical symbol processing

At this stage, on the one hand, there is the suggestion that a mental state involves a relationship of the organism with a symbol having propositional content; and, on the other hand, there are computers which can manipulate symbols in a purely mechanical way. The crucial question now is how a computer can be made to manipulate symbols in a causal sequence which is coherent in terms of the contents of the symbols. Turing has provided the key idea (Fodor, 1987b, pp. 18–19; 1991a, p. 277). He indicated that causal relations between mental states can be made to respect the semantic/ intentional properties and relations of these states by construing them as *syntactical* symbol manipulation processes.[16] This, in essence, constitutes the answer to the mechanical rationality problem that classical cognitive science has further expanded and examined.

Symbols can be processed by rules that are sensitive to the syntactic form of the symbols, and not to their content. The form of a symbol is an abstract feature of its physical instantiation. The syntactic form of a symbol correlates systematically with its content (by way of convention: this specific form symbolizes such and such).[17] It is the syntactic form of the symbol that determines what causal effects it will have, just as the shape of a key (and not its actual physical constitution[18]) determines what lock it will open. Rules that determine how the symbols are manipulated have to be sensitive to the structure of symbols.[19] One can visualize the structure-sensitive processing of symbols by comparing symbols with pieces of a jigsaw puzzle; symbols have to 'fit' into the rule in order to be processed. And though the pieces of the puzzle can carry content, the content itself does not determine whether the symbol pieces will 'fit into the rule'. If the structure-sensitive rules that process the symbols are well devised, the end result will be that the syntactical symbol manipulation will remain coherent while being interpreted. The processing of information will then be seen to be rational. So, according to the computational theory of thought (CTT), cognitive processes can be modeled as syntactic transformations of symbols that can be made to respect logical relations between their contents, such as implication and confirmation.

The importance of syntax also clearly comes to the fore in Haugeland's (1985, p. 106) remark that computers are interpreted automatic formal systems. The computer is a formal automaton taking care of the syntax in a way that (given the right program and the right interpretation of the symbols) will respect the semantic constraints on the content of the symbols. It is clear that formal logic plays an important role in classical cognitive science. Yet, to avoid misunderstandings it should be kept in mind that Fodor is not committed to the view that cognition is *strictly* logical. From Fodor's perspective, logic is merely a useful tool because it is reasonably well understood. It presents a good *example* of a well-structured language with an ordered syntax and semantics but it need not be part of the actual models of cognitive processes. Specifically, there is no suggestion that every cognitive system has a propositional logic at its disposal. As Fodor and Pylyshyn state:

> It needn't . . . be strict truth-preservation that makes the syntactic approach relevant to cognition. Other semantic properties might be preserved under syntactic transformation in the course of mental processing – e.g. warrant, plausibility, heuristic value, or simply *semantic non-arbitrariness*. The point of Classical modelling isn't to characterize human thought as supremely logical; rather, it's to show how a family of types of semantically coherent (or knowledge-dependent) reasoning are mechanically possible. Valid inference is the paradigm only in that it is the best understood member of this family; the one for which syntactical analogues for semantical relations have been most systematically elaborated. (1988, p. 29, n. 19; see also Fodor, 1975, p. 29)

Logic, then, plays an important role in providing classical cognitive science with 'a medium of expression' (Loewer & Rey, 1991, pp. xvi, xxxiii, n. 22), not by prescribing cognitive science deduction as the only means of symbol transformation.

2.3 The constituent structure of the language of thought

Fodor has investigated the nature of the representational system in greater detail. He suggests that in order to explain certain pervasive cognitive phenomena, the representational system must necessarily have specific characteristics. In this section I will investigate these characteristics and the arguments concerning their necessity. Fodor (together with Pylyshyn) phrases the central claim as follows:

> Classical psychological theories appeal to the constituent structure of mental representations to explain three closely related features of cognition: its productivity, its compositionality and its inferential coherence. (1988, p. 33)

In the ensuing discussion of this claim, however, it has become clear that the exact phrasing of this thesis is somewhat misleading. In a later article, Fodor and McLaughlin (1990, p. 185, n. 1; see also Fodor, 1994a, p. 106) indicate that the principle of compositionality is meant to provide an explanation of the productivity and systematicity of cognition. Complex representations have a combinatorial syntax and semantics which is based on the constituent structure of complex representations.[20] This leaves us with the following reconstruction of Fodor's thesis: in order to explain certain characteristics of cognition that are referred to by the terms 'productivity' and 'systematicity' it is necessary for the representational system to be compositional, meaning that representations have a combinatorial syntax and semantics, which is made possible by their constituent structure. Let us now see how this thesis should be fleshed out and why Fodor thinks it is an unavoidable one.

Productivity refers to the thesis that, in principle, a cognitive system can entertain an infinite number of thoughts. This indicates that the representational capacities of a cognitive system are, in principle, unbounded. The only way to achieve this by finite means, Fodor argues, is through a representational system that has a combinatorial syntax and semantics (1975, pp. 31–32; 1981b, pp. 29–30; 1987b, pp. 137, 147–148; Fodor & Pylyshyn, 1988, pp. 33–37).[21]

The *systematicity* of cognition forms the central issue in the debate about the necessary characteristics of representational systems. The term 'systematicity' refers to the fact that the ability to understand and/or produce certain thoughts is intrinsically related to the ability to think other thoughts. If a person is capable of entertaining a thought like 'John loves the girl', he or she is bound to be able to have the thought 'The girl loves John' as well.

This can be explained by means of the compositionality principle in the following way. The elementary mental representations (atoms) that together represent the content of the thought have a structured relationship (e.g. subject – predicate – object) to one another. The structural relations are the same in both thoughts, only certain atoms have changed place. Understanding or entertaining the first thought means that both the atoms and the structural relations are understood, hence the other thought must be understood as well.

Usually the arguments considering systematicity center on language (as in the illustration above), which is the most direct example of systematicity.[22] Yet, systematicity can be noted in non-linguistic organisms as well. As Fodor and Pylyshyn put it, if one denies systematicity in non-linguistic animals,

> It would have to be quite usual to find, for example, animals capable of representing the state of affairs aRb, but incapable of representing the state of affairs bRa . . . So that, though you could teach the creature to choose the picture with the square larger than the triangle, you couldn't for the life of you teach it to choose the picture with the triangle bigger than the square. (1988, pp. 40–41; see also Fodor, 1987b, pp. 152–153)

Although arguments about the precise extent of systematicity are possible,[23] it seems reasonable to accept that cognitive systems display systematicity to a significantly high degree.

In order to explain productivity and systematicity, Fodor argues that thoughts are relations to structured entities instead of unstructured atoms. This is comparable to the difference between sentences and words. Most words (as they appear in a dictionary) are unstructured atoms without a combinatorial syntax and semantics, as can be noted by the fact that knowing one word does not imply knowledge of any other word. In sentences, word-atoms are combined in a structured way to form complex expressions.[24] Thoughts, or rather the representations that form their objects, have a *constituent* structure, just like sentences. The term 'constituency' refers to the part/whole relationship between atoms and complex representations. The simple elements out of which complex representations are construed are literally present in the complex representation.[25] In a symbolic representational system, the constituent structure of complex representations is utilized to closely match the structure of the information represented. The relations between elementary representations explicitly represent the relations between parts of the information.

Thus, certain features of this representational system can, lacking alternative explanations, be inferred from certain characteristics of our cognitive capacities.[26] The systematicity and productivity of cognition can be explained by means of the compositionality principle, i.e. by assuming that the representational system has a combinatorial syntax and semantics, which is made possible by the constituent structure of its complex representations.[27] It is because of these properties of the representational system that Fodor speaks of a '*language* of thought' (LOT).

Unfortunately, Fodor's use of the term 'language' has given rise to certain misunderstandings concerning the exact content of his proposal. One obvious question is how there can be sentences in one's head. This can be countered by pointing out that sentences can be entokened in many different ways: in the form of, for instance, sound-waves in the air, ink on paper, or electro-magnetically on hard disks. Once one realizes this, the suggestion that sentences can be entokened neurophysiologically in the brain becomes quite comprehensible (Stich, 1983, pp. 35–38; Loewer & Rey, 1991, p. xxxiii, n. 25).

A different intuitively plausible objection to Fodor's language of thought has been put forward by Patricia Churchland:

> there is something deeply mystifying in the idea that all of our cognitive activity, including cognitively dependent perception, pattern recognition, and the cognitive activity of infants, is language-like, in the sense that it consists of sentence manipulation. (1986, p. 388; see also Churchland & Churchland, 1990, p. 302)

She speaks of an 'infralinguistic catastrophe' which results from the fact that many organisms display no linguistic capabilities, yet behave in an obviously intelligent way (very small children, deaf-mute people, monkeys, pets). According to the LOT thesis, these organisms should engage in 'sentence-crunching' just like linguistically capable organisms, but Churchland finds this hard to believe.

However, it should be kept in mind that the phrase 'a *language* of thought' only underlines certain similarities between the representational system and natural languages. As we have seen, the reason why Fodor calls the internal representational system 'a language' is that mentalese shares with languages certain syntactic and semantic characteristics (complex representations have a constituent structure which allows for a combinatorial syntax and semantics), thereby providing the organism with the ability to display systematic behavior. It certainly does not imply that there is a *direct* relationship between having such a representational system and having a natural language capacity. The point of the LOT is not that language capacity is the basic module for all intellectual/cognitive activity. Indeed, Fodor (1983) explicitly distinguishes between a language module and the more central processes. As he says elsewhere:

> you should not tie having beliefs to talking a language. (1981b, p. 19, see also pp. 190, 192)

In short, having a language of thought is something quite different from having a natural language capability. There is, therefore, no need to speak of a catastrophe (as Churchland does) if non-linguistic organisms have cognitive characteristics that make the attribution of an LOT to them plausible.

By way of summary, the following theses form the core of Fodor's version of classical cognitive science.

1   Mental states are individuated on the basis of their causal relations with input, output and other mental states (functionalism).
2   Mental states are physically instantiated, but are not type-identical to neurophysiological states (token identity theory).
3   Mental states such as beliefs and desires (i.e. the propositional attitudes) involve a relationship between a system or organism and mental representations (the representational theory of thought: RTT). The relationship between an organism and the content of its thought as specified by a proposition is mediated by a tokening of a symbolic expression that functions as the object of the attitude.
4   Mental representations are symbols with formal (syntactic) as well as semantic properties. Mental representations can play a specific causal role because of the formal characteristics of their physical instantiation (namely through their syntactic shape). Mental states get their semantic properties from the semantic content of the symbols that are their objects.
5   Mental symbols are syntactically processed by structure-sensitive computational rules (the computational theory of thought: CTT). Thus, the

rationality of the ensuing process can be ensured without resorting to homunculi.

6   The productivity and systematicity of cognition can be explained on the basis of compositionality: a combinatorial syntax and semantics that is made possible by the constituent structure of the representational system (which Fodor refers to as 'the language of thought': LOT).

All in all, classical cognitive science has developed a computational and representational theory of cognition that is closely connected to folk psychology according to the literal interpretation. A belief or desire can be interpreted as involving a computational relationship between an organism and a symbolic structure with propositional content. As symbols are physically (i.e. neurophysiologically) instantiated, the causal-explanatory role of mental states is no longer a mystery. Semantic coherence consists of truth functional links between propositions. By manipulating symbols on the basis of their syntactic properties, a purely mechanical yet rational processing of information can be achieved. The functional discreteness of mental states poses no problem either for classical cognitive science as the mental states that play a causal part in the production of behavior or thoughts can be identified by a specification of the symbolic structures and rules that are involved in the cognitive process. Furthermore, the symbolic representational system is compositional; its combinatorial syntax and semantics is made possible by having basic symbols as literal constituents of well-structured, more complex representations.[28]

However, even though classical cognitive science is 'folk psychology compatible', it cannot yet be said to have vindicated folk psychology, because this would, to a large extent, depend on its empirical success in modeling cognitive processes. As stated in the introduction, I intend to use the frame problem as a benchmark for the evaluation of classical cognitive science.

Before doing so, however, I will first examine the alternative connectionist approach to the study of cognition. Connectionism has developed a representational theory which is entirely different in character from the LOT and it claims that it is more adequate from a scientific point of view, especially with respect to the frame problem. In the next two sections, I will investigate the nature of this alternative representational scheme and its relationship to folk psychology.

2.4   A neurocomputational perspective: the importance of distributed representations

In 1986, connectionism received a strong boost by the publication of two volumes on parallel distributed processing (PDP) (McClelland, Rumelhart, & the PDP group, 1986; Rumelhart, McClelland, & the PDP group, 1986). According to some authors, this new development in AI resulted in a radically different model of cognition, inspired by our knowledge of the structure of the human brain and the processes taking place in it (Rumelhart, 1992, p. 70). The nature and variety of connectionist networks has been explained by many writers (see Bechtel & Abrahamsen, 1991; Churchland, 1989, pp. 159–188; 1995; Churchland & Sejnowski, 1992; McClelland et al., 1986; Rumelhart et al., 1986). In this section I will examine the most important aspects of these networks, which, in the current context, concern the nature and function of activation patterns and the weights attached to the connections between units.

A network consists of a set of units with connections between them.[29] Each unit has a certain level of activation and is connected to one or more other units. Importantly, the connections between units have weights attached to them which modulate the propagation of activation along the connection and determine whether the input received will be of an excitatory or inhibitory character (i.e. by changing the polarity of the signal). The pattern of connections and the weights attached to them can be represented in an array of values which is sometimes called 'the connectivity matrix'. Each unit receives input of the units that connect to it, on the basis of which it calculates its *net input*. The receiving unit determines its new level of *activity* on the basis of its net input and its own former status. On the basis of its new level of activation it then calculates what *output* it will propagate to the units it connects to.[30]

Though there are many different kinds of connectionist networks, a short description of a standard example of a feedforward network[31] will suffice in order to understand the function and nature of activation patterns and weights. A simple version of such a network consists of three layers of input, hidden and output units, respectively.[32] Input units, sometimes called 'sensory neurons' by Churchland (1989, p. 123), encode the stimulus received by the network. In other words, the pattern of activity across all input units represents the incoming information. This activation pattern renders a specific output of the layer of input units, which is propagated further into the network. The output of the input units is modulated by the weights attached to their connections with the hidden units. On the basis of this modified pattern of activity, a net input for the hidden units is calculated. On the basis of this net input, the hidden units compute their new activation pattern which eventually results in an activation pattern of the output units of the network. The output of the output units represents the response of the network to the stimulus.

During a supervised training phase, a network receives a specification of the output that it should have produced. In the learning stage, the network uses this information to determine the proper setting of the weights according to a learning rule.[33] At a certain moment the weights will be set in such a way that the network in total has reached its error minimum. The output will be as close to the desired output as the network is able to produce and the network can then be said to have learned the task at hand.

If one tries to understand the functioning of a network on a more abstract level, the following picture emerges. A pattern of activation can be mathematically represented by a vector, specifying a point in the activation space of the units. The activation space of a set of units is constituted by a set of axes equal to the number of units, along which the amount of their activity can be presented (for instance, ranging from 0 to 1 in steps of 0.1). Thus, for a set of three units, a three-dimensional activation space can be envisaged. Every point in that space, for instance, the point indicated by the vector < 0.5, 0.2, 0.9 >, will represent the activation pattern of the set (i.e. the simultaneous activity of the three units). Of course, the more units a set contains, the more dimensions the activation spaces will have. This is why activation spaces are sometimes referred to as 'hyperspaces'. The activity of the whole network can be understood as the transformation of activation patterns, or mathematically as vector transformation.

The weights collectively determine the nature of the activation pattern transformation (Churchland, 1989, pp. 201–202). The setting of all the weights of a network can be represented by a vector in a weight space, analogous to the representation of an activation pattern by a vector in an activation space. The change of weights in a network can be described by outlining the path followed by this vector during the learning phase. When an extra dimension, representing the error rate of the network's performance, is added as the *y*-axis, this trajectory can be seen to 'descend' towards an error minimum. It is important to realize that the weights represent the enduring knowledge of the network. They determine how the network will react to incoming stimuli and can be thought of as constituting the *theory* about the domain (1989, p. 168; Churchland & Sejnowski, 1992, p. 165). A theory, then, is a point in weight space:

> An individual's overall theory of the world, we might venture, is not a large collection or a long list of stored symbolic items. Rather, it is a specific point in that individual's synaptic weight space. It is a configuration of connection weights, a configuration that partitions the system's activation-vector space(s) into useful divisions and subdivisions relative to the inputs typically fed the system. 'Useful' here means 'tends to minimize the error messages'. (1989, p. 177)

The function of the weights can be thought of as a *partitioning* of the activation space of the hidden units. The weights attached to the connections between the input and hidden units determine that a certain activation pattern of the input units will be transformed into an activation pattern of hidden units that occupies a specific region in the hidden unit activation space. When a specific input is received, the hidden units respond by producing an associated pattern of activity. This association is the result of the learning process and is implemented in the setting of the weights attached to the connections between input and hidden units. Hidden units actually function as complex feature detectors in that they react to specific characteristics (not necessarily humanly intelligible or even detectable) of the input activation pattern, which, so the network has learned, are important for the determination of the activity of the output units. Output units respond to the activity pattern of the hidden units by becoming active in a way that has been associated with that pattern through previous learning. In a sense, the output units only have to 'observe' in which part of the space the hidden unit activation vector is located in order to respond appropriately.[34]

The clearest cases learned ('prototypes') will be gathered around a specific place inside a partitioning (a so-called 'hot spot'); the least clear cases will occupy places near the border between partitionings. The network will react most unambiguously to prototype cases. In Churchland's view, the knowledge possessed by an organism consists mainly of a substantial set of prototypes:

> The picture I am trying to evoke, of the cognitive lives of simple creatures, ascribes to them an organized 'library' of internal representations of various prototypical perceptual situations, situations to which prototypical *behaviors* are the computed output of the well-trained network. (1989, p. 207)

Input that results in hidden unit activation patterns close to the hot spot will evoke prototypical reactions. That is, the activation space can also be interpreted as a similarity space in which similarity is grounded in the proximity between vectors. Similar activation patterns cluster together in activation space. From this perspective, learning consists of changing the similarity gradients (Churchland & Sejnowski, 1992, pp. 168–170).

Different weight configurations can lead to roughly the same partitioning of the activation space. Therefore, Churchland (1989, pp. 177–178) suggests identifying a theory with the partitioning it produces, instead of with the weight configuration itself. The response of the output units can be interpreted as the result of an application of the theory. It is to be remembered, though, that the development of a theory computationally takes place through the changing of weights. The partitioning itself has no causal powers but depends on the setting of the weights. The notion of a partitioned activation space merely provides a useful way of understanding the functioning of the network.

It is clear that, by determining the transformation of activation patterns, weights play an essential role in neurocomputational models of cognition. We can now investigate the precise representational function of these causally decisive elements of networks. A specific set of weights, as embodied by a trained network, is a prime example of *distributed representation*. The notion of distributed representation is a fundamental one in connectionism, yet its precise meaning long remained obscure.[35] Van Gelder (1991b) has written a survey of the concept of 'distribution' as it occurs in the literature.[36] He concludes that the notion of *super(im)position* of representings[37] over a portion of representational resources is the most common theme in discussions on the nature of distributed representations (1991b, p. 42). A representation is distributed if it is representing many items while using exactly the same resources (1992, p. 176). No part of the representation should by itself be able to represent a distinct content. No matter how the representational resources are sliced, each content item must be represented over the same extent of the resources as the others (1992, p. 178). To put things differently: the representings of distinct items are superposed if they occupy the same set of representational resources (1991b, p. 43). The greater the total content that is represented by the same amount of representational resources, the more superposed the representing is (1991b, p. 44), and the more distributed the representation. Distributed representations, then, are essentially characterized by the superposition of representings.

In the case of the network described above, all the input–output associations the network can produce are represented in a single set of weights. That is, the representings of all associations are superposed in this one set of weights (1992, pp. 176–177). A single point in weight space represents in a fully distributed way all possible activation pattern transformations the network is able to accomplish.

Van Gelder (1991b, p. 55) notes that distributed representation (as characterized above) is deeply affiliated with the connectionist approach in that neural networks provide a natural medium for implementing them. Furthermore, distributed representations are theoretically significant because they are radically different from symbolic representational approaches where specific representations correlate with specific represented elements:

distributed representations are formally, semantically and computationally *incompatible* with symbolic representations. (1991a, p. 373)

Generally, in a symbolic representational scheme the structure of the domain is mirrored in the constituent structure of the representation. Different items are represented by different symbol structures. This is clearly not the case with distributed representations. In consequence, the nature of computational processes is radically altered as there is no more need for structure-sensitive rules. Semantically, the configuration of connection weights embodies the knowledge the network possesses, yet it *cannot* in any straightforward propositional sense be semantically interpreted. In fact, since a specific configuration of weights determines every reaction to every input the network is capable of, its meaning would be the total of all the potential reactions to incoming stimuli which the network is capable of, i.e. the sum of all interpretations of all possible activation pattern transformations taken together.[38] Van Gelder (1991b, p. 54, see also pp. 34, 45 and 55), therefore, rightly speaks of a 'fundamental gulf in kinds of representation'. This fundamental difference between distributed and symbolic representations provides, I think, an adequate focal point for a comparison of classical and connectionist models of cognition. It constitutes a basic disagreement about the *nature* of the states that are taken to encode the information an organism possesses, and the *way* this information can be utilized in the production of behavior. Especially with respect to the debate about folk psychology, this difference is more important than, say, the incorporation of parallelism or soft constraint satisfaction mechanisms in cognitive models, as these are more concerned with speed and implementation aspects than with cognitive architecture.

The fundamental difference between distributed and symbolic representations leads to several questions. First of all, what is the relationship between neurocomputational models, utilizing distributed representations, and folk psychology according to the literal interpretation? Second, how are behavioral phenomena like systematicity to be explained without representations possessing constituent structure? And third, how can semantic coherence be modeled without recourse to the syntactic structure of symbolic representations? I propose to end this chapter with an investigation of the first question. The second and third questions will be dealt with in Chapter 5, which will explore how neurocomputational models address the issues concerning systematicity, rationality and the frame problem.

2.5   Neurocomputational models and folk psychology

As we have seen, the neurocomputational theory of mind holds that the best way to understand cognition is in terms of the transformation of patterns of activation sustained by sets of units, describable as vector transformations. The information an organism possesses and which determines its reaction to input is represented in a distributed way in the set of weights. The obvious question is how the resulting model relates to the literal interpretation of folk psychology outlined in Chapter 1. According to this interpretation, folk psychology posits functionally discrete, causally operative mental states, which can be interpreted as involving attitudes towards a propositionally specifiable content. For a neurocomputational theory at least one aspect of folk psychology seems difficult to respect: functional discreteness.

Classical cognitive science has no problem modeling functional discreteness since specific mental states can be located computationally by pointing at the rules or concepts representing them.[39] In networks utilizing distributed representations, however, this is problematic as in every cognitive episode all weights collectively are involved:

> It simply makes no sense to ask whether or not the representation of a particular proposition plays a causal role in the network's computation . . . commonsense psychology seems to presuppose that there is generally some answer to the question of whether a particular belief or memory played a causal role in a specific cognitive episode. But if belief and memory are subserved by a connectionist network . . . such questions seem to have no clear meaning. (Ramsey et al., 1991, p. 109)

A different way to indicate the incompatibility between connectionist models using distributed representations and folk psychology is the following. According to folk psychology, people having the same belief are similar in a relevant way. Generalizations about them are possible and useful. In classical computational models these folk psychological generalizations can be preserved by supposing that all people sharing a belief have something computationally relevant in common: a symbolic string representing the content. However, in neurocomputational models nothing can play a role similar to the one performed by symbolic strings. In other words, folk psychology and classical cognitive science can see people sharing a belief as a natural kind. Connectionist models using distributed representations cannot do so; from their perspective there is, computationally speaking, only a chaotic disjunctive set (1991, p. 111).

Contrary to the above claim, it has been argued that the functionally discrete states posited by folk psychology can be identified in connectionist models after all. In particular the activation patterns themselves are suggested to be identifiable with mental states as discerned by folk psychology (O'Brien, 1991, pp. 168–169). In other words, the vector specifying a point in activation space is to be identified as the content bearing state that is causally operative in a functionally discrete way in a cognitive process. This suggestion is unconvincing, however. According to the literal interpretation of folk psychology, beliefs and desires are relatively stable states that determine our responses (including our occurrent thoughts) to incoming information. In neurocomputational models, this causally determining role is played not by activation patterns but by the set of weights of a network. Neurocomputationally speaking, the 'unit of cognition' is a point at any given time in the multi-dimensional weight space, representing the total set of weights. This point determines the nature of the activation pattern transformations and it is this which changes during learning. Therefore, the set of weights should figure in the laws of cognitive science (Churchland, 1989, pp. 177–178). As a result, activation patterns are not the right kind of phenomena to be considered comparable to folk psychological states.

O'Brien (1991, p. 169) has acknowledged that according to folk psychology beliefs are enduring states and not transient ones (see also Ramsey et al., 1991, pp. 114–115). I have had the belief that Amsterdam is a great city for a long time and even though I do not continuously actively entertain this belief (I do, from time to time, think about other things), I have actually always believed it. In other words, once one has made up one's mind, the resulting beliefs tend to 'stick a while'. In networks, by contrast, activation patterns subsist only for a short period. Therefore weights, not activation patterns, are the connectionist elements to be compared with folk psychological states.

A way to counter this rebuttal is by suggesting that a belief can be identified with a *disposition* to produce an activation pattern (O'Brien, 1991, p. 170). The network is organized in such a way that, on encountering a certain input, it will reliably produce an activation pattern that could be taken to function as the active belief. The connections and the weights associated with them together form a connectivity matrix which represents the network's disposition to generate activation patterns.[40] Mental states could then be instantiated by a combination of the activation patterns and the dispositions to generate them, as represented by the connectivity matrix (1991, p. 171). Yet, Ramsey et al. point out that this suggestion is still incompatible with the folk psychological requirement of functional discreteness:

> commonsense psychology requires that belief tokens be functionally discrete states capable of causally interacting with one another in some cognitive episodes and of remaining causally inert in other cognitive episodes. (1991, p. 115)

As indicated in Chapter 1, in folk psychological explanations of behavior or inferences, the causally relevant mental states are identifiable. But in connectionist modeling the *complete* knowledge of the network as represented in its set of weights determines the outcome. This makes it impossible to specify *which* mental states played the crucial role in the cognitive process.[41]

By way of summary, the following theses form the basis of Churchland's position:

1 Mental states as currently conceived do not exist (eliminative materialism).
2 There are no syntactically structured representations, or structure-sensitive processes.
3 Instead there is a distributed representation of information by weights.
4 Cognition consists of the transformation of (prototypical) activation patterns (theses 3 and 4 constitute the core of the neurocomputational theory of mind).

Concluding the second part of this chapter, then, I think that Churchland's suggestion that folk psychology is incompatible with the neurocomputational theory of mind is justified. If this theory is shown to be more adequate than classical cognitive science, the interpretation of mental states as propositional attitudes (computationally modeled as relations to symbolic structures) must be rejected. Rational thought would then be seen not to consist of deriving propositions from other propositions in a semantically coherent way.[42] Learning consists not of the addition or improvement of rules and concepts, but of adjusting the weights towards a minimum error level.

2.6   Conclusion

In this chapter, Fodor's interpretation of classical cognitive science and Churchland's neurocomputational perspective on cognition have been introduced. I have examined how classical cognitive science models mental states as relations to symbolic representations which can be syntactically processed in a semantically coherent way by structure-sensitive rules. The main characteristics of mental states, according to the literal interpretation of folk psychology, are preserved by such scientific theories of cognition. Thus, classical cognitive science, if empirically successful, would vindicate folk psychology. In contrast, neurocomputational models of cognition, as defended by Churchland, are incompatible with the literal interpretation of folk psychology. In these models the system's knowledge is represented by a set of weights in a distributed way. Distributed representations are fundamentally different from their symbolic counterparts. Since the weights collectively determine every cognitive process, it is impossible to say which informational states have played the crucial role in the production of behavioral output. Thus, there is no neurocomputational equivalent for functional discreteness. In order to assess the relative merits of both approaches, I will now turn to an examination of the frame problem, which is held to be a major stumbling block for the classical strategy but which is claimed to be easily solvable on a neurocomputational basis.

Notes

1 Fodor refers to Descartes and Locke (Fodor, 1981b, p. 26) as well as to Hume, Berkeley, Kant, John Stuart Mill, and James (Fodor, 1981a, p. 131). See also Haselager (1992).

2 It is interesting to note the similarities with Churchland's use of the analogy with alchemy to indicate the problematic status of mental states as ordinarily conceived. See also Meijsing (1993, pp. 66–68).

3 Mentalistic expressions were thought to be respectable only in as far as they were translatable into expressions referring to behavior, otherwise they could be discarded as being unnecessary or meaningless (Skinner, 1974, p. 19).

4 Intervening variables are completely reducible to empirical facts, or, to put it differently, they summarize the facts. This is in contrast with hypothetical constructs which are not reducible to empirical facts but should be interpreted as postulated unobserved entities, processes or events (MacCorquodale & Meehl, 1948; Sanders, 1972, pp. 232–252).

5 Ryle disapproved of the 'intellectualist legend' according to which intelligent behavior is the result of the execution of propositional rules. His argument provides a good illustration of Haugeland's paradox of mechanical reason, given above. Ryle says: 'The consideration of propositions is itself an operation the execution of which can be more or less intelligent, less or more stupid. But if, for any operation to be intelligently executed, a prior theoretical operation had first to be performed and performed intelligently, it would be a logical impossibility for anyone ever to break into the circle' (1949, p. 31; see also Fodor, 1981b, p. 16).

6 There are parallels between Ryle's approach and Dennett's instrumentalism, as Rorty (1982) has indicated.

7 Natural kinds are taken to be properties referred to by predicates that are used to formulate natural (in this case neurophysiological) laws. The adjective 'natural' indicates that the taxonomy thus achieved is, at least to a considerable extent, not interest related but rather based on nature 'as we find it'. The latter suggestion is, of course, not without opposition (Putnam, 1981; 1992), but it is still common practice to distinguish between natural and artificial kinds, even though the distinction might not be as clear-cut as to form a dichotomy.

8 Compare: what causes the closing of a door? A 'door closer'. What is a door closer? Something that causes a door to get closed. Criticisms of this kind concerning the 'emptiness' of functionalism have been put forward by, among others, Skinner (1986, pp. 88–89), Churchland (1989, pp. 12–15) and Searle (1992, pp. 42–43, 53). Although these criticisms of functionalism are essentially correct, they are somewhat beside the point with respect to classical cognitive science. They do not constitute a valid criticism of classical cognitive science as long as it can provide the story behind the causal powers of the functionally individuated

mental states. It should be noted that Fodor (1981b, p. 12) explicitly mentions the circular character of 'pure' functionalism.

9 Turing machines are theoretical specifications of a certain kind of computer, though they can be (and have been) actually implemented. A Turing machine consists of a storage medium (a tape) and an active part (the head) that reads, writes and moves along the tape. At each moment the head is in a particular state which specifies what it will do in response to the information it will find on the tape. The complete set of possible internal states is specified in a so-called 'machine table' (Haugeland, 1985, pp. 133–140). The standard computers of today are of a different architecture (attributed to Von Neumann). These Von Neumann machines have the same theoretical capabilities as universal Turing machines but are far more useful for practical purposes (1985, pp. 140–146).

10 Indeed, it has to be noted that Putnam (1988b) no longer defends any version of functionalism.

11 It is not necessary to combine the notion of a computer with symbol processing. It is sometimes suggested that, in a general sense, any physical system that can be seen to compute a function could be called a computer. Thus, even threshing machines or the stone constellation at Stonehenge would qualify as computers (Churchland & Sejnowski, 1992, pp. 65–69; Haugeland, 1985, pp. 258–259, n. 6). However, Kirsh (1990, pp. 341, 364, n. 2) points out that some way of tracking the trajectory of informational states must be possible, if we want to be sure that we are dealing with computational instead of merely complex causal systems.

12 The word 'book' consists of, for instance, ink on paper, or sound-waves in the air. If I write the word 'book' twice, I have created two tokens of the single symbol type 'book'.

13 A proposition is not to be equated with a sentence, but is expressed by it. It is abstract in the sense that it is not in space and time like a sentence is. The existence of a proposition is objective since it does not depend on it being thought, i.e. a proposition is mind independent. It is language independent in the sense that sentences in different languages that have the same meaning express the same proposition. Within a language, the same proposition can be expressed by different sentences as long as they have the same content.

14 Fodor sees a strong connection between computation and propositional content: 'the notion of computation is intrinsically connected to such semantical concepts as implication, confirmation, and logical consequence. Specifically, a computation is a transformation of representations which respects these sorts of semantic relations. It is, however, a point of definition that such semantic relations hold only among the sort of things to which propositional content can be ascribed; the sorts of things which can be said to *mean that* P' (1983, p. 5).

15 Fodor has provided a criterion on the basis of which to separate organisms and/or systems for which a representational theory of thought is plausible from those for which it is not. Only systems that can respond selectively to non-nomic properties of the stimulus are candidates for the ascription of mental representations (1986c, pp. 10–11).

16 It should be noted that showing how the manipulation of symbols can be made to respect the semantic relations between their contents is not the same as explaining how the semantic content of symbols arises. That is, questions concerning mechanical rationality should not be confused with questions concerning intentionality (Fodor, 1981b, pp. 20–24). Turing answered the former, not the latter. He indicated, to borrow a phrase from Dennett, how syntactic machines can mimic semantic ones.

17 According to Fodor and Pylyshyn, classical cognitive science is based upon two central ideas. '*The first idea* is that it is possible to construct languages in which certain features of the syntactic structures of formulas correspond systematically to certain of their semantic features. Intuitively, the idea is that in such languages the syntax of a formula encodes its meaning; most especially, those aspects of its meaning that determine its role in inference. All the artificial languages that are used for logic have this property and English has it more or less. Classicists believe that it is a crucial property of the Language of Thought' (1988, p. 28). See note 19 for the second idea.

18 There are, of course, certain limiting conditions, which in the case of keys have to do with their solidity.

19 In addition to the first idea (see note 17), a second one is crucial to cognitive science: '*The second main idea* underlying the Classical treatment of mental processes is that it is possible to devise machines whose function is the transformation of symbols, and whose operations are sensitive to the syntactical structure of the symbols that they operate upon. This is the Classical conception of the computer: it's what the various architectures that derive from Turing and Von Neumann machines all have in common' (Fodor & Pylyshyn, 1988, p. 30).

20 An additional distinction can be made between a component, referring to a part of the represented item, and a constituent, referring to a part of a representation. Furthermore, there can be symbol constituents and token constituents (these reflect the semantic and physical aspects of the constituent, respectively). These notions will play only a minor role in what follows.

21 It should be kept in mind, however, that the suggestion of productivity is based on an idealization and presupposes a competence–performance distinction (Fodor, 1994a, p. 107). After all, during one's lifetime one can only entertain a finite number of thoughts due to non-cognitive causes such as death. It is not entirely certain that there really is no upper limit imposed by inherently cognitive constraints. This use of an idealization does not form a major problem for the claim of compositionality, as, first of all, it does seem to be quite reasonable and, secondly, systematicity forms another and more important argument for constituent compositionality.

22 This tendency is strengthened by the fact that sentences are normally taken to be expressions of (underlying) thoughts (although this is contested by e.g. Dennett, 1992, pp. 244–246, who holds that no definite, concrete thoughts have to be present 'behind' linguistic expressions).

23 Sterelny (1990, p. 183) doubts that animal cognition is completely systematic. However, the examples he gives to illustrate his doubts are, as he himself acknowledges, far from decisive. Somewhat more forcefully, Dennett (1991a, p. 27) has remarked that Fodor's claim of full non-linguistic systematicity is 'pretty obviously false'. As he says, there may be organisms that we might consider to be able to have the thought that a lion wants to eat them, but not that they want to eat the lion. However, though it may be granted that it is almost unimaginable or extremely unlikely that the organisms referred to will ever have a thought like the latter, this is not the same as showing that it is impossible for the organism to have such a thought. Still, I think that Sterelny and Dennett are right in pointing out that one should not accept the claim of full systematicity without reservation. I will return briefly to this point in Chapter 5.

24 For instance, in logical and natural languages tokens of expression types (i.e. physical instantiations of them) are concatenated in time (speech) or in space (text). It is essential to a concatenative mode of combination that the token constituents can be linked or ordered without altering them in any way. The mentalese formulas in the mind are like sentences in that they consist of concatenations of symbol types. These formulas are physically represented in the brain through a systematic concatenation of their tokenings.

25 A representation x is a constituent of representation y if the content of x is semantically part of the content of y, and if the token of x is syntactically part of the token of y.

26 However, it is not beyond doubt that a representational system that can explain productivity and systematicity really has to have a constituent structure. It is at this point that recent investigations of distributed representations enter the debate, which I will discuss in Chapter 5.

27 There are strong similarities with Newell and Simon's conception of 'physical symbol systems', also with respect to the constituent structure of complex symbols (e.g. 1981, p. 40). This is not to deny substantial differences between Fodor on the one hand and Newell and Simon on the other, as they disagree with respect to the innate character of the representational system, for instance.

28 It bears emphasis that the syntactic structure of the LOT is of primary importance for the explanation of rationality, whereas its constituent structure is important for explaining systematicity.

29 Connectionism allows for a great variety in the pattern of connections between units. Usually, units are connected not to all others but only to subsets of the complete network.

Also, it is not always the case that units have incoming as well as outgoing connections with other units. For instance, in feedforward networks some units have only outgoing and others only incoming connections with other units.

30 Different, linear or non-linear (e.g. sigmoid) functions can be utilized for the calculation of the net input, the activation, and the output. Collectively, these three calculations determine what output a unit produces in response to the received input. The total computation (when non-linear) is sometimes addressed as a 'squashing function' (Churchland & Sejnowski, 1992, pp. 109–110, 168). The connectivity matrix and the squashing function together can be thought of as a kind of pasta or mincing machine that is fed with activation patterns and produces other activation patterns.

31 Feedforward and interactive networks form two main classes of networks in connectionist modeling (recurrent networks can be thought of as constituting a third class). In feedforward networks, the activation flows in one direction only, from input to output units. Recurrent networks are characterized by a feedback loop, through which a certain layer of units direct their output back into a part of the network that will eventually activate them again. In interactive networks, the activation flow follows no general direction. The output is represented by the pattern of activity into which the network as a whole stabilizes. As far as the nature and function of distributed representations is concerned, there are no qualitative differences between these classes of networks.

32 Of course, more levels are possible. In the brain, Churchland (1989, p. 202) suggests, the number of levels that jointly operate as one network lies somewhere between 5 and 50.

33 This learning rule (for instance, the delta rule) is a general mathematical specification of how to adjust weights, and has no connection with the task at hand, or with the representational content of the activation patterns or weights. The learning rule, or any other rules governing the calculations performed by the units in the network (like the propagation rule calculating the net input of a unit, the activation rule calculating the new activation of a unit, and the output rule calculating the output of a unit), should therefore not be confused with rules as used in computational models in classical cognitive science. There are many different learning rules currently being studied.

34 It is, of course, the setting of the weights attached to the connections between the hidden and output units which makes these 'observational' powers possible in a non-homuncular way.

35 Feldman says about the notion of 'distributed representation': 'The problem is that people have been using this term to denote everything from a fully holographic model to one where two units help code a concept; thus, the term has lost its usefulness' (1989, p. 72; see also Van Gelder, 1991b, p. 35).

36 Van Gelder discusses extendedness, microfeatural semantics, coarse coding, equipotentiality, holism, and superposition as suggested characteristics of distributed representations.

37 Van Gelder refrains from speaking of superposed representations, and prefers the phrase 'superposed representings' to stress that there is only one single representational item representing all content (1991b, p. 43).

38 Compare Haugeland's formulation of this point: 'the notion of separate tokens for distinct contents is undermined by distributed representations, to the extent that *there is just one "big" token representing many different contents at once*' (1991, p. 65, n. 4, my emphasis; see also Van Gelder, 1991b, p. 46).

39 This functional discreteness of classical computational models is put to good use in expert systems which can be made to answer 'how' and 'why' questions about their reasoning processes rather easily. They only have to produce the rules and symbols used by the system at the indicated moment.

40 In Churchland's terminology, the connection matrix embodies the theory possessed by the neural network.

41 Heil has suggested that even though there is a separation between the computationally and representationally relevant elements in a network, it is still possible to *describe* the operations of a network in folk psychological terms: 'Networks . . . might mimic systems described folk theoretically. Their doing so, however, would be explicable by reference not to propositions encoded but, rather, to (something like) the obtaining of various connection

strengths over the system . . . Hence, although it might operate in accord with familiar folk principles, it would not act *on* those principles' (1991, p. 130). However, this would imply that a folk psychological explanation of behavior (as in: 'he hit you because he thought you had betrayed him') is not to be taken literally. The functionally discrete mental states identified by folk psychology do not, as such, play a causal role (it was not literally the specific thought that you had betrayed him that made him hit you). Vice versa, you can speak about the actual causal processes going on in the network, but then it is impossible to indicate functionally discrete states. Either way, connectionist models using distributed representations are incompatible with this aspect of the literal reading of folk psychology.

42 Churchland says: 'In place of propositional attitudes and logical inferences from one to another . . . we can conceive of persons as the seat of vectorial attitudes and various nonlinear transformations from one vector to another' (1989, p. 127).

3

The Frame Problem

Among the many problems classical cognitive science encounters in its project of explaining rationality in a mechanical way, an interesting and hotly debated one is the so-called 'frame problem'. Simply put, people have an amazing ability to quickly *see* the *relevant* consequences of certain changes in a situation. They *understand* what is going on and are able to draw the *right* conclusions quickly, even if this means retracting earlier beliefs and adopting new ones. The problem is how to model this ability computationally. What are the computational mechanisms that enable people to make common-sense inferences? In particular, how can a computational model be prevented from fruitlessly engaging in time-consuming, irrelevant inferences? The frame problem, as originally understood, refers to the wearisome point that it seemed necessary to explicitly specify everything that would *not* change after an event, in order to enable computational systems to deal adequately with a changing world.

As Pylyshyn notes in the introduction to a collection of important essays on the frame problem (*The robot's dilemma*, 1987), many objections to classical cognitive science are based on the more or less philosophical arguments that computers cannot 'genuinely' have beliefs or desires, that they cannot 'really' understand or have feelings. But the frame problem is different from these philosophical worries in that it is 'a real *technical* problem', raising a more empirical issue: it questions whether the attempts to model general intelligence will achieve a satisfactory level of *performance* (1987, pp. vii–viii).

The discussion about the frame problem has been somewhat chaotic and even perplexing, as there seems to be little agreement on what exactly the frame problem is, what the main reasons for its emergence are, how it should be solved, and what would count as a solution. I will not discuss every possible (mis)interpretation of the frame problem as this would only result in a dizzy-making display of names and shades of meaning. To indicate the variety of labels, it should suffice to say that the question has been raised whether or not the frame problem can correctly be interpreted as (being related to), in alphabetical order: the bookkeeping problem, the extended prediction problem, the inertia problem, the problem of the metaphysical adequacy of representations, the problem of non-demonstrative inference, the problem of ordinariness, the problem of persistence, the prediction problem, the qualification problem, the ramification problem, the truth-maintenance problem, and the updating problem. Rather than creating a catalogue or dictionary, I will trace the main strands in the debate in a way that is relevant to cognitive science and the problem of mechanical rationality.

A first step towards clarity has been made by Janlert (1987, pp. 3–6) who claims that two general approaches to intelligence can be distinguished: a *deductivist* and a *non-deductivist* one. This division lines up quite well with the familiar distinction between 'neats' and 'scruffies' in AI, respectively (Thagard, 1988, p. 3), where the neats (like McCarthy and McDermott) give a central role to deductive logic in investigating intelligence, while the scruffies (for instance, Minsky and Thagard) favor a more psychological and less formal approach.

Hard-nosed deductivists prefer to see the frame problem as a purely technical issue in *logic* and reject any more general interpretation of it. The frame problem initially manifested itself in the work of the deductivists, which I will, therefore, analyze first. The non-deductivists view the frame problem as an obstacle encountered when trying to understand the *psychological* mechanisms involved in common-sense reasoning. I will argue that the psychologically oriented strategy is a more fruitful way of addressing the frame problem than the exclusively logical approach. I will claim that within the non-deductivist group, two different interpretations of the frame problem can be discerned. The first subgroup sees the frame problem as something to be solved by the development of a good *representational* format, whereas the second subgroup expects progress from a better understanding of non-demonstrative *inference*.

3.1 The deductive approach to modeling intelligence

The emphasis on a good model of the world and the use of a simple logical language (FOPC: first order predicate calculus) are characteristic of what Janlert (1987, pp. 4–5) calls the 'deductive approach'. Since its focus is on intelligence in general, not specifically on human intelligence, it is only tangentially related to psychology. It is relevant to our investigation, however, because the frame problem originally (and clearly) showed up in the deductive approach.

The approach of McCarthy and Hayes (1969) is a primary example of the deductive strategy, and it is in their work that the frame problem was discussed first. McCarthy and Hayes (1969, p. 463) wanted to design a general, flexible intelligence: a computational system that decides what to do by inferring that a certain strategy will lead to a certain goal. They state that general intelligence consists of an epistemological and a heuristic component (1969, p. 466; see also Janlert, 1987, p. 3).[1] The epistemological component contains a representation or model of the world. They indicate that in modeling intelligence a precise choice of what to represent is of primary importance (1969, p. 467). This common-sense view or model of the world is to be represented by sets of sentences in a suitable formal logical language.[2] The heuristic component contains the problem solving and planning mechanisms necessary to engage in goal-directed reasoning. Its way of inferring consists of proving a conclusion deductively valid in a formal language (1969, p. 468).

A central role in McCarthy and Hayes' construction of an adequate epistemological component is played by the concept of 'situation': a situation is a complete state of the universe at an instant of time (1969, p. 477; see also Janlert, 1987, p. 5). A situation cannot, of course, be specified completely, but it can be described sufficiently in terms of facts. A set of sentences describes a situation. McCarthy and Hayes also introduce 'fluents', which specify partial information about situations, for example: time(s), which specifies the time associated with a situation s; in(x,y,s), which indicates that x is in location y in situation s; has(x,y,s), signifying that x has y in s; and result(p,a,s), meaning that action a performed by person p undertaken in situation s will yield a certain result (e.g. a new situation). Fluents can be interpreted as indicating that it is true that in a certain situation a certain fact is the case (1969, p. 478; see also McDermott, 1987b, p. 114).

Situations can change because of actions or events. The effects of an action or event in a certain situation are specified in rules, which take the form of conditionals. A description of the facts of the new situation can be deduced from the facts of the previous situation and these rules. The effect-specifying rules are sometimes referred to as 'laws of ability' or as 'hypotheses' (1969, pp. 480, 487).[3] For example:

$$\text{has}(p,k,s) \wedge \text{fits}(k,sf) \wedge \text{at}(p,sf,s) \rightarrow \text{open}(sf,\text{result}(p,\text{opens}(sf,k),s))$$

This rule states the following: if person p has key k in situation s, and the key k fits the safe sf, and person p is near the safe sf in situation s, then the safe sf will be open as a result of the action open undertaken by person p with the key k on the safe sf in situation s.

Now, the frame problem in the original sense is that in order to deduce a new situation from an old one after an action or event, one has to specify through these kinds of rules not only what changes because of an action or an event, *but also what remains the same*. For instance, in order to know that the color of someone's hair has not changed after using a key, the system has to deduce that this fact is (still) the case in the new situation. But it can only deduce this fact if there are rules explicitly stating that using a key does not result in a change of hair color. Since most events or actions leave most facts unchanged, it follows that a great number of rules are needed to specify non-changes (Hayes, 1987, p. 125). These 'frame axioms', as they are usually called, not only are often difficult to formulate (Ginsberg, 1987, pp. 5–6), but also consume most of the processing time of the system: it will spend valuable time deducing non-changes. In reasonably complex (i.e. normal) situations the number of frame axioms is overwhelming (in the case of m actions and n fluents one would need $m \times n$

frame axioms (McCarthy & Hayes, 1969, p. 487; see also Hayes, 1987, p. 125). As a result, the system gets lost in performing irrelevant computations. This, in essence, is the frame problem as originally encountered.[4] In order to clearly separate it from other interpretations, I will follow McDermott (1987a, p. 106) in addressing the original frame problem as the *inertia* problem: how to make a computational system decide efficiently what does *not* change after an event or action.[5]

In this sense, the frame problem has been an important issue for the logicists in AI. Indeed, McDermott thinks that the frame problem, properly understood as the inertia problem, is interesting only to the group of people working in a purely logical approach to AI,[6] i.e. for those who believe that inference should be reduced to deduction (1987a, pp. 105, 109; 1987b, p. 116). However, McDermott, being a main representative of this group, has concluded that a *strictly* deductive approach to common-sense rationality fails on the inertia problem:

> The lesson we should draw is that logic has severe limitations as a theory of inference, in spite of its tremendous appeal as a unifying theory of knowledge representation . . . in fact almost all inference is nondeductive . . . What we must avoid is the 'tyranny of technicality'. (1987a, p. 116)[7]

But this has not led to an abandonment of the logical approach to common-sense reasoning.

An important suggestion with respect to the inertia problem is to condense all frame axioms into one general rule stating that if a fact is true in a situation and cannot be proven to be untrue in the situation arising after an event, then it is still true (McDermott, 1987b, p. 115). Standard first order logic is unable to deal with this, however, because of its *monotonicity*: as a result of adding new axioms, the number of valid conclusions can only increase and, once established, truths cannot be withdrawn. But a logical system incorporating the suggested general rule is no longer monotonic because it is possible that on the arrival or production of new information something that formerly could not be proven untrue now *can* be proven untrue. Hence, truths can turn into falsities. Many common-sense beliefs and inferences are defeasible in the sense that their truth values regularly do change on the basis of new information.[8] In order to deal with this defeasibility, intelligence must be flexible. An intelligent being must be able to retract conclusions that turn out to be wrong (Ginsberg, 1987, p. 1).

It has, therefore, been proposed to strengthen the deductive approach by extending it with non-monotonic logic (McDermott, 1987b, p. 115).[9] A logical system is non-monotonic if adding axioms to it can make theorems disappear (1987a, p. 108). As Kyburg, Loui, and Carlson comment:

> It is only a small exaggeration to say that non-monotonic reasoning was invented to deal with the Frame Problem. (1990, pp. ix–x)

Non-monotonic logic has been heavily studied in recent years and is generally accepted as an interesting area of research. Serious doubts, however, have been raised about the value of purely logical investigations for cognitive science.[10] There are very few examples of interesting applications of non-monotonic logic to psychologically realistic and interesting phenomena (however, see Hoenkamp, 1987). Indeed, it is stated in the introduction to a volume on non-monotonic reasoning that formal work in non-monotonic logic is unlikely to lead to immediate advances in the actual modeling of common-sense reasoning (Ginsberg, 1987, p. 15). Non-monotonic logic will contribute general purpose solution finding methods (so-called 'weak methods') to AI. However, Ginsberg claims that AI is not mature enough to have much use for such methods. Most problems it deals with are just too difficult for general solutions to be practical. It is, in my view, perhaps better to refrain from using such normative notions as 'maturity'. A less suggestive way of indicating the value of weak methods for AI is given by Laird, Newell, and Rosenbloom (1988/1993). They argue that weak methods do play a central role in attaining intelligence because they are used as 'a last resort' whenever the situation becomes 'knowledge-lean' (1988/1993, pp. 510–511). When all knowledge available for solving the task has proved to be unhelpful, a solution might still be found by weak methods. However, people normally do seem to use what they know. Although valuable in themselves, general or 'weak' methods are of little help, therefore, in attempts to model abilities that depend upon the use of a large amount of knowledge.

Along similar lines, Forbus has claimed that it is 'inappropriate and inadvisable' to understand common-sense reasoning purely in terms of non-monotonic logic mainly because

> if one is serious about formalizing commonsense reasoning, one must necessarily focus on that which commonsense is about. (Forbus in Etherington, Forbus, Ginsberg, Israel, and Lifschitz, 1989, p. 501)

A similarily sceptical judgment concerning the value of non-monotonic logic for AI's attempts to understanding common-sense reasoning is given by Krause and Clark (1993, pp. 191–192). They state that the formal models of practical reasoning developed by non-monotonic logic are extremely complex and generally computationally intractable. They indicate that non-monotonic logic is as distinct from common-sense reasoning as the way current chess programs operate is alien to actual human thought processes in chess. In other words, non-monotonic logic is psychologically *unrealistic*, a 'cognitive wheel' (Dennett, 1987a, pp. 58–60).[11]

To round off this section, it can be concluded that the frame problem emerges most clearly in the purely deductive approach as the inertia problem. Non-monotonic logic, being an important extension of the deductive approach, is of limited use to AI because it neglects the importance of domain-specific knowledge and lacks psychological plausibility.

Since McCarthy and Hayes' (1969) article, the frame problem has become known outside the field of logic and is discussed within cognitive science as a serious problem for any approach to modeling intelligence. In this discussion the frame problem is interpreted in a more general sense than the inertia problem. Within cognitive science the frame problem is perceived as I described at the beginning of this chapter: how are we able to respond adequately, by virtue of our knowledge and reasoning capacities, to a changing world? How to explain our ability to quickly see the relevant consequences of an event? In this sense, the frame problem is no longer strictly related to the question of non-change, which led to the difficulty of how to avoid a multiplicity of frame axioms. Indeed, I would like to suggest that from the perspective of cognitive science the problem of change *is* the heart of the matter. The fact that the difficulties involved in answering these questions first showed up as the problem of inertia is, in my view, merely a *coincidental* consequence of the fact that McCarthy and Hayes pursued a purely deductive approach. I believe that cognitive science is justified in broadening the original interpretation of the frame problem. In this broad sense, the frame problem has also been addressed by non-deductive approaches.

3.2   The non-deductive approach to modeling intelligence

The non-deductivist approach to modeling intelligence addresses the frame problem as an issue of dealing with change and is more psychologically oriented in that (obviously) it allows for non-deductive reasoning methods.[12] The problem of coping with a changing world is a difficult one and can easily seem unsolvable. After all, the number of potential changes seems infinite and the idea that we must always examine all, and rule out most of them, is clearly preposterous (McDermott, 1987b, pp. 116–117). From this perspective, even the question of how a system can be made to predict *all* the possible consequences of an event,[13] let alone predicting the *relevant* ones, seems unanswerable.

A different perspective on the issue can be achieved by considering reasoning about action. There are any number of possible conditions whose actuality would prevent an action from being successfully carried out.[14] We seem to know about these conditions, for we immediately gather the imminent failure of an intended action if we find that one of these conditions obtains. Yet, the number of possible conditions that could cause a simple action to fail is enormous. We do not contemplate each and every one of these conditions, but instead are able to avoid this problem by reasoning on the basis that everything is normal. As Hayes (1987, p. 127; see also Dennett, 1987a, p. 56) says: if we could specify what 'everything is normal' meant, then 'we would have the frame problem licked.'

McDermott has argued that the frame problem, though challenging from a logical point of view, is not a significant obstacle to AI precisely because AI is not committed to finding general and deductive solutions. The frame problem is *computationally* (as opposed to logically) negligible because it can be solved efficiently in concrete cases by the so-called 'sleeping dog strategy' (McDermott, 1987b, pp. 115–116; see also Haugeland, 1987, pp. 84–85).

In this strategy, only the specified direct consequences of an event are processed, while everything else (the sleeping dogs) is simply ignored.

As McDermott says, in practical AI research *specific* models are developed and used to make inferences. That is, the context in which they operate provides additional information and thereby forms a useful constraining factor on the inferences which can be made (McDermott, 1987a, pp. 106–107; 1987b, pp. 116–119; Van Bendegem, 1991/1992, pp. 37–38). Because appropriate and restricted knowledge-representing structures are present, the problem of avoiding an infinite number of irrelevant inferences does not arise. McDermott (1987a, p. 107) admits, though, that there are 'interesting technical questions' concerning the selection of the right models and their subsequent use. Still, he claims that thanks to the sleeping dog strategy

> it is still the case, as it has been since 1970, that no working AI program has ever been bothered at all by the frame problem. (1987b, p. 116)

He is scornful of philosophers for not accepting this solution and for unwarrantedly raising the stakes by increasing the complexity of the situations and events to be dealt with to such an extent that he doubts whether even humans would be able to deal with them satisfactorily (1987b, p. 117). In other words, McDermott argues that up to a certain level of complexity the sleeping dog strategy works satisfactorily or at least well enough to avoid talk about a general frame problem in AI. Above that level, it would be unreasonable to expect a computational system to accurately predict all consequences of an event. All in all, McDermott claims, the frame problem as discussed by philosophers is not a genuine problem of AI. Hence the title of his article: 'We've been framed: or, why AI is innocent of the frame problem'.

However, McDermott's position on the computational insignificance of the frame problem is not completely satisfactory. He is correct in pointing out that, contrary to logic, AI need not result in general solutions but can instead address concrete, context-embedded cases. He is wrong, however, in suggesting that this turns the frame problem into a trivial matter and that AI has actually succeeded in modeling common-sense reasoning under ordinary circumstances.

This becomes clear if one realizes that, as Haugeland (1987, pp. 82, 84) has noted, the sleeping dog strategy answers the question of how a system can ignore all the irrelevant updating questions by stating, in effect: 'let everything lie, unless there is some positive reason not to.' This raises the question of how cognitive systems obtain these positive reasons. The obvious reply is that people *use what they know* about the domain at hand in their reasoning about events. The difficult question is *how* people manage using what they know to efficiently guide their reasoning. McDermott (1987b, p. 120) more or less ignores this design question by suggesting that computational systems are able to deal with normal situations and only fail in situations that are so complex or strange that humans would fail as well.

This implies that AI systems should be able to behave at a normal level in common-sense situations. Yet, the problem is precisely that currently there are *no* such systems and that they are not likely to appear shortly. To be sure, AI systems can be impressively successful in restricted domains of application. But with respect to general reasoning about common-sense situations, much remains to be accomplished. As Fodor (1987a, p. 146) remarks with his usual candor, the AI systems that McDermott claims have not been bothered by the frame problem are 'by any standards, ludicrously stupid' (for a similar but more polite dismissal of McDermott's positive evaluation of the sleeping dog approach, see Hayes, 1987, pp. 129–130).

The same point is made in a different way by Lormand (1990, pp. 363–365). He argues that the sleeping dog strategy is merely intended to deal with the original frame problem (the inertia problem, which Lormand calls 'the persistence problem'). This is to be distinguished from what Lormand calls 'the holism of change problem', finding out which facts do change. Thus, Lormand claims, the sleeping dog strategy can solve the persistence (inertia) problem without needing to solve the holism of change problem. Yet, he says, the holism of change problem needs to be solved in order to create intelligent machines to deal with the world.

In my view, the frame problem is relevant to psychologically interested cognitive scientists in as far as it sheds any light on the difficulties encountered in getting machines reasoning intelligibly about a changing world (which was, after all, McCarthy and Hayes' original intent). Because of the specifics of the approach chosen, the problem of inertia showed up. If AI can solve this problem in a way that does *not* really contribute to a solution of the larger problem then, from a cognitive science perspective, nothing much has been achieved. This is why cognitive scientists are so interested to see whether the sleeping dog strategy is of any use for the larger issues. If this is found not to be the case, then the sleeping dog strategy is not even very interesting.

I conclude, then, that the frame problem can rightfully be interpreted as a problem of dealing with change, and that this is a computationally far from solved problem. Seeing the relevant consequences of an event is made possible by an understanding of the situation. One reaches an understanding of the situation by using what one knows. The real difficulty underlying the frame problem is how the *relevant* pieces of knowledge are found and how they influence one's understanding of the situation, i.e. how they guide the generation of explanatory hypotheses and bear on their acceptability.

Regarding this issue, it seems to me that two general strategies can be discerned. First of all, one can see the frame problem as ultimately a question concerning the ontological structure of the world which should then be represented in such a way that the sleeping dog strategy will work. According to the (what I will call) *representational* approach, in order to solve the frame problem one has to (a) find the 'right' ontology and (b) represent it in a computationally convenient way. Secondly, one can see the frame problem as an *inferential* problem concerning non-demonstrative reasoning. That is, how, on the basis of what one knows and perceives, can one quickly generate a plausible interpretation or hypothesis to explain what is going on? This leads to an examination of the problems concerning induction, abduction, and inference to the best explanation.[15]

The difference between these two suggestions is a matter of emphasis because the course of the reasoning process is strongly influenced by the way in which the representation of information is structured (cf. Haugeland, 1987, pp. 80–82). Therefore, any solution to the frame problem should devote considerable attention to representing information about the world in such a way that it can be efficiently *used*. The disparity in emphasis can perhaps best be described as follows. The representational approach is characterized by a strong interest in questions of what kind of information should be regarded as primary and what kind of representation is most suited for representing this information in such a way that the 'right' inferences will follow almost automatically. The inferential approach focuses on the reasoning process itself and investigates how more global characteristics of what one knows can guide the search for plausible inferences.

The frame problem as a representational issue

A good illustration of the representational approach to the frame problem can be found in Janlert (1987). He gives the following description of the frame problem:

> The general frame problem is the problem of finding a representational form permitting a changing, complex world to be efficiently and adequately represented. (1987, pp. 7–8)

That is, instead of trying to capture inference as a form of deductive reasoning with the inertia problem as a result, cognitive science should address common-sense reasoning as the problem of representing knowledge in a usable way. The main issue is how to *correctly* represent the world in a computationally *efficient* manner. In order to explain his definition of the frame problem and to clarify his (what I call) representational approach to it, Janlert uses three conceptual distinctions; explicit versus implicit, primitive versus non-primitive and primary versus secondary.

Explicit representations are represented concretely in the system, or, to put it another way, explicit representations are actually present (i.e. syntactically tokened) in the system. As only explicitly represented information can be processed directly, it is this information that is immediately available to the reasoning process. By processing explicitly represented information the system can derive and explicitly represent formerly *implicit* information. Implicit information is only 'potentially' represented in that it is not yet, but can become, explicitly represented and thereby available for processing.

Primitive information is foundational in the sense that it provides the basic axioms from which *non-primitive* information can be derived. The distinction of primitive versus non-primitive addresses the informational importance of knowledge, whereas the explicit–implicit distinction focuses on the representational status of the information represented.

Finally, Janlert distinguishes between *primary* and *secondary* phenomena.[16] In his use of this distinction, secondary phenomena are mere epiphenomena and in principle completely reducible to primary phenomena (1987, p. 36).

By means of this third distinction, Janlert seeks to specify a metaphysics[17] of the world which can help determine what should be considered as the primitive information. Insight into the structure of the world, its primary entities, categories and principles, fosters a wise choice of a representational format. In other words, the decision as to what information should be regarded as primitive is to be based on an adequate primary–secondary categorization of the world (1987, p. 20, see also p. 36). Thus, Janlert (1987, p. 33) views knowledge representation in AI as 'experimental ontology'. Although finding the ontological structure of the world seems a daunting task, Janlert's analysis is at least implicitly supported by one of the discoverers of the frame problem, Patrick Hayes:

> I don't think the frame problem is unreal or insignificant: it seems to point up a basic error in the way we try to describe the everyday world. We aren't carving up nature at the right ontological joints, if you ask me. But time will tell. (1987, pp. 129–130, see also p. 127)

Other authors have also indicated that the frame problem can be seen as arising out of the difficulties with respect to pinning down what common sense takes to be its natural kinds (e.g. Elgot-Drapkin, Miller, & Perlis, 1987, p. 27).

A decision on *what* has to be represented has to be supplemented by a decision on *how* to represent and process it. The information represented should not only be adequate, but also be efficiently represented. The straightforward suggestion that all primitive information should be repesented explicitly (e.g. by specific symbolic structure) has to be rejected because, as Janlert (1987, p. 36) notes: 'Explicitness is in the end self-defeating.' He therefore suggests that, in order to avoid the frame problem, the non-deductive approach has to find the right metaphysics and represent it *intrinsically* in the system (1987, pp. 2, 37–38). As the notion of 'intrinsic representation' plays an important role in the representational approach to the frame problem, it is worthwhile to examine it further.

As a first clue to understand what Janlert is getting at, the concept 'intrinsicness' should be understood as stressing that any approach to the frame problem should try to refrain from completely describing the world: it should avoid having to 'spell it all out'. For if everything is explicitly represented, this poses great problems in quickly locating a particular represented item (1987, p. 36). An influential and more thorough analysis of intrinsic representations is given by Palmer (1978). A representation is intrinsic if a representation of a relation has the same inherent constraints as the relation itself (1978, pp. 271–272). That is, the constraints are not arbitrary and not imposed from outside but follow from the inherent structure of the representation. Palmer warns that the notion of 'inherent structure' is, philosophically speaking, far from clear, though it is intuitively clear enough to be useful. The idea is that the representationally inherent constraints are similar to the constraints inherent in what is represented. Haugeland (1987) gives the example of a scale model which may help to convey what the notion of inherent structure is intended to capture. A good scale model has a structure similar to the domain it models, the main difference being, of course, the scale. Therefore, every consequence of an event in the actual world will be precisely matched by the consequences of the small-scale event in the small-scale representational world. The result is, as Haugeland puts it, that

> representations of side effects of events are just side effects of the representations of those events. (1987, p. 86)

According to Janlert, the issue of how to represent the right information in the appropriate way is essential to both the deductive and the non-deductive approaches. Perceiving the issue in this way, the main source of problems for logical approaches lies in the expressiveness of propositional logic.[18] Logic in itself has few isomorphies with the world. As many different ontologies can be expressed in logic, all the constraints and relations found to obtain in the world have to be specified explicitly in the representational system. Indeed, as Palmer (1978, p. 296) notes, propositions represent properties and relations not intrinsically but extrinsically. Not only the objects have to be explicitly represented, but also the way they are related to one another. Hence, after an event, representations of these objects as well as their relations might have to be updated. In this way, the frame problem is seen to arise as a result of the use of a propositional-logical kind of representation. As Haugeland says:

> the frame problem may be an artifact of certain theoretical assumptions – specifically, the selection of a certain general form or kind of representation. If the problem arises only when there is an explicit/implicit distinction, and if not all representational systems support such a distinction, then, presumably, some representational systems would avoid the problem entirely. Therefore, the frame problem may indirectly contribute to (or constrain) discussions of mental representations. (1987, p. 91)

A better approach, therefore, is to use intrinsic representations for which a distinction between what is explicit and what is implicit cannot even be made (1987, pp. 88–91). This way, the metaphysics is built into the system by embodying it in the form of the representation, which simply forces the system to 'obey' (Janlert, 1987, p. 37).

Unfortunately, Janlert, Palmer, and Haugeland provide no clear suggestions as to what could reasonably function as an intrinsically representing scheme. However, I think that a clue can be found in Janlert's (1987, p. 37) suggestion that non-deductivist approaches might be thought of as trying to implement knowledge as a kind of *capacity*. It is equally notable that Haugeland (1987, pp. 86, 90) indicates that the *descriptive* aspects of semi-linguistic, propositional representations might very well be the underlying cause of difficulty. Haugeland mentions depictive, imagistic representations as alternatives, while Lindsay (1988b) has also emphasized the functional advantages of imagery in comparison with descriptive propositional representations with respect to the frame problem. In my view, the invocation of a procedural-like characterization of knowledge and the doubts about the adequacy of descriptive representations tally quite well with the criticism concerning the traditional primacy of declarative knowledge that can be found in the work of Dreyfus and Dreyfus. They suggest that procedural knowledge (know-how) is a more fundamental form of knowledge underlying our common-sense reasoning abilities. The apparent intractability of the frame problem is the result of AI's view of intelligent behavior as arising out of the processing of elements of information about the world (that is, of a symbolic representation of declarative knowledge) (Dreyfus & Dreyfus, 1987, p. 97; see also 1986, pp. 82–90).[19] Dreyfus and Dreyfus (1987, p. 105) argue that the frame problem arises precisely because cognitive science has neglected the procedural kind of knowledge that underlies our skills. In their view, a direct recognition of similarity and relevance is an essential ingredient for modeling common-sense intelligence and avoiding the frame problem.[20] A cognitive system must be able to immediately notice relevant similarities with situations encountered before, which subsequently permits it to react accordingly. Dreyfus submits that connectionist models provide a promising way of approaching this ability (1992, p. xiii, but see also pp. xxxiii–xxxix; Dreyfus & Dreyfus, 1986, p. 91; 1990). Bechtel and Abrahamsen (1991, pp. 147–175) have also suggested that know-how is a more basic form of knowledge than its declarative counterpart and that connectionist models might indicate how this kind of knowledge can be understood as encoded in the setting of weights. This implies that a connectionist approach to intelligence, by using distributed representations, might not be troubled by the frame problem. I will investigate this issue in Chapter 5.

At this point, the conclusion is that for those non-deductivists who conceive of the frame problem primarily as a representational issue, investigations of the right ontological structure of the world are essential, together with finding a specific intrinsic way of representing the onto-logically primary information. I have accepted Haugeland's suggestion that an intrinsically representing scheme is characterized by not allowing a distinction between explicitly and implicitly represented information. If intrinsic representations are indeed essential for solving the frame problem, an investigation into the merits of distributed representations would be all the more interesting. Furthermore, the importance of intrinsicness might lead to serious doubts about the adequacy of the classical propositional-symbolic approach to cognition. There is, however, a second non-deductivist way of looking at the frame problem to which we will now turn.

The frame problem as an inferential issue

The second non-deductivist approach interprets the frame problem as an issue illustrating the difficulties involved in understanding non-demonstrative inference. The problem is how, on the basis of a symbolic representation of knowledge and rule-determined processing, higher or central cognitive processes involved in reasoning are to be modeled. In a general sense, this is the task facing classical AI. This issue has also been investigated from a theoretical perspective by Fodor, who claims that classical cognitive science, despite giving a solution in principle to the problem of mechanical rationality, seems unable in practice to model non-demonstrative reasoning because certain 'key ideas' are lacking. In this section I will describe the general nature of Fodor's analysis, as well as the negative response from scientists working in AI. I will argue that Fodor's analysis of the frame problem as closely related to issues concerning non-demonstrative reasoning is valuable and needs to be taken into account in AI attempts at modeling intelligence. I will assert that it is important to distinguish descriptive from normative aspects of the problem of non-demonstrative inference, and will conclude this chapter by giving a brief recapitulation of the argument so far. In the next chapter, I will examine Thagard's computational work which, in accordance with Fodor's analysis, addresses the issue of non-demonstrative inference. There I will, on the basis of the examples provided by Thagard, investigate and evaluate in greater detail Fodor's thoughts on AI and its potential to deal with non-demonstrative inference.

To obtain a clear picture of Fodor's thesis, it is necessary to take a brief look at his theory of the modularity of the mind (Fodor, 1983). There is widespread debate about the correctness of the modularity thesis (see, among others, Garfield, 1987; Meijering, 1994; Putnam, 1984). I would, therefore, like to stress that I am using Fodor's modularity thesis here to *elucidate* his thoughts on the frame problem and reasoning, not as an argument for the correctness of these views.

Fodor argues that the cognitive architecture of humans is ultimately threefold. Transducers transform proximal stimuli into neural signals that contain the informational content originally residing in the proximal stimuli. This is a psychophysical process that specifies differences in intensity in the incoming array of stimuli. Perceptual systems transform these neural signals into fully developed perceptions. These systems are modular in the sense that they are domain-specific and informationally encapsulated (their processes only use restricted and fixed background information). The modules do not report facts but merely deliver (perceptual) suggestions and hypotheses about the world, formulated in the LOT, as their output (Fodor in Pylyshyn & Demopoulos, 1986, p. 138).

Rationality is primarily operative during belief fixation, when a system arrives at conclusions by attending to all the evidence that is available and relevant. The actual belief fixation process is performed by the so-called central system. It decides what to think about the world given the perceptual input it receives and everything it knows (Fodor, 1983, p. 102; see also Fodor in Pylyshyn & Demopoulos, 1986, p. 132). As Dennett (1987a, p. 44) has claimed, a central if not defining feature of intelligent beings is that they 'look before they leap' and that they use what they know in order to frame further hypotheses. In Fodor's account, this 'looking' is the responsibility of the central system. This system examines, so to speak, what the input systems deliver, it considers what it knows and then uses all this information to generate a plausible hypothesis about the world. Central systems typically perform their tasks not by deduction but by other, non-demonstrative, forms of reasoning. In non-demonstrative reasoning the conclusion does not follow necessarily from the premises but contains more information than originally provided. This is in contrast with deductively valid reasoning, which by way of conclusion merely rephrases (part of) the supplied information which is guaranteed to be true if the premises are true.

The frame problem arises when one addresses the question of how central systems manage to make plausible common-sense inferences. Importantly, there is no fixed delimitation of the information that is relevant to the fixation of a specific belief; everything one knows might bear on the inferences made (Fodor, 1987a, p. 140). This, in turn, raises the question of how the central system manages to select and take account of the relevant information. The difficulty of the frame problem demonstrates our lack of understanding concerning non-demonstrative inference.

Seeing the frame problem as an issue in non-demonstrative inference is, in Fodor's (1987a, p. 142) view, essential to avoid confusing a circumvention of the problem with its solution. This mistake, he claims, is made by the proponents of the sleeping dog strategy. Since usually most events influence only a small set of facts and leave the rest unaffected, these proponents' basic suggestion is to find the world's ultimate ontological structure and represent it in the system, so the sleeping dog strategy will work. This representation of the world's ontology is called 'the basic set of frame axioms' by Hayes, 'the system's metaphysics' by Janlert, and 'the canonical notation' by Fodor. We have seen that according to McDermott this strategy already works, which is why he thinks the frame problem is computationally not very important. Hayes holds that though it is the right way of looking at things, we have not yet succeeded in finding the basic set of axioms specifying the world's ontology. The representational approach to the frame problem has followed a similar line of reasoning but has expressed doubts about whether the world's ontological structure can be adequately represented in a descriptive, semi-linguistic or symbolic medium.

Now, first of all it has to be noted that speaking about 'the' right ontology might be underestimating the difficulties. An inadvertent illustration of this can be found in Hirst (1989) where it is claimed that an approach to knowledge representation has many different kinds of ontology to worry about. Hirst identifies at least nine different kinds of existence to be taken into account.

But even apart from such complexities, Fodor argues that the sleeping dog strategy does not *solve* the frame problem but merely *changes* it from an issue concerning belief fixation into a problem about ontology or canonical notation. As the sleeping dog strategy only works when most facts do not change over events, the difficulty therefore becomes how facts are to be individuated.

> The canonical representations of most of the facts must be unchanged by most events. By definition, a sleeping dog algorithm *won't work* unless the canonical notation does have this . . . property. The problem is – indeed, the *frame* problem is – that such notations are a little hard to come by. Oh yes, indeed they are. (1987a, p. 143)

Fodor (1987a, p. 144) suggests considering the notion of a 'fridgeon', which denotes every particle of the universe that exists at the time that Fodor's fridge is on. He indicates that it is remarkably easy to come up with such 'kooky concepts', but that it is hard to avoid these obviously ridiculous notions in a principled way.[21] For the sleeping dog strategy to work there must be a notation that represents only those facts that really count as facts, i.e. a notation that would not allow 'fridgeons' to be represented (1987a, p. 147). Since the sleeping dog strategy is empty without the 'right' ontology and canonical representational notation, those in favor of this strategy have taken it upon themselves to find such a notation (1987a, p. 144). The sleeping dog strategy, then, is not a solution to the problem but merely its relocation. In Fodor's view, there is no easy way to avoid having to tackle the problem of non-demonstrative inference.

Fodor's interpretation of the frame problem as ultimately an issue concerning non-demonstrative inference has met with some strong opposition. In particular Hayes (1987, p. 132) has ventured some harsh criticisms: 'Fodor doesn't know the frame problem from a bunch of bananas.'[22] Hayes' main point is that what Fodor calls the frame problem is in fact the much more general issue of getting a computational system to reason sensibly about the world. This 'generalized AI problem' (GAIP) is not a well-defined problem but an area of study, comparable to the problem of making better plastics or improving international relations. For that reason, there are no clear answers to the GAIP (1987, pp. 131–132) and it would be unreasonable (and unilluminating) to expect any. The term 'frame problem' should be used in its original sense (i.e. the inertia problem: see Section 3.1).

At first sight this may seem a mere quarrel about names, but ultimately, I think, there is a difference of opinion about the role of philosophy in cognitive science and the way problems in cognitive science should be dealt with. Hayes objects to using the name 'frame problem' for issues relating to modeling intelligence in general. To Fodor, the point is that when one tries to model general reasoning (as performed by central systems) one runs into difficulties as *exemplified by* the frame problem. So, even though one may grant that the name 'frame problem', properly speaking, should not be used to refer to the generalized AI problem, it is still important to keep an open mind on the relation between the two. Treating the frame problem as a well-defined problem which can be addressed independently of this larger issue is unilluminating because the frame problem is a *symptom* of the difficulty of modeling central systems. It is precisely because cognitive science tried to find the mechanism behind intelligence that it discovered the frame problem (Dennett, 1987a, pp. 44–46). Not only is trying to solve the frame problem while ignoring this larger issue likely to lead to a mere relocation of the difficulties to other areas, it is also beside the point to try to find an isolated technical solution because the larger issues *are* the ultimate targets of cognitive science. If cognitive science is interested in studying the nature of rationality and reasoning, the frame problem is not *just* a problem, but rather a *valuable* problem precisely because it directs attention towards more general concerns such as the holistic nature of general rationality. In this sense, the frame problem *is*, as Dennett (1987a, p. 43) puts it, 'the whole pudding'. Perceiving the frame problem in this way does not mean that philosophy attempts to disparage work in AI, prescribe how it is to be done, describe what it can and cannot do, or give it unsolvable tasks. Instead, philosophy tries to see how AI relates and contributes to the study of cognition. Treating the frame problem as a technical issue is missing a chance to deepen our understanding of these more general matters. And this deeper understanding is, ultimately, the aim of cognitive science in general. It would seem unproductive, therefore, to address the frame problem in isolation from the more general issues surrounding non-demonstrative inference.

Fortunately for those who want to investigate non-demonstrative inference as performed by central systems, there are interesting parallels with non-demonstrative reasoning in science and, because scientific reasoning is generally more explicit and intersubjective in nature, this might help shed light on the issue (Fodor, 1983, p. 104; see also 1990, p. 202). This does not, of course, mean that common-sense reasoning as performed by central systems is in every respect similar to scientific reasoning. It is simply the observation that humans typically engage in non-demonstrative reasoning, that well-documented examples of non-demonstrative reasoning can also be found in science, and that it is reasonable to examine whether what we know about the latter can help to elucidate the former. Fodor (1983, p. 114) notes that the question which central systems have to answer is rather like the one facing a scientist after an experiment: 'What, in general, is the optimal adjustment of my beliefs to my experiences?' In science, the non-demonstrative fixation of belief has two characteristics that might illuminate the most obnoxious features of central processes. Fodor calls them 'isotropy' and 'being Quineian'.

Isotropy means that every established fact can be of importance to the evaluation of a theory or hypothesis. Everything you know may help determine what else you ought to believe. Isotropy stresses the potential relevance of each individual belief and is closely related to the importance of analogical reasoning (1983, pp. 105–106).

Being Quineian means that the degree of confirmation of a hypothesis depends on characteristics of the whole belief system in which it is embedded. The notions of simplicity, conservatism and plausibility are often mentioned in this respect as important but poorly understood criteria for evaluating a given body of belief (1983, pp. 107–108). The 'Quineian' feature emphasizes the global character of justification of our knowledge.

Fodor's main suggestion is that the frame problem is an example of the kind of difficulty ensuing from these global, holistic features of our reasoning process (1983, pp. 114–115, 128–129; see also Fodor in Pylyshyn & Demopoulos, 1986, p. 166; and Pylyshyn, 1987, p. viii). Witnessing an event, we effortlessly generate plausible interpretations of what is going on and what the likely results of the event will be. Solving the frame problem requires insight into how the global characteristics of the knowledge we possess guide our non-demonstrative inferential practices. The frame problem can be seen as a computational version of the difficulties surrounding non-demonstrative inference as found in induction, abduction and inference to the best explanation.[23]

The severity of the frame problem: philosophy and AI   At first sight, Fodor may seem somewhat unclear in his evaluation of the severity of the frame problem (interpreted as an issue of non-demonstrative inference). When defending the classical approach to cognition, he calls the frame problem one of the '(ahem!) certain residual technical difficulties' (1987b, p. 156, n. 6), which indicates that he thinks the frame problem is not insoluble in principle but something to be settled by *technical* progress. When arguing with AI experts, however, he is considerably more gloomy:

> Once you get into the central processor you have what is fundamentally an induction problem. I think that every problem in AI reduces to that in about two steps. You have that problem and nobody has any ideas about it. (Fodor in Pylyshyn & Demopoulos, 1986, p. 138)

The reason for this pessimism is that Fodor sees the frame problem as a philosophical problem which can only be solved by a breakthrough in inductive logic. There is no serious psychology of central cognitive processes for the same reason there is no serious philosophy of scientific confirmation:

> Both exemplify the significance of global factors in the fixation of belief, and nobody begins to understand how such factors have their effects. (1983, pp. 128–129; see also 1991a, p. 201)

Fodor is supported in both his diagnosis and his pessimism by Putnam, according to whom existing AI models do not work because they do not adequately address the problem of induction, which is a 'very obscure and dark problem' (Putnam in Pylyshyn & Demopoulos, 1986, p. 137, see also p. 164). Indeed, Putnam (1988a; 1992, pp. 8–14) has argued that the whole AI enterprise is 'much ado about not very much', since it has not resulted in any serious insights into inductive reasoning and the influence of background knowledge on it. In a similar vein, Fodor (1983, p. 107; see also Fodor in Pylyshyn & Demopoulos, 1986, pp. 136–138) has spoken about 'Fodor's first law of the nonexistence of cognitive science'. It is, therefore, not surprising that some have claimed that Fodor argues that the frame problem is in principle unsolvable (Ross, 1990).

However, I think that this interpretation is mistaken.[24] Classical cognitive science is, in Fodor's view, not a hopeless enterprise, even if he clearly thinks that the current work in AI is of little value to modeling non-demonstrative inference. Fodor has expressed his thoughts quite transparently in the following quotation:

> My view about the psychology of central processes is not that it's impossible in principle . . . My view is this: there are some problems you can't solve because key ideas are missing . . . if you look at what passes for the psychology/AI/ neuroscience of central processes, it is just *obvious* that there's been asymptotically close to no progress; and that there isn't likely to be any until somebody has some key ideas that nobody has had so far. (1991a, p. 280; see also 1986a, pp. 115–116; and 1986b, p. 14)

It may be clear then that on Fodor's account, the frame problem is a painfully vivid illustration of the fact that classical cognitive science has so far proven unable to explicate the processes involved in performing non-demonstrative inference. Since these are the very processes that are responsible for our common-sense rationality, it follows that one may wonder, first of all, whether the mechanism of syntactic symbol manipulation that Fodor proclaimed to be the solution to the problem of mechanical rationality (as outlined in Chapter 2) is really a solution at all; and, secondly, in what way this inability affects his intentional realism (as outlined in Chapter 1). The allure of Fodor's interpretation of classical cognitive science as providing a defense of folk psychology depends, after all, on the empirical successes it achieves. We will return to the issue of 'missing key ideas' and its possibly destructive consequences in Chapter 4. At this moment, it suffices to have observed that in Fodor's account the underlying difficulty of the frame problem is the issue of non-demonstrative reasoning which presents very difficult, though not in principle unsolvable, obstacles to cognitive science.

Descriptive and normative issues surrounding non-demonstrative inference
The task of comprehending non-demonstrative inference is an ambiguous assignment. Suppose one encounters puzzling phenomena and ventures a hypothesis to explain them. Many hypotheses can be formed, so questions can be raised as to how, *in actual practice*, plausible hypotheses are generated and how it is determined which is the best. This concerns the *psychological-descriptive* issue of how people actually arrive at conclusions in a non-demonstrative way. Entirely different questions arise regarding how the choice of a theory or hypothesis can be *justified*, and whether it can be accepted as true. This is the *philosophical-normative* problem of how to be

assured of the acceptability (the validity or probability) of the conclusion arrived at.

From the seventeenth century onward, there has been a strong tendency in philosophy to consider that these two issues should be separated. Epistemology was seen as an exclusively normative enterprise, whose task it was to develop, independent of empirical considerations, a prescriptive method of reasoning to be followed by science (Descartes' first philosophy). However, in recent times a 'naturalized epistemology' has come to be defended (Quine, 1969), according to which psychological theory can be of value to normative issues. Descriptive and normative issues are no longer thought to be completely separate.

In order to gain a better understanding of Fodor's views on the relationship between normative and descriptive issues, as well as on his position concerning non-demonstrative reasoning, I propose to take a brief look at Hume's problem of induction. Hume (1739/1978, I, iii, 6) indicated that there is no satisfactory way of justifying inductive generalizations or laws. No matter how many confirming instances are found, there is always the chance that a disconfirming case will show up. There is no way to justify the inductive principle that the future will resemble the past. First of all, as a logical *a priori* principle it fails since its denial does not result in a contradiction. Secondly, as an empirical *a posteriori* principle it begs the question: the fact that in the past everything has stayed more or less the same is only relevant to the future if the principle at issue is assumed to be correct. Hume concluded that our inductive practices are ultimately based on psychological habits, and do not have a rational foundation.

As Watkins (1965) has stated, Hume's induction problem results from the conjunction of the *logical* point that inductive inferences cannot be justified and the *psychological* claim that, in everyday life as well as in science, we do make these inferences. Using these terms, Fodor's position seems to be that important progress with respect to the logical point is necessary *before* any advances in psychology can be made. He specifically states that certain key ideas in logic and the philosophy of science concerning theory confirmation have to be developed before cognitive science can grasp central processes (see Fodor, 1983, pp. 128–129; Fodor in Pylyshyn & Demopoulos, 1986, p. 163). Advances in the logic of confirmation should indicate when and, if so, to what extent we are justified in accepting a conclusion arrived at through non-demonstrative means. Since the frame problem is essentially a problem of non-demonstrative inference, progress in the modeling of central systems can be expected only after a formal model of inductive justification is developed. For instance, only *after* we know what constitutes the correct method of weighing the evidence can we devise and implement mechanisms carrying out this method. In other words, the results of normative investigations should guide descriptive modeling attempts. And since Fodor is of the opinion that advancement in inductive logic is not imminent, he is pessimistic about the prospects of cognitive science as regards making important progress shortly.

I will not argue against Fodor's pessimism concerning breakthroughs in inductive logic. But I do want to investigate and challenge his judgment that progress in psychology is *dependent* on progress in logic. Psychology (or cognitive science, of which AI is a central part) is interested in different answers to the questions surrounding non-demonstrative inference from logic and epistemology. Whether human reasoning can ultimately be shown to be rational is of no inherent concern to psychology. It 'merely' aims at modeling our *actual* cognitive processes. Psychology is interested in how we, in fact, reason, irrespective of how rational these processes are.

This is *not* to claim that logical analysis can never be of value to psychology, but merely to observe that logical theories are primarily directed at formal correctness, whereas cognitivist theories aim at psychological plausibility. Indeed, I would like to suggest that the *problems* inductive reasoning poses for logical analysis are of value for psychological investigations. Two famous problems (to be examined in Chapter 4), i.e. Hempel's (1965, pp. 12–15) raven paradox and Goodman's (1954/1983, p. 74) grue riddle, both point at the divergence between what we intuitively take to be relevant in our inferential practice and what can be logically proven to be so. This way, logic has provided psychology with an abstract indication of some salient aspects of human reasoning, and these can serve as guides and benchmarks for modeling attempts. Logical paradoxes and riddles can be important to psychology regardless of the availability of their logical solutions. There is no reason to suspect that psychological answers to the descriptive problem of non-demonstrative inference can only be given once logical answers concerning the normative problem of non-demonstrative inference are available.

So, even though Fodor is right in diagnosing the frame problem as closely related to non-demonstrative reasoning, and in pointing out that there are severe problems with modeling this kind of reasoning, it is far from obvious that advances in logic are necessary to make progress. Hence, his pessimism concerning the capabilities of classical cognitive science to model central processes is at least partly based on too restricted a perspective. Moreover, much work in cognitive science and the computational philosophy of science is based on the belief that progress in these matters *is* possible without great advances in inductive logic. An important example of these attempts, the recent computational work of Paul Thagard on the issues involved in non-demonstrative inference, will be investigated in the next chapter.

3.3 Conclusion

This chapter has discussed the main interpretations of the frame problem. The deductive approach, with its 'narrow' interpretation of the frame problem as the problem of inertia and its emphasis on the strengths and limitations of logic, has been rejected as ultimately of limited value to cognitive science because of its neglect of domain-specific knowledge and its psychological implausibility.

The non-deductive approach perceives the frame problem as the issue of dealing with a changing world. It raises the question of how to determine what the relevant consequences of an event are, without having to check every possibility. Two points of view have been discussed. From the representational perspective, the frame problem demonstrates the need to engage in ontological investigations and to carefully reconsider the adequacy of a semi-linguistic representational system. That is, one has first to investigate what a system has to know about the *world* and then *represent* this knowledge intrinsically, in order for the system to be able to deal adequately with a changing world. An important point proved to be the fact that no distinction between explicitly and implicitly represented information should be allowed. On the basis of suggestions made by Haugeland, Dreyfus, and Bechtel and Abrahamsen, the thesis has been put forward that connectionist models using distributed representations might not be troubled by the frame problem. This issue will be investigated further in Chapter 5.

According to the inferential approach, the real problems underlying the frame problem have to do with non-demonstrative inference. Establishing what information is relevant to a specific hypothesis and determining how global characteristics of one's knowledge bear on the evaluation of a hypothesis are poorly understood aspects of this kind of reasoning. Some have resisted this more general interpretation of the frame problem, but I have argued that this position (if it constitutes more than a mere quarrel about names) is unsatisfactory because it leads to a disintegrated view of cognitive science. Furthermore, work in symbolic AI has increasingly focused on issues concerning non-demonstrative inference. To this work, and to Fodor's perception of it, we will now turn.

Notes

1 I would like to point out that this use of 'epistemological' has only very little to do with epistemology in philosophy. It is merely a name given to a specific component of a computational model containing knowledge about the world.

2 McCarthy and Hayes stress that, with respect to the epistemological component, the choice of a certain kind of internal structure (i.e. the representational format) is very important. The epistemological component, therefore, includes syntactic aspects of the representational system as well (i.e. it encompasses not only *what* knowledge is represented, but also *how* it should be represented). Since in the approach of classical cognitive science information is processed on the basis of the syntactic form of its representing elements, it follows that the choice of a specific syntactic format for the epistemological component strongly influences the effectiveness of the computational processes as specified at the heuristic level (Dennett, 1987a, p. 48). The problem, then, is that the distinction between an epistemological and heuristic component is not as clear-cut as at first sight it may seem to be. A more practical distinction, therefore, might be made between semantic and syntactic-cum-heuristic aspects of

knowledge and reasoning. In other words, one has to distinguish between *what information* an intelligent system capable of common-sense reasoning about the world has to possess, and *how* this information has to be *represented and processed*.

This way of viewing things is vindicated when one considers an explicit attempt to model common-sense knowledge and reasoning. The Cyc project (Guha & Lenat, 1990; 1993; 1994) has retained the traditional terminology, but the problem with this distinction becomes clear when one realizes that Cyc's heuristic component needs a translation of the information represented in the epistemological component into a different syntactic format in order to be useful to the heuristic reasoning mechanisms. That is, the epistemological component contains the kind of information needed for common-sense reasoning in a more or less syntactically 'neutral' way. Only when the actual reasoning processes become involved is a suitable syntactic format chosen. So, although Guha and Lenat keep the old labels, the components actually embody a distinction between the purely semantic and the syntactic-structural and processing aspects of knowledge.

3 A small terminological matter should be addressed here. Janlert (1987, pp. 5–6) speaks of the result-specifying rules as 'laws of motion', but, although it is true that McCarthy and Hayes (e.g. 1969, p. 477) speak of laws of motion, they use this notion not to refer to rules like the one above, but in a more general way to establish determinism (laws of motion determine, given a particular situation, all future situations).

4 It is interesting to note that in the section entitled 'The frame problem', McCarthy and Hayes (1969, p. 487) present frames as a possible solution to the difficulty of avoiding a multiplicity of rules specifying non-changes. This observation coincides with a comment by Hayes that the frame problem received its name from the idea of 'frames of reference', denoting categories for which it is possible to specify in general terms whether they can influence each other or not (e.g. no concept falling within the category of 'movement' can change a concept falling within the category of 'color': cf. Hayes, 1987, p. 130). The task, then, is to find the right frames.

5 For a time, it was thought that the inertia problem could be solved by finding good alternatives to McCarthy and Hayes' 'situation approach' outlined above (McDermott, 1987b, p. 116). As Hayes says: 'Once a relation or term is given a temporal parameter, there is no *logical* reason why it might not change wildly in value at every moment . . . so of course it is no wonder that the stability which we want has to be explicitly stated somehow in our axiomatic theory' (1987, p. 130). However, refraining from a time-sliced representation of the universe does not solve the frame problem, as both McDermott and Hayes admit, since it reappears in different guises. The details do not concern us here, but see Hayes (1987, p. 130) and McDermott (1987a, p. 108; 1987b, p. 116) for short descriptions of the problems faced by alternative approaches.

6 McDermott does acknowledge that there are two other aspects of the frame problem: a computational and a metaphysical one (I will return to them later). Yet, in his view, these aspects are not essential.

7 McDermott's continuation is also of interest: 'It is an implicit assumption of some work in this area that an inference is completely unwarranted unless it can be shown to be deductively valid – even if we have to change the concept of deductive validity! Hence the Herculean effort to get logical machinery to solve the inertia problem. At some point one has to ask, why bother?' (1987a, p. 116). Similarly, Davis (1990, p. 96) states: 'Deduction does not adequately characterize commonsense inference.'

8 As Haugeland (1987, p. 82) has put it: 'When things start moving around . . . propositions that were once true may not stay that way.'

9 It seems, however, that the allowance of non-monotonicity cannot properly be viewed as a 'mere' extension of deduction. For instance, Davis (1990, p. 101) notes that monotonicity is a main or even defining difference between sound deductive and plausible inference. However, Hanks and McDermott (1987) indicate that default reasoning still resembles deductive reasoning more closely than, for instance, inductive generalization or abductive explanation. For this reason it was thought that mere extensions of deductive logic might suffice (1987, p. 390).

10 An interesting but short discussion about the problems and merits of non-monotonic logic by prominent logicians can be found in Etherington et al. (1989). A similarly short assessment of the accomplishments of non-monotonic logic is provided by Reiter, who observes a 'general ambivalence within AI about the relevance of logic or even, these days, of symbolic processing' (1992, p. 789), but nevertheless stresses that non-monotonic logic has provided important insights. Lormand (1990, p. 373, n. 6) speaks of the 'mixed successes' of non-monotonic logic, and suggests that it might not be needed by AI, as non-monotonic reasoning could be understood as a case of ordinary heuristic search. In other words, modeling non-monotonic reasoning does not require the development of a non-monotonic logic. Oaksford and Chater (1991) undertake a detailed investigation of the potential of non-monotonic logics to model common-sense reasoning and conclude that, first of all, these logics are not able to capture everyday inference and, secondly, even if they could, this would be of little use to cognitive science because the algorithms over such logics are computationally intractable (see also Chater & Oaksford, 1993; Garnham, 1993).

11 As Dennett says (1987a, p. 59), a cognitive wheel is any design proposal in cognitive theory that is profoundly unbiological, however clever it may be from a technological point of view.

12 Janlert (1987, p. 3) mentions the general problem solver (GPS: Newell & Simon, 1972) as a prime example because the GPS uses not deduction but means–end analysis as its basic reasoning mode. There are, of course, many more examples of non-deductive approaches to reasoning: see for instance Holland, Holyoak, Nisbett, and Thagard (1986), Johnson-Laird (1983), Minsky (1986), and Newell (1990).

13 McDermott (1987a, p. 106) has called this 'the ramification problem'.

14 This is called 'the qualification problem' (Ginsberg, 1987, p. 4). As the standard example goes: if you want to start the car you do not first wonder whether there is a potato in the tailpipe.

15 These notions and their interrelations will be discussed in Chapter 4. In this chapter I am only addressing the relationship between the frame problem and non-demonstrative reasoning in general.

16 Although Janlert (1987, p. 20) explicitly refers to Galileo and Locke while introducing the metaphysical distinction between primary and secondary properties of the world, he does not discuss their views. I think it is best in this context to forget about the philosophical discussions of the seventeenth and eighteenth centuries concerning primary and secondary qualities and just keep in mind the interpretation Janlert is giving it here: secondary phenomena are reducible to primary phenomena.

17 The metaphysics of a system addresses questions concerning the ultimate ontological structure of the world, e.g. what the fundamental entities and basic categories and principles are. Janlert indicates, by the way, that it does not matter whether we take metaphysics in the classical absolute sense of 'the way the world actually is' or in the modern more relative sense of 'the way we conceptualize the world'. In both cases, the world (as it is or as it is conceptualized) should be represented in the system.

18 De Champeaux puts it thus: 'The predicate calculus is uncommitted to any ontology. Consequently it has a nearly boundless domain of application. The price for this generality is that some pervasive properties of a domain are represented at great implementation costs. The frame problem is an example *par excellence*' (1987, p. 311).

19 On the page referred to, Dreyfus and Dreyfus specifically mention Dennett. Yet it is clear that they are actually arguing against what they call 'cognitivists' assumptions' and the 'AI line'. It is, in fact, not entirely justified that they turn specifically against Dennett, because Dennett himself (in the same volume and only a few pages away from their own remarks) explicitly suggests that the frame problem might indicate inadequacies of the propositional characterization of knowledge at the semantic or knowledge level, and that this issue might even be prior to questions at the syntactic level (1987a, p. 61). Furthermore, from an early stage Dennett has pointed to this possibility: 'It seems that our entire conception of belief and reasoning must be radically revised if we are to explain the undeniable capacity of human

beings to keep their beliefs roughly consonant with the reality they live in' (Dennett, 1978, pp. 125–126).

20 As Dreyfus and Dreyfus state: 'Unless AI scientists can produce programs in which representations of past experiences encoded in terms of salience can directly affect the way current situations show up, they will be stuck with some version of the frame problem and be unable to get their computers to cope with change. The outlook is grim for AI, however, since the way human beings use past experience to cope with the future seems to require two capacities unavailable to heuristically programmed digital computers: pictorial representation and direct recognition of similarity' (1987, p. 109).

21 Sometimes Fodor is thought to see the frame problem as being the difficulty of avoiding kooky concepts (Dunn, 1990; Lormand, 1990). Yet I submit that these kooky concepts are only used by Fodor to indicate the emptiness of the sleeping dog strategy as a possible solution to the frame problem proposed by the representational approach. It should not be considered as Fodor's diagnosis of the ultimate nature of the frame problem, which, in his view, is intimately related to the problem of non-demonstrative reasoning.

22 Hayes seems to be particularly disturbed by those who attempt to address the frame problem from a more general, philosophical point of view, instead of seeing it as a technical issue in AI. See, for instance, the exchange between Fetzer (1991a; 1991b) and Hayes (1991), where Hayes at one point remarks: 'Fetzer's article illustrates much of what is wrong with quite a lot of philosophical comment on AI. It mis-states the problem, reveals a disturbing ignorance of its subject-matter, argues by assertion rather than analysis, and offers no help with our problems' (1991, p. 71). However, as I point out later in this chapter, I do think that much is to be gained by adopting a somewhat wider perspective on the frame problem.

23 In the literature, the names 'induction' and 'non-demonstrative inference' are sometimes used interchangeably. Yet, not only induction but also abduction and inference to the best explanation are forms of non-demonstrative reasoning. As indicated, these notions and their interrelations will be discussed in Chapter 4. As far as this chapter is concerned, it is best to keep in mind that the term 'induction' should be interpreted in the general sense of 'non-demonstrative inference'.

24 Undoubtedly, Fodor's preference for unqualified statements is partly responsible for the misunderstanding. As Fodor himself once remarked with an uncharacteristic sense of understatement: 'I am not much interested in truth values between zero and one. What I want to know is what is the right idealization' (Fodor in Pylyshyn & Demopoulos, 1986, p. 141).

4

The Problem of
Non-Demonstrative Inference

In Fodor's account, classical cognitive science is, among other things, in the business of proving folk psychology, literally interpreted, right. There really are beliefs and desires, which can be understood as propositional attitudes and computationally modeled as relations to functionally discrete symbols. Semantic coherence is the result of structure-sensitive processing of these symbolic configurations. Thus classical cognitive science provides an answer in principle to how rationality is mechanically possible. However, when one looks at 'folk rationality', i.e. common-sense reasoning, it appears that the 'principled answer' presented by classical cognitive science leaves much to be desired. I have focused on the problem of how human beings are capable of quickly understanding the situation they are in, which in turn enables them to respond reasonably to a changing environment. I have argued that this issue of dealing with change constitutes the essence of the frame problem. In addition, I claimed that Fodor's further interpretation of the frame problem as a clear example of our lack of understanding with respect to non-demonstrative inference is a valuable way of looking at it, because it places the problem firmly in the context of classical cognitive science's larger enterprise.

In this chapter, I will look more closely at non-demonstrative inference and the problems it has raised. I will outline some general constraints on any approach that attempts to address these problems in a way that makes it a legitimate part of classical cognitive science. I have chosen the work of Paul Thagard as an illustrative example of such an attempt, and, after explaining my main reasons for this choice, I will examine several of his theoretical suggestions and computational models in some detail. Although I will complete this examination with a number of critical comments concerning Thagard's work, my main intention at the end of this chapter is to investigate Fodor's response to this *kind* of work in AI and evaluate its consequences for the attractiveness of classical cognitive science and Fodor's intentional realism.

Ultimately, then, the question in this chapter is whether, within the framework of classical cognitive science (i.e. on the basis of a propositional theory of knowledge and a symbolic theory of cognition), it is possible to work towards a solution of the problem of non-demonstrative inference *without* being guided by developments in logic. If classical cognitive science is unable to model how cognitive systems proceed in performing non-demonstrative inference, it seems that Fodor's interpretation of the frame problem leads to enormous difficulties. This in turn would indicate that the classical approach to rationality and cognition, as well as Fodor's defense of folk psychology, is in serious trouble.

4.1 Non-demonstrative inference and hypothetical induction

An inference can be characterized psychologically as an act of thought by which one passes from one state of mind to another and the latter appears to be true if the former is (Tragesser, 1992, p. 206). Generally speaking, the main form of non-deductive or non-demonstrative reasoning is induction. Upon closer examination, two modes of inductive (or non-demonstrative) reasoning can be discerned. These separate forms are sometimes referred to as enumerative and hypothetical induction (Harman, 1992, pp. 200–201). In *enumerative induction*, one concludes from the fact that certain encountered phenomena have certain characteristics that all phenomena of that kind have these characteristics, or at least that the next instance will have them. That is, one generalizes on the basis of encountered evidence. In *hypothetical induction*, one reasons that something must be (or have been) the case as that would explain an encountered phenomenon. Hypothetical induction is sometimes also referred to as abduction or inference to the best explanation. However, I will use the latter two labels only in cases where specific and distinct aspects of hypothetical inductive reasoning have a central place.

A few simple examples may help to illustrate the distinctions. In *deduction* one concludes (validly) from $p \rightarrow q$ and p, that q. In *enumerative induction*, one argues from (several sequences or co-occurrences of) p and q, to $p \rightarrow q$. In *hypothetical induction*, one inferences from q and the assumption that $p \rightarrow q$, to p; that is, on encountering a phenomenon q, one (a) generates a hypothesis or rule such as $p \rightarrow q$, that would explain the phenomenon's occurrence given the antecedent p, and (b) concludes on the basis of this that p must have been the case, which in this example is of course the logically fallacious affirmation of the consequent (Van der Lubbe & Backer, 1993, pp. 119–120). In AI, hypothetical induction is generally referred to as 'abduction'. The two steps involved in abductive reasoning are sometimes distinguished as (a) 'abductive rule generation' and (b) 'abductive rule inference', respectively (1993, pp. 126–127). The focus of research is usually on the generation of rules or hypotheses such as $p \rightarrow q$. Following Thagard (1988, pp. 53–54), who claims to be following Peirce,[1] I will use the term 'abduction' in contexts where the actual *generation* of an explanatory rule or hypothesis plays a central role.

In philosophy, hypothetical induction is sometimes referred to as 'inference to the best explanation' (Harman, 1965/1989; Lipton, 1991). Normally, more rules or hypotheses with respect to the occurrence of q are available or can be generated (e.g. $p \rightarrow q$, $r \rightarrow q$, $s \rightarrow q$). Given these and given q, one concludes (by hypothetical induction) to either *p, r* or *s* on the basis of which hypothesis seems most likely, in the sense that it best explains the occurrence of *q*. I will speak of inference to the best explanation in contexts where issues surrounding the *evaluation* of hypotheses (in order to determine which one is the best) have a central place, again following Thagard (1988, pp. 75–76). To be sure, in philosophy further questions are raised (for instance in the context of discussions concerning scientific realism) as to whether and, if so, to what extent we are justified in believing that the best hypothesis is also true. However, these questions will not be addressed in this chapter.

As a last terminological point, one should keep in mind (as already indicated in the previous chapter) that some authors use 'induction' as a general term encompassing all forms of non-demonstrative reasoning. Fodor, for instance, sometimes uses the term in this general sense, e.g. when he claims that the task of the central system is basically to perform inductive reasoning (Fodor in Pylyshyn & Demopoulos, 1986, p. 138).

So, whenever the term 'induction' appears it refers to non-demonstrative reasoning in general. Enumerative induction is spoken of when discussing the creation of generalizations on the basis of several instances of a certain regularity. Hypothetical induction refers to the kind of reasoning in which a hypothesis is accepted on the basis that its obtaining would explain the phenomena encountered. When discussing hypothetical induction, if I focus on its hypothesis generating aspect, I will speak of abduction. When I examine its hypothesis evaluating aspect, I will sometimes speak of inference to best explanation.

When one reconsiders the nature of the frame problem, it is clear that the interpretation of it as a problem in non-demonstrative reasoning is more closely connected to hypothetical than to enumerative induction. After all, the main difficulty is to get a computational system to generate a reasonable interpretation of what is going on in its surroundings. It concerns the ability of people to quickly engender a good hypothesis that makes their experiences intelligible, and not, in general, the ability to create rough-and-ready generalizations on the basis of numerous instances of a certain phenomenon. I have, then, proceeded from the analysis of the frame problem as closely connected to the problem of non-demonstrative inference to the problem of hypothetical induction and its two aspects: abduction (hypothesis generation) and inference to the best explanation (hypothesis evaluation).

4.2 The work of Paul Thagard: preliminaries

Three works by Paul Thagard (*Induction*, co-authored as Holland, Holyoak, Nisbett, and Thagard, 1986; *Computational philosophy of science*, 1988; *Conceptual revolutions*, 1992) will form the main subject of this and the next three sections. Thagard's work is relevant here because it explicitly addresses issues in non-demonstrative inference as it occurs in both human thinking and scientific theory development. It constitutes a research project extending over many years that has resulted in several computational models and examples, and it is continuously being elaborated, while certain essential characteristics remain the same. Furthermore, this work is optimistic precisely where Fodor is pessimistic:

> In our view, central problems in the philosophy of science are continuous with key issues in cognitive psychology and artificial intelligence. Fodor (1983) has also noted such connections, but where we see mutual illumination, he finds gloom. Using an argument based on the holistic character of inductive confirmation, he suggests that the aims of cognitive psychology and artificial intelligence for a general account of the central processes of thought may be unattainable. In reply, we contend that a sophisticated cognitive view of induction undermines such a skeptical assessment of the possibility of understanding mental processes. (Holland et al., 1986, p. 335)

Thagard's optimism is based on a strong belief in the virtues of a pragmatic approach. Pragmatism, in this context, means that there is no general, abstract, logical way of dealing with all kinds of non-demonstrative inferences normally performed by cognitive systems. Instead, specific ways of dealing with specific problem situations are required, explicitly taking into account *the goals and the context* of the system performing the inferences, as well as the influences exerted by the way in which the knowledge is *organized* in the system (1986, p. 7; Thagard, 1988, p. 39).

Constraints on proposed solutions

Let us be clear about the issue at hand. From a general point of view, as Fodor argues, systems that perform non-demonstrative inference are hypothesis projecting and confirming devices. They must have knowledge or a data-base, a source of hypotheses, and a way, relative to the data-base, of evaluating a hypothesis (Fodor, 1983, p. 121). Even though, in Fodor's modularity thesis, an important difference between modules and central systems lies in the restricted data-bases of the former, as opposed to the latter, Fodor stresses that the size of the data-base of the central system is not, in itself, the biggest problem. The difficulty lies not in finding the relevant pieces of information in a huge data-base, but in finding out how the information in the data-base influences the probability of the hypothesis at hand (Fodor in Pylyshyn & Demopoulos, 1986, p. 130). Matters of scale, then, will be of secondary importance in what follows.[2]

If one looks at Fodor's characterization of non-demonstrative reasoning, one can localize two issues that are of primary importance to attempts to create psychologically plausible models. Both the creation of a set of (plausible) hypotheses, and the criteria on the basis of which the best hypothesis from a set of alternatives can be selected, need to be better understood. So, two 'epistemic filters', to use Peter Lipton's (1991, p. 61) terminology, are essential in solving the frame problem and understanding the mechanisms involved in central systems. The first filter generates plausible candidate hypotheses. The second filter is responsible for the evaluation of the candidates, and selects the best one from the set.[3] Fodor's discussion of the frame problem makes it clear that both filters pose a problem. Specifically, there must be a mechanism that is potentially able to use every little thing one knows, no matter how far afield, in generating and evaluating a certain hypothesis ('isotropy'), and a mechanism to determine how holistic characteristics of relevant information in relation to a hypothesis influence the latter's acceptability ('being Quineian').

An important restriction on acceptable designs consists of the requirement that a computational model should not basically depend on an external and *a priori* structuring of the information it possesses. In making and structuring the system's data-base ourselves, *we* decide, *a priori*, what will be relevant to what, so the system does not even have the chance of finding that out for itself. In other words, the system does not meet the frame problem. Obviously, if we are to understand how humans can see what is relevant, it is not illuminating to let humans do the hard part (of building the structure into the data-base) instead of letting the model do it. Approaching non-demonstrative reasoning on the basis of an *a priori* structuring of knowledge is not satisfactory because this does not solve but merely evades the frame problem. It is important to note, however, that this does *not* imply that there can be no knowledge structure to start with. A computational system need not start as a *tabula rasa*. But it does imply that for any solution to be acceptable, mechanisms should be specified through which the system itself is able in a reasonable way to *expand* and *modify* its knowledge structure.

The points considered so far indicate that there are important constraints on any approach in cognitive science that tries to deal with the problem of non-demonstrative inference. Since I examine the problem of non-demonstrative inference in the context of the discussion concerning folk psychology, the requirement that the approach should be recognizable as part of classical cognitive science (as outlined in Chapter 2) should be added to these constraints. After all, it was seen in Chapter 1 that classical cognitive science seems in principle capable of upholding a view of cognition that allows a literal interpretation of folk psychology. Models that attempt to address the problem of non-demonstrative inference are only relevant to this issue as long as they use symbolic representations and structure-sensitive processing mechanisms. For only then would their success show that the frame problem does not constitute insurmountable difficulties for the chances of classical cognitive science to vindicate a literal interpretation of folk psychology.

All in all, then, it seems to me that the following five constraints can be identified. An approach to the problem of non-demonstrative inference is acceptable *if*:

1   It stays within the framework of classical cognitive science, that is, if it makes use of a symbolic representational system that allows for a compositional syntax and semantics and a truth related interpretation of knowledge (see the next section).

2   It explains how a system can generate plausible and relevant hypotheses instead of a large set of random ones. That is, it should give a general mechanism for implementing the first, abductive filter. As a further specification of this constraint, I will use Goodman's riddle of induction as a test case. The proposed mechanism should be able to avoid the generation of awkward hypotheses (see Section 4.3).

3   It is able to accept certain (classes of) phenomena which intuitively count as confirmatory evidence for a hypothesis, while it rejects other phenomena that, though logically equivalent to the accepted phenomena, are generally deemed irrelevant. That is, the proposed mechanism implementing the second, evaluative filter should be sensitive to relevant information and avoid using irrelevant data. Here, Hempel's raven paradox illustrates the difficulties involved in the selection of evidence relevant to the evaluation of a hypothesis, and it will be used as a test case (see Section 4.4).

4   It succeeds in getting a grip on holistic characteristics of a body of knowledge, such as simplicity and coherence, that are important in selecting the best hypothesis. It should, in other words, propose a mechanism to implement the holistic sensitivity of the second, evaluative filter (see Section 4.4).

5   It does not try to solve the issues involved in points 2, 3, and 4 by a fixed *a priori* structuring of knowledge (by stipulating in a general way what is connected to what), but instead allows the system itself to manage the structure of its knowledge. In other words, can the proposed computational system produce, to borrow a phrase from Boden (1990, p. 190), 'a fundamental change in its own conceptual structure'? I will not treat this issue in a separate section, but instead deal with it when discussing points 2, 3, and 4.

I will not give a complete review of Thagard's work, but I will concentrate on those elements of it that are relevant to the task of understanding non-demonstrative inference from a descriptive point of view. The computational model that I will consider is PI (for 'processes of induction'). The question will be whether Thagard has succeeded in developing ideas that can provide at least an *indication* of how to address non-demonstrative reasoning in accordance with the five points mentioned above.[4] This would mean that it is possible to make progress in the modeling of central aspects of human cognition on the basis of a symbolic representational scheme without having to wait for the development of key ideas in logic.

Thagard, scientific inference and classical cognitive science

In Chapter 3, it was seen that Fodor and others discern some basic similarities between scientific and common-sense reasoning as far as non-demonstrative inference is concerned. Scientific reasoning merits study as it is usually better documented, and performed more 'openly' or inter-subjectively and more systematically. Thagard has worked especially on scientific non-demonstrative reasoning as it is thought to occur within the individual scientist. The representation of information as well as the processing mechanisms are basically the same for common-sense and for scientific knowledge and reasoning. In this section, I will briefly introduce Thagard's general outlook on the nature of science. This should provide sufficient theoretical background for a proper understanding of his computational proposals.

Thagard calls for a pragmatic account of scientific theories in the tradition of Kuhn and Laudan from a practical, historical and philosophical perspective.[5] Practically speaking a (scientific) theory should be *psychologically realistic*, in the sense that it describes how a scientist uses the theory in explanation and problem solving. A description of how theories are formed and evolve must moreover *fit historical cases*. A large part of Thagard's work is, therefore, dedicated to the modeling of historical examples of theory formation and comparison. Finally, a philosophically adequate account of scientific theories must be *capable of generating insights into the nature of explanation and justification*.

Thagard's work can be located within the tradition of classical symbolic AI (Thagard, 1992, p. 29), even though he is open-minded about incorporating 'foreign' elements into his models. It might perhaps be best to describe him as an agnostic with respect to the debate that forms the context of this book (see for instance Thagard, 1989, pp. 491–492).

His research is an example of the 'scruffy' approach in that it rejects a purely logical approach to cognition. This is, of course, quite in line with the idea that reasoning must be looked at from a pragmatic perspective (Holland et al., 1986, p. 8; Thagard, 1988, pp. 4, 28). Induction is studied within a realistic problem solving context, e.g. in normal, complex, and ill-defined problem situations. A system uses what it knows in order to clarify the ill-defined problem (1986, p. 11; 1988, pp. 27–29). For Thagard, the basic question here is how a cognitive system can use stored knowledge in the processing of environmental input, without being bogged down by everything it knows. This leads to a search for constraints on the processing of information that can ensure that only plausible and relevant inferences are drawn. The guiding idea of Thagard's work is that these constraints arise through the structure of the representation of the knowledge which a cognitive system possesses (1988, p. 39; see also 1986, pp. 3–5).

The knowledge of a system is primarily represented by a complex structure of messages, concepts, rules and generalized problem solutions (1988, pp. 12–19, 38–42). Specific facts are represented by *messages*: lists containing a predicate, an argument, its truth value, a measure of its confidence, and its identifying name, e.g.:

(has_life(Mars), projected to be false, 0.7, hypothesis-26)

Concepts are computationally represented by frame-like structures (Minsky, 1977; 1981), containing slots with (default) values. Representational schemata or stereotypes like frames and scripts play an important role in AI. The basic idea is aptly described by Dennett:

> An artificial agent with a well-stocked compendium of frames or scripts, appropriately linked to each other and to the impingements of the world via its perceptual organs, would face the world with an elaborate system of what might be called habits of attention and benign tendencies to leap to particular sorts of conclusions in particular sorts of circumstances. (1987a, p. 57)

Dennett notes that these representational schemata are unsatisfactory in that they are rigid (they do not degrade gracefully when unusual things happen) and externally provided and updated. Janlert (1987, p. 16) notes an additional difficulty in the problem of deciding when to change from one frame to another. However, as we will see, Thagard has indicated ways of meeting these problems. The representational structures he suggests go beyond frames because they have rules attached to them which are more complex than simple slot-fillers (normally default values). These representational frame-like structures do not provide a definition of the concept but give something rather more like a description of what is typical about it (Holland et al., 1986, p. 18; Thagard, 1988, p. 18; 1992, pp. 24–30).[6]

Together, concepts form a *conceptual hierarchy* (1986, p. 19; 1988, pp. 16–17; 1992, pp. 30–33). Concepts are connected to one another primarily through kind and part links, but instance, property and rule links are also possible. Once a concept is activated, it can, in turn, activate other concepts to which it is connected through these links.

For the representation of *rules*, the format of production rules is chosen. These if – then – (or condition – action) rules can become operative when their conditions are satisfied, and then execute the action part. Like concepts, production rules also have added structure, e.g. a strength measure, indicating their history of successes and failures, and connections to related concepts (1988, p. 16).[7]

Useful problem solutions are represented by abstract *problem solving schematas* or exemplars. These explanatory schemata are basically sets of principles of an abstract nature, making application in several different domains possible. They can arise through repeated use of similar exemplars in different domains (1988, pp. 40–43). Adequate exemplars are retrieved by exploiting their analogy with current problem situations (1986, pp. 287–319; 1988, pp. 22–25).

Even though almost everything represented is expressively equivalent to what can be formulated in FOPC, Thagard stresses that the extra structure indicated above is extremely important from a procedural point of view, since it gives PI its processing efficiency (1986, p. 321; 1988, p. 31; 1992, p. 32). As we will see below, it is because of this structure that the spreading of activation through the information is *directed*. Thus, important constraints are imposed on the reasoning process, something which is lacking in a purely logical approach.

PI's problem solving or explanatory activity consists in firing rules that will lead from starting conditions to a goal. A rule can fire when its activation exceeds a certain threshold. The level of activation is based on several factors, including: fulfilment of its conditions (match), its past history of usefulness (strength), its compatibility with other active information (support), and its relation to the current goal (1986, pp. 49, 129). Many rules compete in their struggle to become active and more than one can be fired at the same time. Parallelism is an important aspect of PI (1986, p. 132; 1988, pp. 19–20; 1992, pp. 56–58).

> By tending to fire the strongest and most goal-appropriate rules, and by spreading activation only to the new concepts in fired rules, a constrained search through the space of relevant information can be carried out. (1986, p. 336)

The above should suffice as an outline of the fundamental characteristics of Thagard's computational work. It is clear that his approach falls squarely within classical cognitive science. Symbols are structurally organized into more complex wholes, allowing a compositional syntax and semantics, and can be processed by structure-sensitive rules. I will now examine his ideas concerning the hypothesis generating and evaluating aspects of non-demonstrative inference, which come to the fore in abduction and inference to the best explanation, respectively.

4.3   The first filter: generating hypotheses

Suppose a cognitive system witnesses an event or encounters a puzzling situation, which presents it with a problem to be solved or a phenomenon to be explained. In principle, an infinity of explanatory hypotheses can be proposed and, as a result, a first obstacle to the system's attempt to make sense of its surroundings lies in the production of one or more plausible hypotheses. This process of abduction presents a major challenge to modeling attempts. I will use Goodman's (1954/1983, pp. 72–81) new riddle of induction as an illustration of the inconveniences abduction causes for a purely logical or syntactical approach and as a test case for Thagard's work. Even though Goodman introduced the example in the context of enumerative induction, it clearly depicts the importance of avoiding irrelevant explanatory hypotheses, which is a central issue in hypothetical induction as well.

The thesis that all emeralds are green is confirmed by all green emeralds found. Yet these same instances of green emeralds can also be taken to confirm the thesis that all emeralds are grue, where the predicate 'grue' is defined as: x is grue when it is green before time t (say the year 2000) and x is blue after that time t. The problem is to explain why the first hypothesis should be taken seriously to be confirmed by instances of green emeralds, while the second should not. Alternatively, why do we generate a hypothesis like 'all emeralds are green' on encountering an instance of it, instead of the hypothesis that 'all emeralds are grue'?

As Goodman (1954/1983, p. 80) himself has put it, the new riddle of induction is 'the question what distinguishes law-like or confirmable hypotheses from accidental or non-confirmable ones', where the latter can arise through the use of strange concepts such as 'grue'.[8] Goodman (1954/1983, pp. 94–99) suggests that the past history of a term plays an important part in deciding which hypotheses are to be taken seriously. Hypotheses using well-entrenched terms (concepts that have played a frequent role in previous successful hypotheses) are projectable to future cases and should, therefore, be preferred. The entrenchment of a concept depends to a great extent on its previous use (or the use of other terms that are coextensive with it) in the formulation of hypotheses. The task facing Thagard is to make this suggestion more concrete by giving a computational under-pinning of the ability to generate projectable hypotheses.

The basic idea behind Thagard's approach is that the mechanism of directed spreading of activation avoids the investigation of numerous unnecessary hypotheses. Because inference is primarily studied in the context of problem solving, the concepts involved in the specification of the problem and the goals can start the spreading of activation. Other concepts can be active too, for instance because of previous cognitive processes or because of current incoming information. Once started, the spreading of activation is directed mainly through the connections between concepts and rules and through the structure of the conceptual hierarchy, where activation can spread to subordinates and superordinates.

> The system is computationally efficient because only plausibly relevant rules – those attached to active concepts – are likely to be considered on a processing cycle. (Holland et al., 1986, p. 132; see also Thagard, 1988, pp. 20–22, 54)

Since the directed spreading of activity keeps the system focused, and prevents it from pursuing irrelevant inferences, the structure of the knowl-edge representation is very important (1988, pp. 26, 29). Using this basic idea, four kinds of abductive processes are implemented in PI: simple,[9] existential,[10] rule forming and analogical[11] abduction, all resulting in explanatory hypotheses (1988, pp. 53–63). Of these four, I will concentrate on rule forming abduction, as it involves complex mechanisms illustrating several aspects of Thagard's work.

In simple and existential abduction, the crucial part of the abductive process is solved by the existence of rules waiting to become active. But, of course, the problem is how these rules come into existence in the first place. Even if the task of locating and matching relevant knowledge items is alleviated through the mechanism of directed spreading of activation, this cannot be the whole story. To paraphrase a critical remark by Thagard himself concerning Schank's script approach,[12] the mechanisms outlined above work only if we have ready-made rules for every explanatory task. Assuming the availability of all these rules obviously begs the question and it would, furthermore, be wrong since it would leave our ability to deal with new and strange situations unexplained (1988, p. 45).

So, to escape criticisms concerning the *a priori* character of standard AI approaches included above as the fifth constraint on acceptable approaches to non-demonstrative inference, it should be made clear how connections between concepts and rules are made or changed by the system itself instead of being specified in advance by the programmer. That is, a computational system should be capable of modifying the structure of its own knowledge representation in relevant ways. In the same vein, in many cases no adequate concepts or rules are available and the system itself should be able to create useful new ones. Both points indicate the urgency of the problem of the generation of new, useful rules and concepts, and of (other) ways to autonomously alter the structure of the conceptual hierarchy. Thagard explicitly accepts this (what I have listed as the) fifth constraint as an important one:

> The basic knowledge structures of the system should be derivable by the system's own inductive principles. Few artificial intelligence systems can satisfy this constraint; most expert systems, for example, depend entirely on having rules written by their programmers. But we see it as an important constraint, necessary to avoid brittleness and the use of arbitrary internal symbols with no pragmatic significance. (1986, p. 143, see also p. 350; 1988, p. 71)

To see whether the issue of abduction is addressed in a way that honors this fifth constraint, I will look at the mechanisms proposed by Thagard to (a) implement rule forming abduction, and (b) create new concepts and change the structure of the conceptual hierarchy in substantial ways.

Rule forming abduction

Assuming for the moment that relevant concepts are available (I will discuss their actual generation in the next section), how are useful connections (in the form of propositional rules) established between them (Thagard, 1992, p. 52)? That is, how is *rule forming abduction* to be understood? A mere random 'evolutionary mutation' or blind 'cross-fertilization' of existing rules is not constrained enough to explain the human ability to come up with reasonable hypotheses:

> Any account of rule generation must address Peirce's problem of generating *plausible* new rules. The space of *possible* rules is effectively infinite, and the islands of potential utility are widely scattered. (Holland et al., 1986, p. 79)

A potentially useful but computationally dangerous way of creating explanatory rules is to trigger abduction when several active messages specify different properties of the same individual, since this way too many new rules would be generated. If you know two specific facts about a person, one of which is puzzling you, it is generally no good to infer the rule that the second property explains the presence of the puzzling first one, since they might well be totally unrelated (if you notice that a particular psychologist has red hair, it would be quite rash to conclude abductively that all psychologists have red hair and that this general rule explains the particular case). A way to constrain this process is the requirement that only if there is knowledge of a general relation between certain properties, can a specific rule forming abduction start.[13]

At this point, an example might help to illuminate several aspects of Thagard's ideas. First of all, it will help to illustrate the importance of rule firing and of directed spreading of activation through a conceptual hierarchy in influencing the reasoning process. Second, it will indicate how several abductive processes might be involved in a reasoning process. Finally, it will show how rule forming abduction takes place in PI, and thus explain how PI can generate new rules on its own.

Suppose one notices that sound propagates and reflects, what could explain this phenomenon? This is a problem discussed by Stoic philosophers, and most explicitly by the Roman architect Vitruvius (second half of the first century BC), who tried to describe the acoustic principles utilized in the design of Greek amphitheatres. So, picture Vitruvius standing in an amphitheatre and shouting something. He receives a signal from someone standing at some distance, indicating that he has been heard, and also hears his echo coming back at him. I will concentrate on the propagation of his shout. There is a specific x (his shout) that is an instance of S (sound) and has the characteristic P (propagates). How can we explain that for $S(x)$ it also obtains that $P(x)$? To put it more pontifically: how did Vitruvius uncover the wave theory of sound, and how did he use it to abductively explain its propagating and reflecting characteristics?

In a passage quoted by Holland et al. (1986, pp. 339–340), Vitruvius explicitly notes an analogy between the propagating characteristics of sounds and water waves. From a modeling point of view, the question therefore is how Vitruvius noted the similarity with water waves *in the context* of explaining the characteristics of sound. Exactly how this association between sound and waves took place in the mind of Vitruvius is, of course, unknown, but PI has simulated several ways of doing it. Basically, the approach followed by Thagard is to create a conceptual hierarchy and a rule base representing the knowledge of the person whose reasoning is being modeled, as far as can be established on the basis of historical texts.[14] One possible line of reasoning that may have led Vitruvius to his abduction can be depicted as in Figure 4.1 (Thagard, 1988, p. 22, see also pp. 209–224). Horizontal arrows indicate firing rules, vertical lines indicate activation flow to superordinates or subordinates in a conceptual hierarchy.

As a result of rule firing and the spreading of activation through the hierarchy, the concept of 'wave' is activated in PI and with it the general rule that waves propagate. This general rule has thus become available for PI to infer that this specific instance of a sound (i.e. Vitruvius' shout) is a wave, since this would explain its propagation (1988, p. 55). By this process (which Thagard calls 'simple abduction'), PI has acquired the information that the examined instance of a shout is a wave and a sound. From this, PI

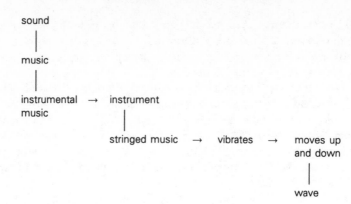

Figure 4.1

abduces to the rule that all sounds are waves and that this explains their propagating and reflecting characteristics (1988, pp. 59–60). The activity of the general rule that waves propagate licenses PI to abductively form this new rule; if it were absent, no rule forming abduction would have taken place.[15] Rule forming abduction is accomplished through a generalization from hypotheses (abduced simply or otherwise), not from observed instances (1992, p. 54).

At this point, it can be concluded that the mechanisms outlined above at least indicate how a computational system could generate new, plausible explanatory hypotheses. As Thagard cautiously puts it:

> Obviously, directed spreading activation and abduction are not guaranteed to find a potentially explanatory hypothesis. In PI, as in people, activation may spread to areas of memory that are irrelevant, while possibly explanatory rules remain dormant. Nevertheless, PI's spreading activation and abduction are techniques for making the finding of explanatory hypotheses more likely than chance. (1988, p. 64)

With respect to the fifth requirement of not reverting to *a priori* relevance determination, it can be said that even though information has to be available to start with, the resulting rule is created, in a genuine sense, by the system and can be used in the formation of yet other rules. This at least goes some way towards meeting the fifth requirement. Furthermore, as we will see in the next section, PI has methods of changing and expanding its conceptual resources as well.

Concept generation and the changing of conceptual hierarchies

When one looks at science, one finds that discovery is not just a matter of collecting data and then trying to find laws which account for them. A crucial aspect is reconceptualization, the formation of new and useful concepts. Usually a restructuring of the input and a conceptual combination of knowledge already possessed are necessary in order to deal with difficult, vague or puzzling input. Conceptual change takes place primarily through the creation of new concepts or by changing the structure of the arrangement of concepts in a conceptual hierarchy. Both cases can be understood by looking at the representational structure underlying our concepts (Thagard, 1992, p. 39)

Thagard indicates that at a basic level concepts can originate 'bottom up'. From simple concepts, new, more complex or theoretical ones can be generated through conceptual combination. For instance, when rules with the same set of features as conditions are simultaneously active, this could lead to the generation of a concept combining the characteristics specified in the antecedent part (1988, p. 69). Another triggering mechanism is to create a new concept when two active concepts have instances in common. An unrestricted use of this principle would lead to the formation of a great many uninteresting concepts (like 'yellow banana'), which could just as well be handled by simple inheritance mechanisms in the hierarchy. Therefore, a new concept is only formed when the combination of its 'parents' results in conflicting expectations (an often used, yet somewhat outdated example is 'feminist bankteller'), as determined by the rules attached to them. In the example of the discovery of the wave theory of sound (given above), a conflicting expectation of the newly formed concept 'sound-wave' arises because in water waves propagate in a single plane, whereas sound propagates spherically. Conflicting expectations can be reconciled through the addition of rules specifying the peculiarities of the new concept, in this case that sound-waves spread spherically (Holland et al., 1986, pp. 138–144; Thagard, 1988, pp. 65–66). These new concepts can then be used in the further development of yet other concepts. In his later work, Thagard (1992, pp. 35–36, 51–52) calls the combination of concepts into a new one that is added to the conceptual hierarchy 'coalescence'.

A wide variety of conceptual changes or indeed conceptual revolutions can be understood computationally as changes in the *structure* of a conceptual hierarchy. Relations between concepts can be specified by indicating their superordinates and subordinates or by various kinds of rules attached to them. Apart from simple expansion of a hierarchy, effected by inserting new concepts into the hierarchy, more radical changes are possible. For instance, when a previous distinction is abandoned because what were thought to be separate phenomena are now found to be similar, a part of the kind hierarchy collapses. Branch jumping occurs when a concept is relocated to another part of the hierarchy, as when Copernicus reclassified the earth as a kind of planet, or when Darwin placed humans among the animals. The most substantial change is brought about by reorganizing the entire hierarchy, for instance through the use of a new organizing principle. Thagard (1992, pp. 34–37) again mentions Darwin as an example; by making ancestry an important determining factor for species instead of surface similarity, he changed the entire conceptual hierarchy of living creatures. Since the system itself is capable of enhancing and modifying its knowledge structure, there is no need to specify everything *a priori*, thereby adopting extreme nativism (1988, p. 72).

This approach, Thagard feels, is capable of dealing with Goodman's 'grue' puzzle. The concept 'grue' is not available and will not be generated unless it is needed by the cognitive system and turns out to be of value. The entrenchment of a concept or proposition is dependent on its having a place in the conceptual hierarchy, its utility in processing and its coherence with other parts of knowledge, and all these factors can be made computationally precise (1986, p. 235; 1988, p. 36; 1992, p. 94).

To draw a few interim conclusions: I think that Thagard has indicated ways of understanding and modeling mechanisms that together constitute in a rudimentary way the first, abductive filter. The ideas and models presented so far clearly stay within the approach of classical cognitive science. They show how, on the basis of a symbolic, well-structured representational format and structure-sensitive rules, the creation of plausible hypotheses in the context of explaining or understanding events might be possible. Thagard has at least indicated how the notion of entrenchment can be computationally operationalized. Furthermore, mechanisms have been pointed out by which a system can to some extent itself expand and modify its knowledge, thereby escaping the criticism of standard AI approaches of relying too much on *a priori* specifications of knowledge structure. However, it is also clear that much remains to be done. I think that the value of Thagard's work lies primarily in the *theoretical* analysis of the pragmatic applicability of the presented computational principles and mechanisms. At this stage, the actual model PI merely provides an illustration of this analysis. PI is operative on far too small a scale to provide a genuine demonstration of the effectiveness of the implemented computational processes. Furthermore, the psychological plausibility of the mechanisms implemented in PI remains a largely uninvestigated issue.

There remains another task that, according to Fodor, presents enormous difficulties for understanding non-demonstrative inference. This involves the issues surrounding inference to the best explanation and concerns the problem of how to evaluate competing hypotheses in order to find the best one among the alternatives.

4.4   The second filter: evaluating hypotheses

Evaluating hypotheses presents a difficulty because there is no straightforward way of measuring the level of confirmation of a hypothesis. The crucial question is: 'What probability does this data-base bestow upon this hypothesis?' (Fodor in Pylyshyn & Demopoulos, 1986, p. 130). As Putnam (in Pylyshyn & Demopoulos, 1986, p. 164) has described it, the question concerns the general problem of what makes a theory good. There are two difficulties which should be noted here. Firstly, one has to find what evidence is relevant, and to what extent, to the evaluation of a hypothesis (recall Fodor's 'isotropy'). Secondly, there is the problem of accounting for the way global characteristics of data and theories influence the acceptability of a hypothesis (the 'Quinean' characteristic). I will look only briefly at the first issue, as Thagard deals with it broadly along the lines considered in the earlier section on abductive rule generation. The second issue will be investigated more thoroughly.

Determining relevance

Hempel's (1965) paradox of the raven provides a good illustration of the difficulties involved in characterizing how explanatory hypotheses are confirmed by relevant evidence. According to the approach advocated by logical positivism, a hypothesis is confirmed by observed instances that are in accordance with it. So the hypothesis 'all ravens are black' is confirmed by instances of black ravens. Logically, however, the expression 'if x is a raven then x is black' is equivalent to the expression 'if x is not black then x is not a raven'. Hence, on the logical positivist model, all non-black things that turn out not to be ravens have to be accepted as confirming instances of the hypothesis that all ravens are black. Clearly, this result is unwelcome. There must be a way to exclude certain kinds of evidence as irrelevant to a specific hypothesis.[16]

PI is not modeled to make observations, but it is possible to translate Hempel's paradox into the difficulty of determining what parts of information that one possesses are relevant in the evaluation of a certain hypothesis.[17] In Thagard's computational scheme, the selection of relevant pieces of information is controlled by the spreading of activation, as described above. Concepts, once active, support the rules attached to them, and rules can receive support from more than one concept (e.g. when they are attached to more concepts). The support rules receive as well as the strength they have (an indication of their earlier utility) influence whether they will fire, and thereby contribute their action part to the information the system is considering (Holland et al., 1986, pp. 128–129). Therefore, what is not activated will not play a role in the evaluation of the hypothesis. Here it becomes apparent that the structure of the representation of information plays a vital role in the determination of what information is taken into account. Not the logical relations between pieces of information, but the structural relations between representations determine the selection of evaluatively relevant knowledge. This naturally allows for the possibility that potentially relevant information is ignored in the evaluation of a hypothesis (i.e. there might be a discrepancy between what *is* and what *should* be taken into account), but from a descriptive-psychological perspective this does not constitute a major problem. After all, people regularly fail to take relevant information into account. Of course, computational systems should be tested for their ability to model these failings realistically.

Holistic factors in evaluation

The second difficulty noted by Fodor is that the level of confirmation depends on certain global characteristics of the whole theory.[18] Fodor claims that, especially in these matters, fundamental ideas are lacking. There are no computational formalisms that take the global aspects of a theory into account nor are there any good ideas for developing them (Fodor, 1983, pp. 128–129; see also Fodor in Pylyshyn & Demopoulos, 1986, pp. 158–159).

Admittedly, in the discussion about how to evaluate theories with respect to their global characteristics, certain catch-phrases have appeared. Among them are simplicity, coherence, conservatism, consilience, and analogy. There is general agreement that factors denoted by these terms do play a role in theory selection, but it has proven to be very difficult to explicate both their specific role and the way they should be measured (Harman, 1992; Holland et al., 1986, p. 333; Thagard, 1988, p. 78; 1992, p. 63). Indeed, Giere sees these phrases as largely empty of content and as mere parts of the rhetoric of science (Giere in Callebaut, 1993, pp. 231–232).

Thagard has tried to make these factors more precise within a computational framework. He has developed two computational models for this goal: PI (the main outlines of which I have discussed above) and ECHO.[19] In the context of PI, Thagard examines especially consilience, simplicity and analogy. He stresses that these criteria should be thought of not as necessary or sufficient conditions on acceptable theories, but as evaluation standards which, in some cases, can offer diverging estimates of the excellence of a theory (1988, p. 78). Below I will review Thagard's theoretical and computational ideas with respect to (1) consilience, (2) simplicity and (3) their integration into a single evaluation procedure. Thagard seeks to explain why these criteria are important, and how they can be accommodated in a computational system. With respect to the explanation of the importance of consilience and simplicity, it has to be kept in mind that we are interested in the adequacy of Thagard's theory from a psychological perspective.

Consilience The importance of consilience (scope or comprehensiveness) can be explained from a computational perspective by pointing out that possessing a consilient theory or hypothesis means that a wide range of phenomena can be understood by the same explanatory rules and concept hierarchy (Holland et al., 1986, pp. 330, 333). A consilient theory is of value to a cognitive system because it makes its problem solving methods available to a whole array of problems.

A theory is more consilient than another if it explains more classes of facts, or if it applies its problem solving methods to more classes of problems (Thagard, 1988, p. 78). In order to make the criterion of consilience computationally operative, it must be specified when a collection of phenomena counts as a class of facts, and how the relative importance of different classes of facts is established (1988, pp. 78, 81).

Thagard takes a 'class of facts' as a pragmatic notion. What constitutes a class of facts is decided by the standard organization of knowledge within a scientific discipline about which (to a large extent) there is agreement between scientists (1988, pp. 78–79, 96; 1992, p. 93).[20] Computationally, one can think of classes as represented by nodes at a certain level of abstractness in a hierarchy. The importance of the explananda is indicated by the strength of the rules expressing them, which is a function of the past usefulness of the rule, capturing aspects of both its probability and utility (1988, p. 89; 1992, p. 56).

In addition to this static interpretation of consilience, Thagard speaks of dynamic consilience as being the extent to which a theory can add newly explained classes of facts to its explanatory domain. Predictive success (especially of very unexpected phenomena) is sometimes thought to indicate dynamic consilience, but Thagard prefers to assess the value of successful predictions not in terms of consilience but in terms of simplicity (1988, pp. 81–82). Although consilience is an important factor in evaluating a theory, unrestricted use of it is dangerous. It could lead to the acceptance of a theory that succeeds in explaining everything by giving an *ad hoc* explanation for every phenomenon. An important constraint on consilience is formed by another criterion, that of simplicity (1988, p. 82).

Simplicity A theory is perceived to be simpler than its rivals when it requires fewer special assumptions (which are only used for the explanation of one single class of phenomena) or auxiliary hypotheses (statements not part of the original theory but assumed to explain certain facts[21]) (Thagard, 1988, p. 83). Simplicity does not necessarily refer to ontological thrift, i.e. the number of kinds referred to by a theory (Holland et al., 1986, p. 334; Thagard, 1988, p. 86). Also, simplicity cannot be measured by straight-forward comparison of the number of postulates of two competing theories, since this would ignore the explanatory role the postulates play (1988, p. 85). Computationally, a method of implementing special assumptions consists of attaching exception rules to concepts organized in the default hierarchy (1986, p. 334). The ability to predict new, hitherto unobserved or unnoticed phenomena is best understood as an indication of a significant simplicity (rather than consilience) of a theory. After all, a theory can easily be made consilient after the fact by adding an additional hypothesis. But successful predictions make clear that the theory does not need a large number of auxiliary hypotheses specially arranged for the occasion:

> successful predictions are to be valued as signs of the simplicity of a theory, showing that its explanations do not require *post hoc* additions. (1988, p. 85; 1992, p. 95)

Furthermore, simple explanations, through the absence of *ad hoc* hypotheses, indicate that the available explanatory schemata are powerful enough to deal with many phenomena, thereby increasing the unificatory power of the theory (1988, pp. 84–85).

Since there is no general rough-and-ready way of assessing the simplicity of theories, the assumptions and explanations of each theory have to be carefully considered (1988, p. 84). Yet, once the specific details of the competing theories have been collected, the basic idea of measuring simplicity is the following. First, the number of co-hypotheses, the ones that jointly explain a phenomenon, is determined. Subsequently, one hypothesis H is calculated to be simpler than another if it has a lower ratio of co-hypotheses to facts explained (1988, p. 90). More precisely: the simplicity of H is the number of facts explained by H, minus the number of co-hypotheses of H, divided by the number of facts explained by H.[22]

Integrated evaluation   As indicated above, simplicity and consilience are to be taken into account together, keeping each other in check, as it were. A good theory achieves consilience at a lower cost in terms of special assumptions (i.e. by being simpler) than its competitors (Holland et al., 1986, p. 334; Thagard, 1988, p. 83). For simple cases of assessment, where all elements are of equal value, Thagard suggests the following crude mechanism: the value of a hypothesis H is the value it got for its simplicity times the value for its consilience (1988, p. 91). However, the issue becomes considerably more complicated if the explananda are of different importance, and Thagard admits that a more complex mechanism needed for these cases has not been implemented in PI (1988, pp. 91–92).

In his work *Conceptual revolutions* Thagard (1992) has tried to give a more complex account of hypothesis evaluation. The basic idea behind his theory of explanatory coherence (TEC) is that a hypothesis is more acceptable if it has greater coherence with the theory or body of knowledge in which it is embedded.[23] Consilience and simplicity are considered to be the most important factors contributing to the coherence and thereby to the acceptability of a hypothesis (1992, p. 67). TEC has been implemented in a computational program ECHO that has been tested on an impressive range of scientific cases like Lavoisier's oxygen theory, Darwin's theory, Wegener's continental drift theory, the Copernican, Newtonian and Einsteinian revolutions in physics, and more 'mundane' matters such as conceptual development in children and legal reasoning.[24] However, from the perspective of this book, ECHO is of considerably less value than PI, and it is worthwhile to devote some time to discovering why this is so, as it will shed some light on the nature of the controversy between classical cognitive science and connectionism.

ECHO, the computational implementation of TEC, is quite different from PI in one vital respect. As Thagard says, ECHO is a connectionist network using localistic representations of propositions and its main work consists of multiple constraint satisfaction (1989, pp. 456–457). Contrary to what Thagard himself seems to think, however, the use of parallel constraint satisfaction in itself does *not* imply a departure from classical cognitivist ideas. Indeed, Thagard's claim that ECHO is connectionist is criticized by several commentators as essentially unfounded. They indicate that the computational mechanisms used by Thagard can perfectly well be implemented in classical architectures (Lycan, 1989, p. 480; McDermott, 1989, p. 483). Importantly, Thagard (1989, p. 457; 1992, pp. 27, 242–243) avoids the use of distributed representations, which would place ECHO firmly in the connectionist approach.

In my view, what *does* make ECHO a radical departure from the approach adopted in PI is that its units are taken to represent one complete proposition each. In this way, Thagard denies himself the representational power of the symbolic approach because the representations used no longer have any constituent structure (see also Cheng & Keane, 1989, p. 470). A crucial consequence of this is that an external force must provide ECHO with a specification of the relations between the propositions represented by the units. ECHO is unable to construe these by itself, since for ECHO the different hypotheses are unanalyzed and unanalyzable wholes (see also Simon, 1989, p. 487; Thagard, 1989, p. 497). Furthermore, as Thagard (1992, pp. 83–84) himself admits, it means that ECHO is totally dissected from the representational structure provided for by the conceptual hierarchy,[25] which, in the context of PI, Thagard thought to be of such crucial importance. This voluntary abandonment of the advantages of representational structure is all the more puzzling since, as we will see in Chapter 5, Thagard himself criticizes distributed representations for their lack of representational power. Yet the representational format used in ECHO is even less efficacious. So, even though ECHO is a computationally sophisticated mechanism for evaluating theories, it is separate from Thagard's other main ideas, which seem to have been sacrificed to computational power.[26]

In this section, two important questions were addressed. First, how can a system be made to utilize only 'intuitively' relevant information in the evaluation of a hypothesis, instead of irrelevant but logically equivalent data? Second, how can global factors of one's knowledge influence the evaluation of a hypothesis? Regarding the first issue, the spreading of activation through the conceptual hierarchy and the firing of rules results in the selection of information that is used in a certain context. Consistent with the pragmatic approach, a computational system deals with issues of relevancy on the basis of its context, its goals and the structure of its knowledge representation (a considerable part of which is ultimately created by the system itself). With respect to the second issue, Thagard has indicated how consilience and simplicity may be understood and measured computationally. However, the proposed mechanisms are relatively crude first attempts at dealing with the issues involved.

4.5 Comments on Thagard's work

The frame problem was discussed in Chapter 3 as a general problem encountered by cognitive science when it attempts to model the human capacity to understand its changing environment. It was seen that the essence of the frame problem is intimately connected to the obscurity of the cognitive processes involved in performing non-demonstrative reasoning. In this chapter, we have focused on the difficulties that classical cognitive science encounters when trying to understand and model hypothetical induction (being an important form of non-demonstrative inference). In Chapter 3 I suggested that a normative-philosophical understanding of the logical complexities involved in the justification of the generated hypothesis is not necessary for a computational analysis of the cognitive processes involved in non-demonstrative reasoning. This chapter has shown that Thagard takes his task to be a descriptive-psychological one: how do human beings in actual practice go about making sense of events in their surroundings by generating a plausible hypothesis on the basis of incoming information and their knowledge?

Two aspects of hypothetical induction have been distinguished: an abductive, hypothesis generating aspect; and an evaluative aspect, in which the selection of the best hypothesis has a central place. I have examined Thagard's attempts to investigate, in the context of scientific reasoning, these issues pragmatically, by taking into account the goals, context and knowledge structure of the system. Adopting a pragmatic approach is in line with the rejection of the primacy of logical analysis concerning the frame problem and non-demonstrative inference, as indicated in Chapter 3.

Five criteria have been listed on the basis of which the value of Thagard's work (within the context of this book) can be evaluated. A computational theory of hypothetical induction must (1) use a well-structured symbolic representational system and structure-sensitive processing rules, (2) indicate how plausible hypotheses (instead of random ones) can be generated, (3) demonstrate how a determination of what constitutes relevant information can take place, (4) show how global characteristics of what one knows influence the acceptability of a hypothesis, and (5) explicate how a computational system can accomplish the above-mentioned tasks while it is itself responsible for (changes in) the structure of its knowledge.

On the basis of the material discussed in this chapter, I think that Thagard's ideas as implemented in PI, but not ECHO, qualify for criterion 1 and that he has also provided several mechanisms concerning criteria 2, 3 and 4 that go some way towards meeting criterion 5. Not only has Thagard indicated how the creation of a set of plausible hypotheses is mechanically feasible, but he has also made some progress in explaining in computational terms how holistic criteria can play a role in the evaluation of hypotheses. It is clear, however, that the suggestions considered in this chapter only scratch the surface. It should be acknowledged that Thagard himself is the first to admit this, regularly devoting sections to shortcomings of his ideas and models. I will indicate a few weaknesses that will need to be addressed if further progress is to be made.

Firstly, Thagard's computational models are of far too small a scale to be interpreted as genuine test cases of the frame problem. For instance,

Thagard (1988, p. 29) has mentioned 60 rules or concepts as an upper limit for PI. The model does not run the risk of being overwhelmed by the sheer size of its task, resulting in 'computational apathy', since far too few facts and rules are implemented. As Thagard subsequently mainly concentrated on ECHO, in addition to other projects, it seems that PI has not been increased in size. Yet, more knowledge is needed to make PI more realistic (1988, p. 30) and to improve its reasoning capacities (1988, pp. 47, 72). Secondly, PI does not by itself find problems to solve, these must be given to it from outside. There is no account of when PI should start investigating problems (1988, pp. 175–176). This implies that PI, to a significant extent, is still externally controlled. Thirdly, sometimes the use of certain computational mechanisms seems to be quite disconnected from the theoretical ideas that should form their backbone, as in the case of ECHO. This makes their value debatable.

Despite these criticisms, I think that Thagard has indicated that it may be possible, within a classical cognitive science context, to analyze some salient aspects of the issue of non-demonstrative inference in computational terms and to devise some ways of dealing with them. Having seen some major characteristics of a typical scruffy AI attempt to deal with problems of non-demonstrative inference, we can now ask whether Fodor is justified in rejecting it across the board. Is something basically wrong about the idea of scruffy AI that the structure of knowledge representation plays a vital role in controlling reasoning processes?

4.6 Fodor's position evaluated

In this section I will examine the debate about the value of Thagard's work (and the scruffy approach in AI, which it illustrates) for the chances of classical cognitive science to deal with problems of non-demonstrative reasoning. Before doing so, let us consider briefly what is at stake by reviewing the route that brought us here. In Chapter 1, I have indicated that classical cognitive science provides a model of cognition that is compatible with a literal interpretation of folk psychology. In Chapter 2, it became clear that one important virtue of classical cognitive science is that it shows how, on the basis of a symbolic representational system and structure-sensitive processing rules, an answer to the problem of mechanical rationality can in principle be provided. However, the precise value of this solution in principle is a matter of considerable debate since important problems have been identified concerning attempts to understand and model common-sense rationality and reasoning. As discussed in Chapter 3, investigations of common-sense rationality run into the frame problem which, on the inferential approach, can be diagnosed as intrinsically connected to issues concerning non-demonstrative reasoning. This led, in the current chapter, to an investigation of the mechanisms involved in hypothesis generation and evaluation which turned out to depend to a considerable extent on finding relevant information that can guide these processes. Looking at the philosophy of science helped to further define the problems as global or holistic, in the sense that potentially everything one knows can be relevant, and that global characteristics of one's knowledge in relation to a hypothesis bear on its acceptability. I have claimed that the outline of Thagard's ideas and computational work can be seen as an example of the non-deductive approach to the problem of non-demonstrative reasoning in AI. Having examined Thagard's work in this area, it is now possible to investigate Fodor's criticisms of it.

To put the basic issue as simply as possible: imagine someone thinking about what is happening in his environment, and suddenly something important pops up in his or her mind (either consciously or subconsciously) that helps to make sense of the situation. What explains this sudden appearance of relevant information? How can this be understood in computational and symbolic terms?

Fodor stresses that people possess an enormous amount of information, and that it should be explained how it is possible to use only the relevant parts of it on any given occasion. When a large amount of information is available, the problem is that especially in the case of abductive rule generation a 'creative element', as Van der Lubbe and Backer (1993, pp. 126–127) call it, seems to be involved. One has to discover, among the myriads of connections, a *relevant* relation between certain pieces of information and the phenomenon to be explained in order to generate them into an explanatory hypothesis. Suppose for the moment that the puzzling phenomenon is given (which of course is a substantial simplification, since perceiving something *as* in need of an explanation is itself an important aspect of cognition), and that the explanatory hypothesis has the form $p \rightarrow q$, where q is the explanandum. The problem becomes one of finding relevant facts that can function as the conditional in this explanatory hypothesis.

Translated into the scruffy terminology of directed activation spreading through a structured representation of knowledge, this means that there must be a link (rules or connections in a conceptual hierarchy) between the representations of the conditional and the antecedent facts. If there is no such connection, then the antecedent fact is not available for incorporation in the explanatory hypothesis. If one wants to avoid missing relevant information, this implies that *all* the conceptual structures that *could* be of explanatory relevance have to be linked to the conceptual structure representing the explanandum. As Van der Lubbe and Backer remark:

> It is clear that, in practice, this hinders building expert systems with a performance compatible with human-like reasoning. Whereas a human is superior with respect to the generation of new associations, the expert system should *a priori* include all possible relations and associations. (1993, p. 127, see also p. 132)

An *a priori* connection of everything to everything is computationally unfeasible, and would not help a great deal anyway since the question then becomes which connection should be used.

Thagard's pragmatic proposal is, as we have seen, that the mechanisms responsible for hypothesis generation and evaluation take into account only the information that is active on a certain occasion. Which information is actually used by these mechanisms is, therefore, strongly dependent on the way one's knowledge is structured. The interconnections between elements of knowledge (preferably created by the system itself during its problem solving activities) as represented through the means of frames and conceptual hierarchies provide a structuring of information. This structure together with the mechanism of activation spreading determines which information plays a role in determining the course of reasoning (i.e. which information is 'deemed relevant').

Yet, Fodor rejects this kind of work as unimportant. A first objection of Fodor is that much research in AI of this kind evades the real problem by artificially restricting the models, for instance, by not supplying them with knowledge that is deemed beforehand to be irrelevant to the kind of tasks to be confronted by the model. As Fodor told Newell in a related context:

> You don't build the model so that it begins to think about protons when it's worrying about tigers. You don't even put any information about protons in, but people have information about protons and they know how not to use it. The question is how do they know how not to use it. (Fodor in Pylyshyn & Demopoulos, 1986, p. 167)

Although this is, of course, a valid criticism in its own right, it is also a somewhat frustrating one, since AI is not yet at the stage where 'everything one knows' can be put into a system[27] (not to mention the fact that no one – AI researcher, psychologist or philosopher – knows what 'everything one knows' concretely amounts to). An interesting attempt to create a 'common-sense encyclopedia', i.e. Lenat's Cyc project (Guha & Lenat, 1990; 1993; 1994), has not yet provided running models that are easy to evaluate. At the present stage of inquiry, therefore, it is better to leave actual empirical models behind and to focus instead on the question whether something is fundamentally wrong with the basic idea that the structure of information representation is essential in determining to a large extent the course of reasoning.

With respect to this question, Fodor has specifically claimed that the idea that relations between chunks of information can guide the inferential process is fundamentally misguided. Allowing the representational structure of a computational system to control to a large extent its inferential processes does not solve the problem. This objection of Fodor is specifically directed against the use of frames and scripts as representational devices. As he says, these are merely notational or representational devices that might become useful only once one knows what is relevant to what. Having these representational suggestions does not help in finding answers to the relevancy question, and, lacking this answer, frame and script approaches remain an empty promise (Fodor, 1983, pp. 115–117). Fodor concludes that using structured representational schemes such as frames and scripts merely changes the interpretation of the frame problem from an issue in confirmation logic into an issue of executive control, which in his view is no change for the better.[28]

However, this objection seems to misconstrue the role schemata play in AI. Although frames and scripts do not solve the issue of what knowledge to specify through these means, they do play an important role in facilitating the computational *use* of whatever information is thus represented. AI takes schemata to be relevant to the frame problem not because they provide a solution to problems in the logic of confirmation but because they are important computational aids in representing information effectively. Moreover, the intent of scruffy AI is not to solve but to circumvent the kinds of problems that logical approaches to non-demonstrative reasoning face, by providing *practical* means of bringing relevant information to bear on the reasoning process (Thagard, 1988, p. 27). From this perspective, turning an issue of logic into an issue of executive control *is* thought to be a change for the better, as it may increase the chances of finding a practical solution to the frame problem.

Yet, Fodor argues, structural relations between complex representational structures are insufficient to capture the true nature of our reasoning processes. The links connecting chunks of knowledge are *mere associations*. If one recalls the example of Vitruvius' reasoning as modeled by Thagard (the path that led Vitruvius from thinking about sound to thinking about waves), then Fodor's objection is that this is not *reasoning* at all. The following interesting exchange between Fodor and Hayes throws substantial light on this issue:

> *Hayes*: In trying to think, in trying to make inferences, the central 'smart box' is going to want to use . . . associations as well; they are useful to it, so if you take them out of there it is in trouble . . .
> *Fodor*: I think that that is false, I think that there is a deep misunderstanding in the field, and that people are still making the mistake that Kant said you shouldn't make: do not think of inference as a special kind of association; they are not the same kind of relation.
> *Hayes*: I am not saying that they are. I am saying that in controlling inference you might use association.
> *Fodor*: You might, but then you would have an awful lot of trouble understanding unexpected tasks. You would only be able to understand a world which does what you expect it to. (Fodor and Hayes in Pylyshyn & Demopoulos, 1986, pp. 136–137)

What this amounts to, then, is first of all that Fodor claims that inference is not association. This can readily be acknowledged, especially if one looks at the history of associationism (Jorna & Haselager, 1994; Warren, 1921). Associationists such as Locke and Hartley only took associative principles into account when explanations of *failures* of reasoning were called for. One of the few outright attempts to provide an account of rational reasoning on associationist principles can be found in the work of James Mill.[29] His approach to ratiocination was unsuccessful and John Stuart

Mill quickly abandoned it, concentrating instead, like most associationists before him, on the synchronous association of ideas into complex wholes.

However, the more modest claim that associations can *guide* the reasoning process is an important aspect of scruffy AI. Thagard's model of Vitruvius' discovery of the wave theory of sound provides, in my view, a clear instance of Hayes' suggestion to use associations to control inference.[30] Fodor's rejoinder, in the exchange with Hayes given above, is that the structure of represented information cannot be *all* that guides inference.[31] Associative links, Fodor argues, are only of very limited use in directing inference as they are only helpful in standard situations, where the world does what one expects.[32] The guidance provided for by links that associate bits of information will be of little value because there is no general way of indicating what is relevant to what. On the basis of the Quine-Duhem thesis, Fodor argues that one cannot once and for all localize the class of data relevant to the fixation of a belief or the confirmation of a scientific hypothesis (1983, pp. 108–109). Quine argued that the first dogma of empiricism, i.e. that there is a distinction between analytic and synthetic statements, has to be rejected since there is no non-circular way to flesh out the notion of analyticity. Because of that the second, reductionist dogma fails as well; the confirmatory instances of a statement cannot be known *a priori* (1951/1980, pp. 40–41). The consequences of assuming that there is no analytic–synthetic distinction is confirmational holism. Our knowledge of 'what confirms what' is *a posteriori* and contingent (Fodor & Lepore, 1992, pp. 37–38). Therefore, the endeavor to make *a priori* or general decisions on structure, on what is relevant to what, is an impossible one.

> What degree of confirmation a given piece of background information bestows on a given . . . hypothesis can't be decided ahead of time because it depends not just on what the information is and what the hypothesis is, but also on a bundle of local considerations that change from moment to moment . . . The moral is that it's just about inconceivable that confirmation relations could be 'hardened in' once and for all in the way that the structure of memory search might be. Our estimates of what confirms what change as fast as our changing picture of the world. (Fodor, 1990, pp. 218–219)

In Fodor's view, then, there is a principled reason to have little faith in the attempt to deal with the frame problem on the basis of a pre-existing structure of knowledge.[33] So, what does underlie our confirmational estimates or intuitions?

The relevancy of a piece of information is, Fodor argues, connected to the configurational or global characteristics of the whole belief system in which the hypothesis is embedded. As he says:

> The closer you get to what we intuitively think of as the highest cognitive processes, real intelligent decision making, the more the variance is taken out, not by detailed connections between specifiable classes of data and hypotheses, but by configurational properties of the whole knowledge system . . . the frame problem is just an example of that. It's not a special problem that was invented in AI; *it's*

just a problem of confirmation that emerges when you try to do a confirmational logic for what's in somebody's head. (Fodor in Pylyshyn & Demopoulos, 1986, p. 163, my emphasis)

Fodor suggests that these configurational properties are denoted by catch-phrases such as simplicity, but that we do not understand how these kinds of characteristics can function as guides to relevant information (or otherwise take away the variance). The global characteristics of the belief system, then, are important not only with respect to the acceptability of a hypothesis, but also help in determining the relevance of a given fact for a specific hypothesis.

> What Quine showed us (as well as Putnam and others working around that period in the philosophy of science) is that almost certainly *what localizes the relevant data is configural properties of the whole belief system,* which we not only don't know how to metricize, but which we don't even know how to identify, except in terms of catch words like 'projectability', 'conservatism', 'simplicity', and all that stuff that philosophers of science use to say, 'I do not know what this phenomenon is'. (Fodor in Pylyshyn & Demopoulos, 1986, pp. 166–167, my emphasis)[34]

In contrast with scruffy AI, Fodor's answer to the question as to what could explain the appearance of relevant information can best be interpreted as that there must be a *reason* for that information to pop up under specific circumstances. There must be reasons for the importance of data instead of merely 'hardened in' associative links between frames. But, Fodor claims, we do not have a clue about *what* reasons could play a role in the 'appearance' of the relevant information, except that they seem to be connected to holistic characteristics of bodies of information. A better understanding of what would constitute such reasons must, Fodor believes, be provided by key ideas in inductive logic. The ultimate reasons under-lying our intuitions as to what is relevant can only be found by means of a confirmational logic. But developments in this area offer little promise as yet. And *that* is, in Fodor's view, the problem of non-demonstrative inference. If this view is correct, work in AI of the kind exemplified by Thagard is not even addressing the right issues involved in non-demonstrative reasoning. For classical cognitive science, then, it seems that there is no alternative but to wait for 'key ideas' in logic.

However, I would like to suggest that if the obstacles are of such magnitude that no one has even a clue on how to overcome them, it follows that both the defense of folk psychology and the principled answer to the problem of mechanical rationality are far from satisfactory. After all, what good is a scientific underpinning of folk psychology if it is not applicable to the kind of phenomena that are preeminently described and explained by that very same folk psychology? And what use is a scientific model of rationality if it cannot account for the kind of reasoning that is the most interesting and pervasive from a psychological point of view? If our lack of understanding in these fields is really as enormous as Fodor suggests, one may wonder with reason whether not only AI but also the whole Fodorian program *with respect to folk psychology* is not just 'much ado about not very much'.[35]

Given that one of the basic assumptions of AI, i.e. that representational structure plays an important role in determining the course of reasoning, is swept aside as severely misguided, it is small wonder that the reaction to Fodor from AI quarters has ranged from perplexity to outrage. Newell has expressed bewilderment at Fodor's diagnosis of work in AI:

> it seems to me that from where Fodor and I sit in cognitive science, we see completely different landscapes. Several times Fodor went emphatically on record as holding that almost all the research I've been involved in has not made the slightest progress or something like that. (Newell in Pylyshyn & Demopoulos, 1986, pp. 153–154)

Also illustrative is Hayes' reaction:

> My reaction to the exchange between Newell and Fodor is that Fodor is reading the wrong literature. What on earth does the history of inductive logic – Reichenbach, Carnap – got to do with it? (Hayes in Pylyshyn & Demopoulos, 1986, p. 163)

At this point I would like to stress that, in my view, it is crucial to make a distinction between two aspects of the problem of non-demonstrative inference. From a *normative* point of view, the difficulty is how to justify the acceptance of the hypothesis arrived at by non-demonstrative means. *Descriptively*, the issue is to find a computational mechanism that is able to perform non-demonstrative inferences in a psychologically plausible way. The importance of the distinction between these two ways of looking at non-demonstrative inference becomes clear when one considers that from a logical-normative point of view the issue is that *everything* one knows influences what one *ought* to believe.[36] But psychological-descriptively, the concern is about how *part* of what one knows influences what one *ends up* believing. Indeed, Fodor (1983, p. 137, n. 36, and p. 115) has noted that decisions about what to believe do not generally succeed in making optimal use of all data available and he has also explicitly acknowledged that there is good evidence for heuristic short-cutting in belief fixation. However, strangely enough he does not attach much weight to these observations. Nevertheless, I think that the discrepancy between normative and descriptive issues makes an important difference and significantly enhances the chances of cognitive science dealing with the frame problem in a satisfactory way.

When one looks at the history of discussions about non-demonstrative inference (traditionally referred to under the general label of 'induction'), one finds that the importance of the distinction between descriptive and normative aspects of non-demonstrative inference is stressed repeatedly. Hume, as was seen above, argued that there is no logical justification for our inductive practices, and suggested we should be satisfied with our psychological 'habits of thought', i.e. the laws of association. More recently, Hempel stressed that one should not confuse issues in logic with issues in psychology:

> While the process of invention by which scientific discoveries are made is as a rule *psychologically guided and stimulated* by antecedent knowledge of specific facts, its results are *not logically determined* by them; the way in which scientific hypotheses or theories are discovered cannot be mirrored in a set of general rules of inductive inference. (1965, p. 5)

In other words, Hempel indicates that if we are to model how cognitive systems generate and evaluate hypotheses, it is futile to look expectantly at confirmational logic and wait for key ideas to be developed there, as Fodor is proposing. It is in this respect that Thagard's work is of value. His work can be seen as an attempt to model what (to paraphrase Hempel) 'psychological guidance and stimulation' amounts to in computational terms. That this 'psychological guidance and stimulation' may seem like 'sleepwalking' (to use Koestler's 1959 terminology) from a logical point of view, is of no *intrinsic* concern to psychology.

Gjertsen compares the state of affairs within inductive logic with respect to non-demonstrative reasoning to the situation mathematical logic was in not too long ago. Mathematical logicians like Russell, Frege and Hilbert tried to provide solid foundations for mathematics, until Gödel showed that this was unachievable. Gjertsen observes:

> So far no Gödel has been able to show that the work of inductive logicians is similarily misguided. Their work, however, has become increasingly complex and artificial, and increasingly divorced from the realities of scientific practice. (1989, p. 98)

It might well be, then, that Fodor's expectations may never be fulfilled. All in all, I submit, even though we cannot be certain that progress of the kind that Fodor is willing to wait for is not achievable in inductive logic, it seems reasonable to try different and more practical approaches.

This is exactly what some AI researchers have suggested. Hayes, for instance, claims that there is a difference in kind between research in AI and philosophy. When Fodor speaks of the problem of induction, Hayes says, he should not expect AI to solve a philosophical problem in a philosophically satisfactory way. Philosophically speaking, the problem of induction is a normative matter of justification. Yet, AI is in the business of making a model that works; hence descriptive adequacy is much more important.[37] As Hayes says:

> The philosophical problem of induction is to find philosophically adequate justifications for the inductive processes people use, not to discover what they are . . . we AI hackers don't have to give any particular philosophical justification for our choice of representational vocabulary. We will use what works, and we will find out, ultimately, by computational experimentation. We might build a complete working robot, induction and all, without making a scratch on the philosophical problem of induction: that's not our business. (1987, p. 134)

> the frame problem is not one of *justifying* certain inferences, but of formulating a succinct and usable way of *expressing* them . . . The problem is not an epistemic

one of 'ascertaining' anything – it is a representational one of how to express the information we want our robots to use. (1991, pp. 72, 75–76)

Hayes insists that a rational reasoner's set of beliefs is not completely shapeless. Even if every element of knowledge were potentially relevant to the formation of a hypothesis, this does not mean that a reasoner is in a constant state of buzzing, blooming confusion. Everything might be potentially relevant to everything, but not everything is relevant to everything at the same time. Hayes (1987, p. 136) argues that precisely the existence of chunks of interrelated knowledge (for instance represented by frames) gives reasoning its efficiency.[38] Along the same lines, Lormand (1990, pp. 365–367) argues that the search for valuable links between elements of knowledge can be guided by a hierarchy of inference rules (established on the basis of their previous usefulness). Confronted with a problem, the computer selects the most promising rule (for instance, the one with the highest strength measure as in Thagard's model). Of course, as Lormand admits, creating these hierarchies of relevant rules is a large and often domain-specific task, but there is no reason to suppose that there are any principled problems involved.

Fodor may try to counter these arguments by claiming that he expects inductive logic to provide a competence specification of our non-demonstrative reasoning capacities, and not a performance description. Chomsky's distinction between competence and performance has provided an influential methodological guideline for empirical research in cognitive science. In the domain of linguistics, Chomsky proposes to make

> a fundamental distinction between *competence* (the speaker-hearer's knowledge of his language) and *performance* (the actual use of language in concrete situations). (1965, p. 4)

Linguistic rules, collectively constituting a linguistic grammar, explain the speaker's ability to recognize and use novel sentences. A competence theory specifies a tacit body of knowledge, describing what we would be able to do under ideal circumstances. An organism's competence outlines 'a space of possible behaviors' of which the actual behavior of the organism provides only a sample (Fodor, 1968, pp. 130–131; see also Chomsky, 1965, pp. 3–4, 9–10). Only under complete idealization is the performance a direct reflection of the competence.[39] Given such a competence specification by linguistic theory, it is the task of cognitive psychology, psycholinguistics and neuroscience to find out how this tacit knowledge is represented in us (e.g. whether the linguistic rules are represented declaratively or procedurally) and what factors cause the 'performative wrinkles' in our competence (Stillings et al., 1995, p. 373, see also pp. 217–218). The idea, then, is that a competence specification *guides* psychological research. The distinction between competence and performance has been applied to other areas of interest to cognitive science as well. As Katz says:

> The linguist whose aim is to provide a statement of ideal linguistic form unadulterated by the influence of such extraneous factors can be compared to the

logician whose aim is to provide a statement of ideal implicational form
unadulterated by extraneous factors that influence the actual inference men draw.
(1974, p. 232)

A competence theory specifies the logical structure of the inferential
principles that reasoners have mastered in being or becoming smart. Fodor
might argue on the basis of this that logic should guide the psychological
research of our reasoning practices by outlining our potential inferential
capacities. As he says:

a theory of scientific confirmation is basically just a model of what a scientist
would do if he was doing what he is taught to do. It's just a model of belief
fixation in a reasonably idealized scientist . . . The general problem of inductive
confirmation of belief is simply not understood, and it seems to me exactly the
same problem in psychology as it is in the philosophy of science. (Fodor in
Pylyshyn & Demopoulos, 1986, p. 158; see also Putnam in Pylyshyn &
Demopoulos, 1986, pp. 164–165)

Yet I submit that resorting to a competence–performance distinction,
though legitimate in itself, does not make Fodor's dismissal of scruffy AI
and his preference for logical solutions more plausible. The issue is what
would constitute a *good* competence theory for psychological investigations
of non-demonstrative inference. Using an 'idealized scientist' as the guiding
standard for psychological theory development would be, in my view, a
crucial mistake. The point is that an idealized scientist is not a psychologically interesting phenomenon as far as investigations into common-
sense reasoning are concerned, but rather an epistemological one. An
idealized scientist is what one could call 'a walking set of normative
standards concerning non-demonstrative reasoning'. But there is no reason
to suppose that the way we actually generate and evaluate hypotheses
conforms to these standards. It would be seriously misleading to take
justificational theories of reasoning as provided by logic as a competence
specification for psychological research[40] (not to mention the fact that it
becomes downright obstructive if there are not even any such theories). The
risk of psychological research being misled by normative competence
theories has also been noted by Simon[41] with respect to the study of our
linguistic capacities:

There is a continuing danger that focus upon an ideal competence that resides in
some kind of Platonic heaven (or a Cartesian one) will impose normative
constraints on the study of actual language behavior. (1981, p. 23)

Cognitive science studies 'satisficers', not 'optimizers'. It studies cognitive
systems that find tolerable, not optimal, solutions to their problems. For
that reason, it is necessary to understand the processes underlying our
actual reasoning capacities, not to infer what optimal intelligence amounts
to.[42] In order to understand 'idealized scientists', standards of how one
ought to reason are important to the philosophy of science. Though it is
not unreasonable to look at confirmational logic for illumination in this

respect, one must be careful in prescribing its findings to psychological research, as this harbors the danger that *normative* issues are 'smuggled' into psychology. Yet, compared to issues in philosophy of science normative aspects play a much smaller, if any, role in *psychology*.

I conclude, then, that Fodor's arguments against the suggestion that structured representation of information plays an important role in guiding inferences are far from decisive and that his alternative holds little promise. Thagard's work shows that AI, instead of being too much programming too soon, provides one of the preciously few ways to actually engage in an investigation of human non-demonstrative reasoning. Therefore, the scruffy approach in AI cannot be rejected on principled grounds, and there is no reason not to engage in the kind of work carried out by Thagard.

4.7 Conclusion

I engaged in this rather detailed investigation of attempts to understand non-demonstrative reasoning and fundamental criticisms of it in order to evaluate the status of the literal interpretation of folk psychology. Taking Thagard's work as representative for scruffy AI, I think the following conclusions can be drawn. A symbolic computational approach to the processes of hypothesis generation and evaluation *is* possible. It provides the means to formulate the problems in a way that allows a systematic and practical method of study. Classical riddles and paradoxes of inductive logic can be translated into computational issues and provided with suggestions as to their *pragmatic* solutions. Similarly, there are computational ways to take evaluation criteria into account. Finally, there are several computational suggestions as to how computational systems can themselves expand and modify their knowledge structures as a result of their reasoning processes.

Yet, I think that one has to acknowledge that work of this kind has only scratched the surface of the difficulties involved in modeling non-demonstrative reasoning. As I see it, Thagard's work is only one of the first steps in the exploration of the possibilities of the kind of work in AI that is based on the structure of knowledge and mechanisms that utilize this structure, rather than a clear sign of its success. In this sense, it paradoxically provides an inspiring as well as a sobering example. Inspiring, because it indicates that the problems can be tackled. Sobering, because a review of the proposed computational models, PI and ECHO, show how much remains to be done before real tests can be confronted. All in all, then, the situation classical cognitive science is in with respect to non-demonstrative reasoning is typical of any empirical science approaching a difficult and largely unexplored terrain.

The position of classical cognitive science would be worse if there were principled reasons why the approach favored is unlikely to yield satisfactory results. Reasons of this kind have been put forward by Fodor, who has shown himself to be both one of the staunchest defenders of the classical approach to cognition *and* one of its severest critics. Although such a dual role is undoubtedly a sign of intellectual honesty, it leaves his defense of classical cognitive science and the literal interpretation of folk psychology in dire straits. Clearly, it is logically possible to insist that classical cognitive science provides the only acceptable solution to the problem of mechanical rationality, while emphasizing at the same time that such a solution has to be strengthened by almost magically good ideas to be of value in the field of folk psychological rationality. Yet, from a more practical perspective, such a diagnosis may well fan the desire to pursue investigations in a radically different direction.

However, I think that if one considers Fodor's arguments carefully, the position of classical cognitive science, and the literal interpretation of folk psychology that depends on it, do not warrant the pessimism expressed by Fodor. The crucial issue concerns the role that mechanisms such as the spreading of activation through a representational structure play in determining the course of inference. These mechanisms are, as Fodor points out correctly, far from logically satisfactory as they only lead to a consideration of a subset of all the information that logically speaking ought to be taken into account in the generation and evaluation of beliefs or explanatory hypotheses. I have argued that though this feature does constitute a deficit from a philosophical-normative perspective, it inflicts no serious damage upon a psychological-descriptive approach to cognition. Idealized scientists are not the proper subject matter for psychology. An examination of these abstract phenomena may surely yield interesting information for psychology, for instance, by indicating points where psychological processes take a different course than a purely logical analysis would allow or where psychological processes typically take a specific route which from a logical point of view remains inexplicable. But precisely for this reason, they do not provide adequate benchmarks for cognitive science investigations of psychologically plausible reasoning. This, I think, has been pointed out in different ways from several quarters.

Ultimately, then, though logic is one of the main inspirations of classical cognitive science through its emphasis on the value of syntactic symbol manipulation for understanding rational cognitive processes, it is of limited value in understanding common-sense rationality. The somewhat para-doxical conclusion must be, therefore, that when it comes to the kind of reasoning that folk psychology is primarily concerned with, the logical inspiration for the answer to the problem of mechanical rationality should not be taken too literally, in order for the literal interpretation of folk psychology to have chances of survival.

Notes

1 It should be noted that Peirce had varying views about non-demonstrative inference and that he changed his terminology over the years. However, I will consistently use the term

'abduction' to refer to the process of generating hypotheses, as this is current practice in AI. See for instance Luger and Stern (1993), Marostica (1993), Paul (1993), Van der Lubbe and Backer (1993).

2 This is not to say that matters of scale are completely unimportant, but to indicate that at the current stage of investigation suggestions with respect to cognitive mechanisms are more important than their immediate application in larger knowledge structures.

3 Note that nothing here is implied about the question whether the hypothesis selected as best is also true. That is, one can view the succession of filters as a series of questions. An event in one's surroundings raises the question as to what to believe (what am I to think of this?), the first filter generates several possibilities (well, this or that might be the case), the second filter selects the best one (I think that is the case). After these psychological issues a further philosophical issue can be raised, i.e. the question whether the selected hypothesis is really true (am I right?). It is with respect to the last question that issues surrounding scientific realism and the like arise. These are not addressed here.

4 The issue, then, is *not* whether Thagard's work contains the definite answer to the problem of non-demonstrative inference, as it would be quite unreasonable to expect so.

5 Thagard's outlook on science is based on Kuhn's notion of a paradigm. The term 'paradigm' is ambiguous (Masterman, 1970) and its meaning can range from something very general like a world view to more specific items like problem solving examples, also known as exemplars. Thagard (1988, pp. 36, 43; 1992, pp. 47–50, 55–58) concentrates on paradigms as exemplars and he aims at making the notion more precise in computational terms. Despite his basically Kuhnian outlook, Thagard adopts the classical distinction between observations, laws and theories as the main elements of science. Laws generalize and systematize observations, theories explain laws and go beyond observations in postulating unobserved, theoretical entities (1988, pp. 12–15). Thagard (1992, p. 53) does not defend an impermeable divide between observables and unobservables, but although he does admit that theories influence the way we perceive the world, he explicitly denies that this leads to the incommensurability of radically different theories. As he says: 'We can admit that observation is theory-laden in a weak sense without adopting the relativist conclusion that it is theory-dependent' (1988, p. 96). An important function of a theory is to explain phenomena. Thagard claims that explanation goes beyond prediction in providing understanding. To understand something is to fit it into previously organized patterns or contexts, which can be specified computationally (1988, p. 44; see also Holland et al., 1986, pp. 328–329). Not only are inferential practices considered in the context of problem solving, but explanation is also regarded in this light. Explanation can be seen as a kind of problem solving, with the difference that instead of it being considered whether a sequence of actions can lead to a goal, a series of hypotheses are weighed for their explanatory value (1988, pp. 45–46).

6 Thagard (1988, p. 17) gives the following representational structure for the concept 'sound' as used by PI:

Name:	sound
Data-type:	concept
Activation:	0
Superordinates:	physical phenomenon, sensation
Subordinates:	voice, music, whistle, animal sounds
Instances:	
Activated-by:	
Rules:	
Rule-0:	if x is heard, then x is a sound.
Rule-1:	if x is a sound, then x is transmitted by air.
Rule-2:	if x is a sound and x is obstructed, then x echoes.
Rule-3:	if x is a sound and y is a person and x is near y, then y hears x.
Rule-4:	if x is a sound, then x spreads spherically.
Rule-5:	if x is a sound, then x is a sensation.
Rule-6:	if x is a sound, then x is a physical phenomenon.

7 Thagard (1988, pp. 17–18) gives the following example of the elaborate structure of rules. The rule displayed is the third one attached to the concept of 'sound' (see note 6) and in effect states that 'if x is a sound and y is a person and x is near y, then y hears x':

Name:	Rule-3
Data-type:	rule
Concepts-attached-to:	sound
Conditions:	(sound($x) true)
	(person($y) true)
	(near(xy) true)
Action:	(hears(yx) true)
Slot:	person-effect
Status:	default
Strength:	0.7
Activation:	0
Old-matches:	nil
Current-match:	nil
Satisfies-goal?:	nil
Projection-status:	nil
Current-value:	0
Action-instances:	nil

A division can be made between synchronic and diachronic rules. In synchronic or atemporal rules, the condition part specifies a category (e.g. if an object is a dog), while the consequence part specifies either another category (then it is an animal) or an association (then activate the 'bone' concept, in other words: think about bones). In diachronic rules, the condition part specifies a situation (if a person annoys a dog) while the consequence part either contains a prediction (then the dog will growl) or the action that should be taken (if a dog chases you, then run away) (Holland et al., 1986, pp. 29, 42). Note that both the conceptual hierarchy and the rules allow directed activation spreading.

8 It is tempting to see Fodor's (1987a, pp. 143–146; see Chapter 3) use of the 'kooky' concept of 'fridgeon' as inspired by and in any case largely analogous to Goodman's example, although Fodor himself makes no reference to Goodman. Lormand (1990, p. 373, n. 8) asserts that any association between Fodor's kooky concept of 'fridgeon' and Goodman's 'grue' would be wrong since, as he claims, 'fridgeon', unlike 'grue', is perfectly projectable. He thinks that this follows from the fact that if one particle is a fridgeon this would mean that Fodor's fridge is on, and therefore all particles are fridgeons. I think 'fridgeon' is not a projectable predicate, however, nor do I think that Lormand's argument shows it to be so. Of course, if one accepts the concept 'fridgeon', then once one particle may be called so, all particles may be called so. This simply follows from Fodor's definition of the concept. But the whole point of projectability is that there must be a way of preventing these ridiculous concepts from entering our hypothesis generating practices. 'Fridgeon' is not projectible because as a concept it is not *entrenched*, as Goodman says, in our practices. The fact that *if* it did apply, it would apply across the board, does not change that verdict.

9 Simple abduction uses existing general rules to construct hypotheses concerning the properties of individual objects.

10 Existential abduction postulates the existence of something hitherto unknown, again using general rules which have become operational because of the directed spreading of activation.

11 Analogical abduction is a more speculative way of inference in that it makes more substantive leaps in the creation of new rules possible. It uses past cases of hypothesis formation to generate new hypotheses. PI models this process in several steps. First of all, a representation of the 'base' hypothesis must exist, so there is something to be exploited. Second, the attempt to form an explanatory hypothesis is started by the spreading of activation from start and goal concepts. Third, the spreading of activation in the conceptual hierarchy and the firing of rules should result in the activation of concepts connected to the base

hypothesis, so its existence becomes noticed. When the activation of the base hypothesis transgresses a threshold, PI initiates the fourth phase. In this phase, PI tries to establish a mapping between concepts of the base hypothesis and the original concepts that started the spreading of activation. It can accomplish this by tracing how the activation spread, determining which original concepts led to the activation of which concepts of the base hypothesis. These are then mapped. The fifth step consists of a translation of the explanatory rules attached to the base hypothesis. If the analogical hypothesis is found to be applicable, then a sixth step becomes possible in which an abstracted, more general form of the base and analogical hypotheses, called a schema, is stored to for future use (Holland et al., 1986, pp. 287–319; Thagard, 1988, pp. 22–25, 60–63).

12 Basically, the idea behind Schank's scripts is that there is a standard representational format in which one's knowledge of stereotypical sequences of events, involved for instance in 'going to a restaurant', is instantiated (Schank & Abelson, 1977a; 1977b).

13 Suppose you know that entities of a certain kind have a specific property and you want to explain this, e.g. why is it the case that a specific x that is S is also P? Immediately abducing to the general rule that all instances of S are also P seems premature, as the co-occurrence of S and P in the case of x might be totally coincidental. But if you can also think of a general rule that is related to the fact you want to explain, e.g. all $W(x)$ are $P(x)$, then you might infer that the specific x must also be W. This allows you to abduce to the general rule that being S implies being W: all $S(x)$ are $W(x)$ and therefore, since all $W(x)$ are $P(x)$, it is explainable why the x that is S is also P (Thagard, 1988, p. 59). In this way, the general rule that all $W(x)$ are $P(x)$ constrains the abductive generation of the rule that being S implies being P. Importantly, though this general rule is part of the knowledge of the system, the fact that it becomes operative in this context is explained through the mechanisms of directed activation spreading and rule firing.

14 At least this is his approach with respect to the knowledge of Stahl, Lavoisier, Darwin, Wegener, Aristotle, Ptolemy and Newton in his book *Conceptual revolutions* (Thagard, 1992). In the particular case of Vitruvius, the knowledge PI was endowed with seems to have been less based on historically reliable information on Vitruvius' knowledge. This 'psychohistorical untrustworthiness' does not detract from the value of the example, however, since I am using it as an illustration of PI's general mode of operation with respect to abductive inference and not of its historical validity.

15 To avert the danger that still too many new rules are created, several additional constraints or triggering conditions are suggested (Holland et al., 1986, pp. 79–83). An important triggering condition for the generation of explanatory hypotheses consists in the failure of a prediction or the happening of something unusual. A second constraint avoiding useless rules is formed by a set of higher-order, relatively domain-independent, inferential rules, comprising pragmatic reasoning schemata (1986, p. 43). Examples are the specialization heuristic which specializes a more general rule when it has failed, and the unusualness heuristic which uses unexpected properties of a phenomenon in the formulation of the condition part of new rules (1986, p. 43; Thagard, 1992, pp. 54–55). These very generally phrased adaptive types of transformation provide for a more directed generation of new rules. A further constraint on rule generation is formed by constraining the process of recombining rules through a preference for successful and simultaneously active rules.

16 It is important in this context to appreciate the inadequacy of Bayesian probability theory to deal with theory evaluation. This approach starts with a given set of relevant evidence and calculates how each piece of evidence contributes to the overall probability of the hypothesis. In order to do so, it must have information concerning the probability of the evidence, the probability of the hypothesis, and the probability of the hypothesis given the evidence (Krause & Clark, 1993, pp. 20–21, 45, 50–51). Although there are problem domains where all this information can reliably be obtained, Thagard (1988, p. 97; 1992, pp. 92–93) notes that in the field of theory evaluation the relevant probabilities are almost impossible to find. Secondly, assuming the availability of detailed probability information is essentially another way of avoiding the main problem. If you have, in advance, a specification of the relevant data, their likelihood, a set of candidate theories and their likelihood given the

evidence, then mechanically deciding between those theories is not a big problem: 'if you say in advance which is the event space and which are the reasonable theories given that event space, then one can mechanize choice among theories; but Mill could already do that, Bacon could already do that' (Putnam in Pylyshyn & Demopoulos, 1986, p. 165). Finally, some have argued that the Bayesian approach is primarily of normative, not descriptive, value since it is known that, in general, humans are bad at estimating numerical probability values and do not engage in complex arithmetic while performing inferences (Krause & Clark, 1993, p. 16).

17 Similarly Hempel (1965, p. 5) speaks of 'antecedent knowledge of specific facts' that psychologically guides and stimulates scientific discoveries.

18 This aspect underlines in a different way why a Bayesian approach is unsatisfactory. It provides a 'local' method for establishing statistical significance, but has no way of assessing how global factors contribute to the confirmation of a hypothesis (Fodor, 1983, p. 139, n. 44; see also Fodor in Pylyshyn & Demopoulos, 1986, p. 159; Harman, 1992, p. 205).

19 ECHO is an acronym for 'explanatory coherence by Harmany optimization'. This is a pun based on conflating Harman (who has done considerable work on the topic of induction) and a well-known mathematical operation, harmony theory (which allows a network to reach an optimal and stable state) (Thagard, 1989, p. 497).

20 This, as we have already seen above, is consistent with Thagard's rejection of incommensurability, although it cannot be considered an argument against incommensurability, as that would obviously beg the question.

21 Auxiliary hypotheses or assumptions are not necessarily bad or *ad hoc*, for instance when they are shared by competing theories.

22 Though Thagard speaks here of the number of facts, I take it that he, in line with his earlier remarks on consilience, actually means the number of classes of facts.

23 Put more psychologically: 'If a proposition is highly coherent with the beliefs of a person, then the person will believe the proposition with a high degree of confidence' (Thagard, 1989, pp. 436, 459–460; see also 1992, p. 64). So TEC, though primarily applied to scientific hypothesis evaluation, can also be taken as an attempt to model common-sense belief evaluation.

24 For some critical remarks see, among others, Giere (1989) and Zytkow (1989).

25 As Thagard says in the context of a specific modeling attempt of Lavoisier's oxygen theory: 'ECHO . . . deals only with relations between propositions, and does not take into account the structure of Lavoisier's conceptual system. It treats propositions as unanalyzed wholes, without breaking them down into their conceptual constituents . . . A full computational analysis of Lavoisier's mental system would specify all its conceptual and propositional components and clarify their interrelationships, but a cognitive system rich enough to do this and incorporate ECHO has yet to be built' (1992, pp. 83–84).

26 See also Dietrich (1989, p. 474), who speaks of 'computational positivism' having disastrous consequences. It should be kept in mind, however, that my criticisms concerning ECHO do not imply a wholesale rejection of TEC, since TEC can be implemented in many different ways. Furthermore, Thagard (1992, p. 84, n. 3; see also 1989, pp. 458, 497; and Zytkow, 1989, p. 490) has indicated that he wants to blend PI's representational abilities with ECHO's evaluation mechanism, and he expects a great deal from the development of hybrid systems. Until this has been achieved, however, it seems that a principled, integrated way of using measures of consilience and simplicity in the evaluation of a hypothesis remains a largely unsolved issue.

27 The same point applies to connectionist models.

28 Fodor further indicates that since frames and scripts can point to other frames and scripts, once a lot of information is represented through these means there will ultimately be connections between everything and everything; only the length of the connecting paths will differ. Then the question becomes once again which connections should be preferred. However, this does not seem to constitute a principled objection. It is standard practice with respect to models that use mechanisms of activation spreading to incorporate a decay parameter that stops activation from continuing endlessly. This effectively prevents everything from becoming activated and allows for 'automatic preference'.

29 For example, Mill tried to explain syllogisms in terms of the underlying associations. Seeing the truth of a premise, e.g. 'all men are animals', is merely the recognition that the meaning of 'all men' is included in the term 'animals', and that recognition is nothing more than a case of association. The same goes for the premise 'kings are men'. The conclusion 'kings are animals' is also reached through association: 'In each of the two preceding propositions, two terms or names are compared. In the last proposition, a third name is compared with both the other two; immediately with the one, and, through that, with the other; the whole, obviously, a complicated case of association' (1829, ch. 12, p. 311).

30 As Thagard says: 'the simulation gives some idea of how an association between sound and waves might occur during an attempt to explain why sound propagates and reflects' (1988, p. 22).

31 Putnam agrees with Fodor on this: 'Mechanisms like association cannot be the whole solution to the problem' (Putnam in Pylyshyn & Demopoulos, 1986, p. 138).

32 Fodor's phrase 'a world which does what you expect it to' may give rise to misunderstandings. After all, common-sense rationality is called for under ordinary circumstances and the frame problem arises during normal events in everyday situations. If association guided inference of the kind investigated by Thagard resulted in a satisfactory model of common-sense reasoning under normal conditions, this would be a great success on any account, despite the fact that more creative reasoning under more unexpected circumstances would not be explained by it. It is clear, however, that Fodor means that associative control of inference is insufficient even to model standard kinds of reasoning that are of interest for cognitive science.

33 Note that the issue here is not whether this structure is created externally or whether it is created by the system itself during its reasoning processes. The point is that once the structure is established, it is not guaranteed to be of the right kind for every possible situation.

34 I do not think that catch-phrases such as simplicity are intended to capture processes of localizing relevant data by the configural properties of the whole belief system. That is, there is the problem that you cannot specify in advance which data help confirm which hypotheses. And there is the different problem that global characteristics of a body of relevant knowledge also count in the evaluation of the plausibility of a hypothesis. But it is, contrary to Fodor's claim, not clear if (and how) these global properties essentially determine which data are relevant. Simplicity is not intended to answer that question. Global factors such as simplicity affect (in an insufficiently understood way) the confirmation of a hypothesis, but not the selection of relevant data. In this sense, the work of Thagard can be taken to shed light on the mechanisms involved in measuring the simplicity of a hypothesis with respect to a certain set of data. But, if the question really is how global factors determine which data are relevant, there are not even catch-words to label the mechanisms.

35 Recently, Pickering and Chater (1995) have followed Fodor in his claim that cognitive science is committed to the view that cognition is mechanized proof theory. They argue that therefore cognitive science can only deal with knowledge-free processes. Because folk psychology concerns knowledge-rich processes, cognitive science and folk psychology apply to entirely separate domains. Cognitive science can therefore not provide theories that will vindicate (or eliminate) folk psychology. As I argue in the remainder of this chapter, however, the idea that cognitive science is dependent on logic is unfounded and not universally supported (see also Morris & Richardson, 1995).

36 As Reichenbach puts it: 'If we want to say that logic deals with thinking, we had better say that logic teaches us how thinking *should* proceed and not how it *does* proceed . . . We know very well that productive thinking is bound to follow its own dark ways, and that efficiency cannot be secured by prescriptions controlling the paths from the known to the unknown. It is rather the results of thinking, not the thinking processes themselves, that are controlled by logic. (1947, p. 1). Logic, in Reichenbach's view, provides a rational reconstruction of thought. Hence his famous distinction between the context of discovery and the context of justification, the former being the domain of psychology, the latter being the concern of logic (1947, p. 2). The difference between logic and thinking is also pointed out by Cummins (1989, p. 167, n. 20): 'Systems of formal logic contain what are called rules of

inference. But such rules don't tell you what to infer; they are only part of a system that determines the validity, not rationality, of an inference already made. They thus have little to do with inference as it is meant here, i.e., with inference construed as the essence of cognition: generating a result that is rational (rational enough) relative to the situation you are in.'

37 Taking my remarks in Chapter 3 about Hayes' interpretation of the frame problem into account, the following picture emerges. I disagree with Hayes about the proper interpretation of the frame problem because I think that Fodor is right in seeing it as strongly related to the problem of induction (non-demonstrative inference). However, I agree with Hayes when he claims, contrary to Fodor, that a philosophical or logical solution to the problem of induction is not required for the purposes of AI and cognitive science in general.

38 Hayes also stresses that he is not advocating a fixed structuring of information. The structure should not be general and principled, and therefore specifiable *a priori*, but idiosyncratic and changeable.

39 As Chomsky says: 'The problem for the linguist, as well as for the child learning the language, is to determine from the data of performance the underlying system of rules that has been mastered by the speaker-hearer and that he puts to use in the actual performance' (Chomsky, 1965, p. 4).

40 Stich (1990, pp. 79–86) discusses and rejects a philosophical argument that an organism's inferential competence must necessarily be normatively impeccable. On the basis of several empirical studies, Jepson, Krantz, and Nisbett (1993, p. 80) have argued against a normative specification of inductive competence.

41 Similarly, Newell, Rosenbloom, and Laird have noted that there can be a large gap between competence and performance (1989, p. 98).

42 Interestingly, Kitcher (1990, p. 191) argues that Kant's work can be seen as a task analysis of the kind propagated by Newell and Simon but that Kant, contrary to Fodor, was careful to keep the normative separate from the descriptive. On the basis of his task analysis, Kant argues that reasoning (as the process of belief formation or fixation) is a two-tiered process invoking the faculties of 'understanding' and 'reason' (1990, p. 200). Understanding, as the faculty of concepts with the power to combine them in a judgment, is subject to the law of association (1990, pp. 200–201; Kitcher refers to Kant, 1787/1956, A100). It finds relevant material by means of its imaginative power though it is, from a normative point of view, far from perfect in doing this. As Kitcher (1990, p. 202) notes, even if the requisite information is available, there is, in Kant's view, no guarantee that it will be found. Reason, the faculty with the power to infer, unifies and systematizes our knowledge. Importantly, Kant pointed out that the systematizing principles of reason are 'regulative' but not 'constitutive'. They represent epistemic ideals, normative principles about how best to systematize knowledge, not empirical accounts of what actually happens when we reason (1990, p. 203; Kitcher refers to Kant, 1787/1956, A642–A644/B670–672). Kitcher explicitly applies her interpretation of Kant to Quine's argument for confirmational holism and Fodor's interpretation of it. As she says: 'What Kant's position shows is that the move from Quinean holism about belief to Fodorian skepticism about a science of belief fixation rests on two confusions. First, and most clearly, this reasoning slides from normative considerations to descriptive claims. Second, it also trades on conflating the roles of understanding and reason in belief formation' (1990, p. 205). Thus, I take Kitcher's interpretation of Kant to support my argument that good competence models should not necessarily be based on normative accounts of reasoning. Even if one accepts confirmation holism as a problem for a logical analysis of the justification of non-demonstrative reasoning, it does not follow that human beings implement mechanisms that have a logically valid way of dealing with it.

5

The Neurocomputational
Theory of Cognition

In Chapter 3, I examined how the representational approach to the frame problem led to a discussion of the disadvantages of the symbolic representational system. Haugeland, for one, suggests that the frame problem is a consequence of the use of semi-linguistic representations and Dreyfus views the frame problem as an artificial one created by the use of a symbolic representational scheme. In line with these views, Churchland (1989, p. 156) claims that the frame problem is a direct consequence of the sentential view of representation because this is 'an appallingly inefficient way to store information'. If knowledge is stored as an immense set of sentences, then the retrieval of the few relevant ones that help to understand an event is bound to become problematic. In Chapter 4, I examined a typical response of classical AI, consisting of attempts to devise a well-structured, and therefore computationally more efficient, organization of knowledge representation by way of frames and conceptual hierarchies. In this chapter we will examine whether a distributed representational scheme provides the basis for an alternative view of human knowledge and reasoning that evades the frame problem altogether. Churchland's neurocomputational model explains an organism's ability to generate an explanatory hypothesis quickly as the result of a process of prototype vector activation. I will investigate his proposals and the related work of other investigators on the basis of three questions.

First of all, how is the hypothesis *generated* by the network? Specifically, what influences the production of the eventually ensuing prototype vector? Can Churchland explain how the relevant knowledge is brought to bear upon the network's response? After considering Churchland's proposed solution to this important aspect of the frame problem in Section 5.1, I will investigate whether it stands up under close scrutiny, by raising two further questions.

The second major question to be investigated in this chapter concerns the exact nature of a prototype vector. Specifically, what are its *representational capacities*, i.e. what kind of information can it carry? In trying to answer this question, I will return to Fodor's discussion of compositionality (considered in Section 2.3) and his claim that a representational system must have a combinatorial syntax and semantics in order to explain productivity and systematicity. In Fodor's view, a representational system that does not utilize constituently structured representations cannot be compositional. In Section 2.4, I noted that distributed representations, by superposing representings, are radically different from symbolic representations and do not explicitly mirror the structure of the information represented. The question therefore is whether distributed representations can handle structured information and explain productivity and systematicity. I will discuss this issue in section 5.2.

The third issue to be investigated concerns how competing prototype vectors are to be compared and *evaluated*. What makes the generated activation vector epistemically valuable (e.g. good, true, useful)? In Section 2.5, I noted the incompatibility between cognitive models based on distributed representations and the literal interpretation of folk psychology. This forms an important basis for Churchland's eliminativism, introduced in Section 1.3. Churchland attempts to draw some strong consequences from his neurocomputationally inspired eliminativism, especially with respect to a propositional interpretation of knowledge and informational states. Section 5.3 will be devoted to the epistemological consequences of Churchland's eliminativism, and to the possibilities his neurocomputational theory of cognition offers for an evaluation of hypotheses.

5.1   The frame problem revisited: distributed representations and prototype activation

In Section 2.4 I investigated the nature of distributed representations. The knowledge of a system was found to reside in its connectivity matrix (i.e. the connectivity pattern and the weights attached to the connections), determining the transformation of activation patterns in a network. In response to incoming information, the network generates an activation pattern that represents its response to the information it has received. The output pattern can be seen as the result of an application of a theory, embodied in the connectivity matrix, with respect to the incoming information as represented by the input pattern.

During the learning phase, the weights are set in a way that results in a partitioning of the activation space of the hidden units. The network has developed, as Churchland (1989, p. 206; 1995, p. 83) puts it, a system of prototype representations for each general category that is of relevance for the task it has learned to perform. A prototype can be thought of as a point or small volume in the hidden unit activation space (a 'hot spot'), representing a family of relevant features that are characteristic for stimuli belonging to a specific kind. Different input vectors can result in the activation of this prototype vector by the hidden units: the network has learned that these diverse inputs are similar with respect to the task it has learned. Previously unencountered input patterns that result in hidden unit activation patterns close to the prototypical region will evoke the prototypical reaction of the network. Activation patterns that occupy a place at a considerable distance from the prototypical region in the activation space indicate that the system is dealing with a murky case.

According to Churchland, it is on the basis of this computational model that we can understand how human beings can see the relevant consequences of events or actions in their environment so quickly:

> Explanatory understanding consists in the activation of a specific prototype vector in a well-trained network. It consists in the apprehension of the problematic case as an instance of a general type, *a type for which the creature has a detailed and a well-informed representation*. (1989, p. 210, see also p. 208)

The network generates an explanatory hypothesis, which effectively says: 'this incoming information is of such and such a type.' The generation process itself can be quite complex. Churchland stresses that the activation of a prototype should not be thought of as a simple affair, a mere behavioristic, reflex-like connection between sensory input and motoric output. Since a network may have many[1] layers of hidden units, there is ample possibility for quite complex processing. Still disparate activation patterns in one layer can result in quite similar activation patterns the next layer. In this way a hierarchy of prototypes can be represented where subordinate prototypes are embodied by activation patterns in early layers, and superordinate prototypes by activation patterns in subsequent layers (1989, p. 216). Furthermore, a network can receive input from other areas of the brain and, through recurrent connections, transmit the results of previous processing back into its earlier layers (1989, p. 208; 1995, pp. 99–108). Therefore, the actual processing taking place in networks can be very complex and, though fast, is far from reflex-like.

Churchland also indicates that the prototype activation model does not instantiate a 'mere' process of classification, but adds information to the incoming activation pattern. The activation of a prototype models explanatory understanding as a kind of *ampliative recognition*. An organism ends up understanding far more about the situation than was originally present in its input since the prototype is the result of the previous complex processing of many examples during its learning stage (1989, p. 212).

Churchland (1989, pp. 212–218; see also 1995, pp. 97–143) illustrates this prototype activation model's range of application by examining six different kinds of prototypes that together give a unified explanation of much of our explanatory understanding. The most obvious application, which has already been noted, is that in which prototypes represent clusters of properties identifying categories. But prototypes can also represent temporal sequences of event types which lie behind our typical causal explanations (etiological prototypes) or our functional explanations (which Churchland refers to as 'practical prototypes' as in: the heart beats in order to pump blood). Superordinate prototypes can represent a specific prototype as an instance of a more encompassing category, thus allowing for the implementation of hierarchies. Social-interaction prototypes constitute our knowledge of legal, moral or social matters. Finally, motivational prototypes depict standard configurations of beliefs and desires in relation to behavior. It is the latter, learned, set of prototypes that particularly constitutes folk psychology.

As a further indication of the potentially broad area of application of this approach, one may note the argument that pattern recognition should be seen as a basic cognitive operation, underlying our learning, choosing, judging, reasoning and even calculating abilities (Aparicio & Levine, 1994; Bechtel, 1993, p. 127; Bechtel & Abrahamsen, 1991, pp. 140–145; Margolis, 1987, p. 43). Margolis, for instance, suggests that judgment can be interpreted as an internal process of pattern generation and recognition, depicting events and actions potentially taking place in the world. Reasoning is a specialization of pattern recognition applied to the language we use in describing our judgmental ponderings, whereas logic is a further specialization of reasoning, utilizing abstract variables (1987, pp. 51–62). Cognition, then, is not a process of syntax-sensitive transformation of symbolic structures, but consists of pattern recognition, leading to the recognition of yet further and deeper patterns. In this view, we are in a continuous cycle of receiving informational cues and recognizing the patterns inherent in them, which themselves become part of the cue for the next pattern recognition, etc. (1987, p. 2). Unfortunately, Margolis' accounts of these cognitive processes are expressed in very general and vague terms (as Bechtel & Abrahamsen, 1991, p. 143 put it: 'he deliberately paints a general view of cognition with a broad brush'). Yet Margolis' remarks are valuable because they at least give a rough indication of how pattern recognition might be of importance to higher cognitive functions.

Rumelhart (1992) has argued that the ability to recognize patterns underlies much of our reasoning capacities. Though he does not refer to Margolis, Rumelhart has sketched a model that, in my view, provides a good illustration of how Margolis' cycles of pattern recognition could be implemented. Rumelhart suggests a system consisting of two sets of inter-active networks. One performs the production of output through a standard relaxation function, which causes the network to settle into the most appropriate state with respect to the received input. It receives inputs from the world, and responds by specifying actions to be undertaken. The other set of units has the same relaxation mechanism, but its input consists of specifications of actions and it responds by specifying results. The state into which it settles represents the situation as if the action was undertaken. The output of this second network might subsequently be given as input to the first, action-specifying, network. This could then provide new actions as output which could be fed back again into the second, result-specifying, network, etc. Thus, a sequence of 'what would happen if I did this' states can be modeled, which, according to Rumelhart (1992, pp. 77–78), can elucidate why we are good at 'perceiving' answers to problems. Acquiring expertise is becoming better in translating problems into pattern-matching tasks (1992, p. 78).

Furthermore, the notion of partitioned activation spaces might shed new light on the riddle of induction. For instance, Gardenfors (1990, p. 79) has argued that the problem of finding projectable predicates (i.e. avoiding irrelevant but possible inferences) is solvable through a representational approach of conceptual space instead of through linguistic or propositional representations. Although his remarks on the insufficiency of linguistic representations are unconvincing (since he falsely presupposes that a linguistic representational format must necessarily use a purely definitional theory of conceptualization), his analysis of conceptual spaces is interesting from a connectionist perspective. A conceptual space is essentially similar to what Churchland calls an activation space, although there are differences with respect to the exact layout of the space and the nature of the dimensions: compare for instance Gardenfors (1990, pp. 84–86) with Churchland (1988, pp. 148–149; 1989, pp. 103–104). A property can be understood as a region within the conceptual space (Gardenfors, 1990, p. 87). A projectable or natural property can be thought of as being a convex region in conceptual space. A region is convex when all points between any two points that are located in the region are also within that region (1990, p. 88). This precludes for instance Goodman's 'grue' as a natural property since many points exist that fall outside the region specified by grue, yet lie between points that are within the region 'grue'. For instance, a point in the color–time region green-before-2000 (grue) and a point in the color–time region blue-after-2000 (again grue) have many points which do lie between them in the conceptual space, yet are not grue (as for instance points in the region blue-before-2000). Gardenfors concludes: 'the notion of a conceptual space and, more generally, "topological" representations of knowledge should be computationally much more efficient than traditional linguistic representations when trying to write programs that perform inductive inferences' (1990, pp. 93–94).

A claim has been made that connectionism provides the architecture for radically new and better models of common-sense reasoning, instead of constituting a 'mere' implementation of classical approaches to cognition (Sun, 1994).[2] Sun describes an architecture (CONSYDERR[3]) that deals with similarity-based inferences. It consists of two components, two networks that are, so to speak, put on top of each other. The first component (CL: CONSYDERR localist) uses localist representations and can implement rules through an excitatory connection from the condition node to the conclusion node. The second component (CD: CONSYDERR distributed) represents information related to the concepts localistically encoded in the first component, in a distributed way by specifying their features at a subconceptual level. Once a node of CL is activated, the architecture operates in a three-step cycle: (1) the top-down phase, in which the nodes in CD connected to the activated node in CL become active; (2) the settle phase, in which the activated nodes of CD in turn activate other nodes in CD and the whole CD network is allowed to settle into a stable state; (3) the bottom-up phase, in which the activated nodes in CD direct their activation back to the nodes in CL with which they are connected.

On the basis of this architecture, GIRO, a model for geographical information reasoning and organization, has been developed. Geographical areas and regional characterizations are localistically represented in CL (e.g. Brazil-north, Ecuador-coast, cattle-country, producing-banana). Each node of CL is connected with a set of nodes of CD (at the 'lower' level, so to speak) representing its features (e.g. tropical, rainy, fertile, prairie, plain). Activation of a specific node of CL will result in the activation of the associated feature nodes in CD. GIRO can be given questions about what products a specific region will produce (e.g. 'What is the main agricultural product of Brazil-north?'). In the event that GIRO does not have a rule specifying the requested information, it is still able to come up with 'an educated guess'. Activation of the node localistically representing Brazil-north will 'flow down' to CD and activate nodes representing the features of Brazil-north (e.g. tropical, rainforest, hilly plateau). These features are, in varying degrees, shared by other areas. Since these other areas might be connected to nodes specifying their agricultural products, these nodes also get activated as the CD network settles into a stable state. The activated nodes of CD are then allowed to activate the nodes of CL with which they are connected (so the activation flows 'back up' again), and the products associated with areas similar to Brazil-north will represent GIRO's answer to the question. CD effectively performs a similarity mapping with other geographical areas to supplement rule-based reasoning (Sun, 1994, p. 257). Sun claims that models of this kind

> are not just implementations of their symbolic counterparts, but better computational models of commonsense reasoning. (1994, p. 241, see also pp. 242, 243)

I think, however, that this is far too strong a claim. In my opinion, the main problem is that the representational theory underlying CONSYDERR and GIRO is at best a hybrid one. Activation of the nodes in CD representing the features tropical, rainforest and hilly plateau does not represent Brazil-north in a genuinely distributed way. These nodes merely specify certain features of Brazil-north, while the content 'Brazil-north' itself is only represented localistically in the other component, CL. This becomes clear if one realizes that the relationship between the features given and Brazil-north must be explicitly represented by connections with the node in CL that does represent Brazil-north. A further indication of the hybrid character of Sun's model is that nodes in CL representing agricultural products are simply duplicated by nodes in CD. For instance, 'cattle-country' is localistically represented in CL *and* in CD. This clearly goes against the account of distributed representations as provided by Van Gelder (discussed in Section 2.4) since it is possible to slice CD in such a way that distinct items are represented by distinct subparts of the representational resources.

In general, Sun does not make a clear distinction between what the nodes represent for the network itself and what the activation of the network means for the user. He stretches his interpretation of the network's activity far beyond what it actually represents. This is obvious when, for instance, Sun (1994, p. 253) takes the activation of the node representing 'Brazil-north' in CL to embody the question 'What is the main agricultural product of Brazil-north?'

Furthermore, it is unclear in what sense CD can be said to perform reasoning as all CD is allowed to do is to make a similarity mapping between regions on the basis of activated features. Finally, since CD does not use truly distributed representations, Sun's model cannot count as a clear instantiation of the connectionist alternative to the classical approach.[4] All in all, then, Sun's model does not substantiate his claim that connectionist architectures provide a better account for common-sense reasoning.

Returning to a more *theoretical* perspective, I think that the essence of Churchland's proposed neurocomputational solution to the frame problem is clear, despite the fact that its practical value remains to be shown. Cognitive systems can quickly see what the relevant consequences of a change in the environment are, because the information they receive results in an almost instantaneous activation of an adequate prototype that constitutes an explanatory understanding of the situation. As all weights influence the emergence of the activation vector, everything the network knows is brought to bear upon its response to incoming information. Churchland argues that because the relevant knowledge is activated automatically, the frame problem does not even arise. As he says:

> Since information is stored not in a long list that must somehow be searched, but rather in the myriad connection weights that configure the network, *relevant aspects of the creature's total information are automatically accessed by the coded stimuli themselves.* (1989, p. 178, my emphasis)

He is supported in this optimistic attitude by several others. Meijering (1993, p. 31), for instance, has expressed great confidence: 'the infamous frame problem is solved in the blink of an eye' (my translation).[5]

Importantly, this proposed solution to the frame problem is made possible precisely because neurocomputationalism forswears the symbolic representational format. As we saw in Chapter 4, the use of symbolic representations as utilized in classical cognitive science allows for a close mirroring of the structure of knowledge as propositionally described. In Thagard's PI, the relationships between concepts as expressed in a proposition are explicitly represented by links between symbolic structures in a hierarchy or through the use of rules. In the terminology of the representational approach introduced in Section 3.2, symbolically capturing a propositional description of knowledge results in its *extrinsic* representation. According to the representational approach, this is the main cause of the emergence of the frame problem. To capture the potential relevance of everything to everything, every possible relation between two concepts which might at a certain point in time and in a certain context become important needs to be represented explicitly through a hierarchical link or a rule. Even if this were feasible, finding the relevant information in the midst of a myriad of symbolic structures and their interconnections quickly becomes computationally overwhelmingly complex.

Modeling information processing on the basis of distributed representations and activation pattern transformation seems to skip these problems because no attempt is made to match closely a propositional specification of information. Instead, a distributed representation represents information in holistic fashion, without its decomposition into constituent concepts and their interrelationships. As the knowledge a system possesses lies embodied in its weights, it directly and automatically constrains the processing of incoming information. There is no need to search for the relevant pieces of information before they can be applied. Moreover, changing the knowledge of a system after an event has occurred need no longer take the form of an explicit reconsideration of all symbolic structures and their interconnections. Changing the setting of one weight automatically influences all the information processing of which the network is capable.

In the terminology of the representational approach to the frame problem, the question is whether distributed representations may be said to represent their information intrinsically. Following Haugeland's analysis the condition is that representations should not allow a distinction between explicitly and implicitly represented information. Claiming that distributed representations represent their informational content explicitly seems rather awkward for, because of the superposing of representings, it cannot even be clearly stated *what* they would explicitly represent (other than: everything the network knows). They also do not represent implicitly because nothing has to be derived before it can be used for processing. The weights directly and immediately influence the processing of information. It is interesting to note that the difficulty of applying these notions to connectionist ways of representing information has led to a reconsideration of the nature of the explicit–implicit distinction (Clark, 1992; Hadley, 1995; Kirsh, 1990). Instead of concluding that these notions are inapplicable, however, attempts have been made to redefine them in various ways. This has led to rather counterintuitive results (e.g. Kirsh's claim that symbolic representations need not be explicit) and contradictory conclusions about distributed representations being explicit (Clark) or implicit (Hadley). Elman (1991, pp. 218–219) has expressed doubts about the usefulness of the distinction and claims that it makes no sense to view networks 'through traditional lenses'. In my view, distributed representations conform to the requirements of the representational approach. They do not allow a clear distinction between explicitly and implicitly represented information but represent their informational content intrinsically. Furthermore, the problem of finding the right ontology, as discussed by Janlert (see Section 3.2), is answered by letting the system learn to partition its activation spaces in response to its interactions with the environment. The system thereby creates a hierarchy of prototypes representing the categories it discerns in its environment that have proven useful in generating adequate responses to incoming information.

However, to see whether the frame problem really is that easily solved, I propose to look at the two remaining issues that lie beneath the surface of the suggestion of resonating prototypes. First of all: are distributed representations really adequate when it comes to the representation of complex information involved in reasoning and understanding? Or is the gain in automatic and direct retrieval of relevant knowledge overshadowed by the substantial loss in ability to represent the structure of information? Specifically, can neurocomputational models adequately represent the structure inherent in information without resorting to a representational format with constituent structure? The second issue concerns the evaluation of hypotheses generated. How can the appropriateness of such an information bearing state be established? This point is closely connected to the epistemological implications of eliminative materialism. If our cognitive states are not propositional attitudes and therefore not truth valuable, what kind of epistemic virtues do apply to them? To paraphrase McCauley's (1993, p. 84) formulation: can normative reflection occur within a non-folk-psychological, non-propositional conceptual scheme?

5.2   The representational capacities of distributed representations

An important question can be raised with respect to the representational potential of distributed representation. In particular, how can more complex information be represented? According to Thagard, for instance, distributed representations are, in this respect, still no match for their symbolic counterparts:

> The concept of distributed representation is powerful and appealing, but the connectionist framework has a long way to go to catch up to the expressive power of the rule and frame approaches. (1992, p. 242)[6]

According to Churchland, however, activation vectors hold great representational promise. A conservative estimate of the representational capacities of the brain indicates that an astronomical amount of entities can be represented. Churchland roughly calculates that given an estimate of 10^{11} non-sensory neurons in the human brain, divided into about 10^3 specialized subsystems, each specialized state space has about 10^8 dimensions. This allows, he claims, for a 'stunning variety' of coding vectors that function as 'stunningly complex and fine-grained representations' (1989, p. 209).[7] Therefore, Churchland concludes, even the most complex or intricate phenomena can be represented, from cell meiosis to a six-course dinner, and from twelve-bar blues to stellar collapses. Activation spaces can encompass categories of great complexity (1989, pp. 191, 210; 1995, pp. 114–121). Churchland explicitly claims that there is a great deal of structure in the activated prototype vector:

> The vector has structure, a great deal of structure, whose function is to represent an overall *syndrome* of objective features, relations, sequences, and uniformities. (1989, p. 212)

It would seem, then, that Churchland thinks that the number of units (embodying the dimensions of a representational activation space) is the decisive factor in the ability to represent complex information. Yet such an assumption would be defective. After all, the issue is not just how many different dimensions a prototype vector can have since that only indicates how *much* information it can represent. Rather, the problem is how the *structure* of information can be represented through activation vectors and how this structural information can be *used* by the weights of the network.

As said, an activation vector specifies a point in activation space, the dimensions of which are formed by the individual units belonging to the set sustaining the activation pattern. A point in this space merely represents the synchronous or simultaneous association of all their activation levels. No structural relations between the informational contents of these activations are herein represented. It would be an error, then, to take the units and their subfeatural contents as the ultimate 'constitutive' representational elements of the activation pattern. As soon as this step is made, the charge of simple associationism becomes hard to counter.

Indeed, the relationship between connectionism and associationism has frequently been noted and discussed (Bechtel, 1985a; Buckingham, 1984; Dellarosa, 1988, pp. 28–29; Jorna & Haselager, 1994; Levelt, 1989; Lindsay, 1988a, p. 41; McLaughlin, 1993, p. 163; Ramsey, 1992). Fodor specifically uses the term 'associationism' in a pejorative sense as a label underscoring the naivety of the connectionist approach to cognition.[8] Its representational theory, he claims, is basically a matter of association, and the difference between localist and distributed representations is inessential in this respect (Fodor & Pylyshyn, 1988, p. 15, n. 10). It does not matter whether the contents associated are, to use Smolensky's (1988, p. 6) terminology, at the conceptual or the subconceptual level since in both cases there is only simultaneous entertainment (which could also be called a contiguity-based association), whereas what is needed is that the contents are 'in construction' with one another. That is, there is a big difference between the simultaneous activation of representations of e.g. 'the body' and 'heavy', and combining them into a structured whole as in 'the body is heavy'. In the former case the only information expressed is that there is a body and that there is something heavy, whereas in the latter case it is represented that it is the body that is heavy. Connectionist vectors (prototypical or otherwise) are just structureless heaps and do not have an internal structure which could be utilized in further processing (Fodor & Pylyshyn, 1988, p. 27). Furthermore, Fodor claims that even if connectionism allowed structured representations, they would be of no use as long as structure-sensitive processes are rejected.[9] Connectionism merely offers sophisticated versions of the old associationist principles of learning and reasoning (Fodor, 1994c, p. 296; Fodor & Pylyshyn, 1988, pp. 30–32).[10] All that happens when the activations of units lead to the activation of other units is the association of their contents. If connectionism does not aspire to implement a classical architecture, it is by its nature committed to associative relations between units; but association is not a structure-sensitive relationship (1988, p. 67).[11] Finally, as soon as one accepts both structured representations and structure-sensitive processes, one is committed to the classical approach to cognition, and connectionism becomes a mere matter of implementation. It seems, then, that connectionism has the unappetizing choice between being a mere implementational (and therefore cognitively irrelevant) theory or a modern version of a refuted associationism.

Not surprisingly, many connectionists have rejected this line of reasoning. In their opinions, connectionism should not be equated with simple associationism (Smolensky, 1989, pp. 5–6), although it might, perhaps, be regarded as 'associationism with an intelligent face' (Bechtel & Abrahamsen, 1991, p. 103). Several attempts have been made to show that connectionism *can* represent and use structured information without thereby succumbing to a mere implementation of the classical architecture.

Although the issues involved in evaluating this claim have become increasingly complicated, and are as yet far from settled, I will examine one project that attempts to validate the connectionist claim. The basic suggestion, advocated by Van Gelder (1990; 1991a) and Chalmers (1990; 1993) among others, is to try to achieve a functional kind of compositionality without constituently structured representations. To address this issue properly, we have to reconsider and expand upon some points discussed in Section 2.3.

As we saw there, the *classical* symbolic representational format can be used to represent the structure of information by allowing tokens of constituent symbolic elements to be arranged into an organized complex whole. The meaning of the complex symbolic structure can be composed of the meaning of its constituents together with their mutual syntactic relationships. The abstract constituency relationships among expression types are directly and physically realized in the relationships among their corresponding tokens. In other words, the representations have syntactic structure (Van Gelder, 1990, pp. 360–361). This constituent structure of representations makes compositionality possible, which in turn explains productivity and systematicity. Although arguments about the exact nature and pervasiveness of systematicity are possible (as was noted in Section 2.3), it is generally agreed that a system must be able to represent complex structured information in order to exhibit interesting cognitive functions. Any representational scheme that is of interest to cognitive science must, at least to a considerable extent, be compositional (Chalmers, 1993, p. 306; Hinton, 1990, pp. 2–3; Pollack, 1990, p. 78; Smolensky, 1991, p. 288; Van Gelder, 1990, p. 350).

Van Gelder (1990; 1991a) has suggested that compositionality can be achieved *without* constituent structure. In fact, he claims that distributed representations can constitute a functionally compositional representational scheme that is, at least in principle, capable of representing in a usable way the structure inherent in information. If this is the case, then Churchland is right, again at least in principle, not to worry too much about the representational capacities of his neurocomputational models.

According to Van Gelder, a representation can well represent a structured item without itself having a constituent structure, as long as there are general, effective, and reliable processes by which to compose complex expressions from constituents, and to decompose a complex expression back into its constituents. Processes are general if they are applicable to arbitrarily complex representations, effective when they can be performed mechanically, and reliable if they always generate the same answer for the same input (1990, p. 361). A functional compositional representation differs from a syntactic or concatenative representation in that its structure is *not* directly reflected in its tokening. There is, in other words, no part–whole relationship between simple and complex representations in a functional structure. However, designing and implementing these compositional and decompositional processes is no easy matter.

The task is especially difficult since there is an important additional constraint on the resulting model. The computational processing of representations which results in behavior must operate directly on the functional structure residing in the representations, without depending on a preliminary decomposition process into constituent elements. It is, for instance, no use performing a decomposition of a complex symbolic structure in order to let the constituents play their causal role, because such an undertaking would simply boil down to an implementation of the classical architecture. Resorting to constituent structure whenever 'real action', as Van Gelder (1990, p. 381) puts it, is called for, is effectively acknowledging that no genuine alternative to classical cognitive science has been provided. So the challenge to connectionism is

> to devise models in which structure-sensitive processes operate on the compound representations themselves *without* first stopping to extract the basic constituents. These processes must capitalize *directly* on the inherent and systematic similarities among the nonconcatenative representations. (1990, p. 381; see also Chalmers, 1993, p. 312; Fodor & McLaughlin, 1990, p. 202, n. 14)

David Chalmers (1990; 1993) has attempted to meet this challenge head on. Chalmers presents a connectionist network utilizing distributed representations that models the transformation of sentences from the active to the passive mode. He makes no claims with regard to the psychological or linguistical plausibility of his model. He uses syntactic transformation as a clear example of structure-sensitive operations (1993, p. 313). For instance, the sentence 'John loves Michael' should be transformed by the network into 'Michael is loved by John.' Note that the information present in the structure of the sentence is that John is the one who loves Michael, and not vice versa. On Fodor's account, a network is incapable of distinguishing between 'John loves Michael' and 'Michael loves John' since it is 'structurally blind' and merely associates 'John', 'loves' and 'Michael'. Providing a transformation into the correct passive mode, then, indicates that the network *is* able to recognize and use the structure in the information represented.

First, syntactically structured sentences (represented by trees) are transformed into distributed representations. This is accomplished by the so-called RAAM network (Pollack, 1990).[12] The RAAM network transforms the concepts, as well as their place in the tree structure, into a distributed representation. This same architecture can be used later to decompose distributed representations of sentences back into their tree structure. The RAAM architecture is general (it applies to tree structures of arbitrary depth), effective (the (de)composing processes are performed mechanically) and reliable (after sufficient training) (Chalmers, 1990, pp. 55–56) and thus effectively provides what Van Gelder refers to as 'functional compositionality'.

The resulting distributed representations are used by the actual transformation network (a basic, three-layer feedforward network, learning through back-propagation) that performs the passivization directly on the distributed representations, without using a decomposition process first. The resulting output is of course again a distributed representation which then is fed into the RAAM, translating it back to its syntactic structure.[13] The question, of course, is whether Chalmers' network is able to use the structure that is implicitly contained in the activation patterns provided by the RAAM network. Can the network create a partitioning of the activation space that allows it to react adequately to this implicit structure?

After training, the transformation net was tested with new sentences. Chalmers (1990, p. 60) reports a 65% generalization rate, which, high in itself, went up to 100% after correction of RAAM errors. Chalmers concludes:

> Not only is compositional structure *encoded* implicitly in a pattern of activation, but this implicit structure can be *utilized* by the familiar connectionist devices of feed-forward/backpropagation in a meaningful way. (1990, p. 60; see also 1993, p. 314)

So, Chalmers claims that his results contradict Fodor's thesis that syntactic constituent structure has to be present in representations in order to be of use to information processing mechanisms. There is no need for an explicit tokening of the simple parts of the representation in the complex one. Chalmers states that his work provides a counterexample to Fodor's claims by indicating that distributed representations *can* have enough formal structure to be functionally compositional and of direct use to the system's processes. Chalmers claims to have shown how a connectionist architecture can provide for systematic cognition. Furthermore, this systematicity has been achieved without resorting to a classical architecture utilizing representations with a constituent structure.

If one looks critically at Chalmers' work, a first thing to notice is that his model does not capture tense and noun–verb agreement. That is, instead of transforming 'John love*s* Michael' into 'Michael is love*d* by John', the network actually transforms 'John love Michael' into 'Michael is love by John' (1990, p. 56). Passivization, then, is represented in a somewhat simplified form by transforming sentences of the form noun-verb-noun into noun-is-verb-by-noun.[14] Yet, McLaughlin (1993, pp. 176–177) remarks that this abstracts away from precisely the things that make the active–passive transformation hard to capture. McLaughlin does not, therefore, consider that Chalmers' model constitutes a counterexample to Fodor's claims. I do not agree with this verdict, however. After all, Chalmers explicitly does not want to model our linguistic abilities, but is attempting to show that structure-sensitive processing is possible in connectionist networks with distributed representations. The structure in his examples resides in the subject–object distinction (who is doing the loving versus who is being loved). The task the network faces and fulfills is to capture this structure by retaining the subject–object roles in the passive mode, not to express it in correct English.

A second point of interest is that McLaughlin accuses Chalmers of taking the fact that the network *represents* items with a syntactic structure for it actually *having* a syntactic structure. In my view, McLaughlin's accusation is misguided. Indeed, the whole point of Chalmers' work is to show, along the lines indicated by Van Gelder, that a network can be sensitive to syntactic structure *without* having syntactically structured representations. Far from confusing the representation of a structure with the possession of a syntactic structure, Chalmers attempts to show that the latter *is not necessary* for the former. It would seem, then, that McLaughlin has missed the important role of Van Gelder's notion of functional compositionality in Chalmers' work.[15]

A more serious criticism has been given by Hadley (1994a, p. 261) who notes that the novel corpus of sentences that Chalmers used to test his network contained no new words (i.e. no words not already encountered during training) or words occupying new syntactic positions (i.e. the network had encountered all words in all syntactically possible places during training). In other words, the novelty of Chalmers' corpus of test sentences is rather moderate. As Hadley says (1994a, p. 262), if a completely new word were introduced in an otherwise familiar sentence, this might result in such disruption of the network that *it would not even recognize the familiar lexical items*. Hadley concludes that Chalmers' model only exhibits a weak form of systematicity and does not succeed in capturing the strong systematicity[16] argued by Fodor as being a clear characteristic of human cognition.

Hadley's criticism raises the important and more general point that one has to be very careful that the structure-sensitive behavior of a network is not simply the result of statistically large similarities between the training data to which the network has become tuned and the test data. This hampers a straightforward assessment of the force of connectionist examples of structure-sensitive processing. To paraphrase Clark (1990, p. 201; see also Christie, 1993, pp. 159–160), the worry is that it is quite possible to create a model that *looks* as if its operations are structure-sensitive by making it perform a suitable function in extension. To remedy this danger, Hadley (1994a, pp. 249–252) proposes to consider the system's ability to generalize by examining the degree of sentence novelty a system can handle.

The matter of distinguishing real systematicity from statistical coincidence (e.g. aptly similar training and test data) also comes to the fore in the discussion about Fodor's repeated claim that merely providing counterexamples is far from sufficient to show that connectionism can deal with compositionality in a completely satisfactory way. As he says, it is a *law* that cognitive capacities are systematic (Fodor & McLaughlin, 1990, pp. 202–203; Fodor & Pylyshyn, 1988, p. 48). That is, it is easy to 'wire up' a non-systematic connectionist network, but it is impossible to create an unsystematic classical system. The point of the law requirement, as Butler (1993, p. 323) notes, is that merely showing that systematicity is *possible* on the basis of a connectionist architecture is not enough; it must be indicated why systematicity is *necessary* given the architecture. Likewise, Butler says, a theory of planetary motion that merely allowed for the possibility of elliptical orbits of planets would be considered as insufficient. To really count as an explanation, it would have to show that the nature of such orbits necessarily followed from the theory. Similarly, connectionists have to demonstrate that systematicity necessarily follows from the architecture.

Two things can be said about Fodor's argument. First of all, one may question whether it is really a 'law of nature that you can't think *a*R*b* if you can't think *b*R*a*' as Fodor claims (Fodor & McLaughlin, 1990, p. 203). The 'lawfulness' of systematicity has indeed been doubted by several writers (Dennett, 1991a, p. 27; McNamara, 1993, p. 114; Wilks, 1990, p. 331). However, though there may be room for argument about the exact extent of systematicity, it is quite clear that children and adults display systematicity in a strong sense (Hadley, 1994a, pp. 252–254, 270). Furthermore, given that we are discussing claims that connectionist models can be functionally compositional and thereby display systematicity, we may concentrate on strong systematicity and let discussions about the lawfulness of this phenomenon rest. Secondly, one can, as does Chalmers (1993, p. 316), quite rightly point out that the fact that 'differently wired' networks could easily be insufficient at best shows that not all possible connectionist architectures are satisfactory. To be acceptable, Chalmers says, the class of rightly wired networks would have to be compositional and display systematicity under many different learning conditions. I think Chalmers is right in stating this, but it only helps to underscore the fact that merely demonstrating that a rightly wired connectionist network with distributed representations can be compositional is not sufficient, since this might be an artificial result of the specific characteristics of the training and testing data. Fodor's requirement that systems *must* be compositional can, I suggest, most beneficially be seen as an attempt to provide a safeguard against too readily taking 'accidental' signs of systematicity for the real thing. With respect to this worry, I think that Hadley's proposed criterion of generalization ability, i.e. the network's capacity to deal with genuinely novel sentences, is adequate. Hadley (1994a, p. 271) notes that in the light of this criterion the work of Chalmers and several other connectionist attempts to answer Fodor's challenge do not succeed in displaying the strong degree of systematicity charactʒristic of humans.

Of course the debate is continuing (see, for instance, Bakker, 1995; Christansen & Chater, 1994; Hadley, 1994b; Niklassen & Van Gelder, 1994), so it would be premature to conclude anything definite about the potential of distributed representations. The representational story to be told, however, will in any case be considerably more complex than Churchland appears to think. Moreover, there are reasons for pessimism regarding the potential of distributed representations to be scaled up to reasonably complex cases. Hummel and Holyoak (1993) observe that distributed representations of, for instance, predicates and objects cannot be combined into larger distributed structures without losing information about which objects are bound to which predicates. That is, there is an 'inherent tradeoff between distributed representations and systematic bindings among units of knowledge' (p. 464) that comes clearly to the fore as soon as several distributed representations have to be combined (they give the example of the sentence 'Jane knows that Ted gave Mary flowers', where a distributed representation of 'Ted gave Mary flowers' is difficult to combine in a distributed fashion with a distributed representation of 'Jane knows that p' without losing information as to who knows what or who gave what to whom). Shastri and Ajjanagadde (1993) make the same point and claim that a purely distributed representational system 'cannot have the necessary combination of expressiveness, inferential adequacy and scalability' (p. 485).

In conclusion, I think that Churchland's remarks about the representational potential of vectors can easily be rejected as insufficient. Merely having many dimensions available is substantially different from having the resources to represent structure in a way that can influence actual cognitive processes. Since dimensions merely represent the activation of a specific unit that is part of a larger set, the end result is a mere conjunction of activation values. Addressing the issue of representing structured information in terms of the number of dimensions available must be rejected as an instance of simple and insufficient associationism. However, more sophisticated work in connectionism has shown that by resorting to more complex architectures, it is possible to create networks that allow some degree of structure-sensitive processing in a non-classical way, i.e. by being functionally compositional. Yet genuine doubts may be raised about whether the results achieved indicate the true capabilities of distributed representations or whether they largely depend on the specifics of the training and testing data. Moreover, serious doubts can be raised about the potential of functionally compositional schemes to be scaled up.

The conclusion at this point (and on the basis of the material considered) must be that connectionism has still no principled and satisfactory way of effectively representing structured information in a distributed way. This, in turn, makes Churchland's proposed solution to the frame problem considerably less attractive. The consequence of that, finally, is that my analysis so far provides little support for the claim that folk psychology in its literal interpretation has to be rejected. It is true that models based on distributed representations are incompatible with folk psychology, but their empirical superiority over classical models has yet to be demonstrated.

5.3   Evaluating hypotheses

From a general point of view, Churchland (1979, p. 125; see also Churchland & Churchland, 1990, p. 302) says, organisms should be considered as 'epistemic engines', devices that exploit sensory stimulation and the information already stored, in order to produce more information with which to guide behavior. Traditionally, and under the influence of folk psychology, the basic units of information were thought to consist of propositions (1979, p. 127).[17] Churchland argues that this is a basic mistake. By uncritically accepting folk psychology as a basis for further inquiries, cognitive science has adopted a wrong characterization of the knowledge of cognitive systems as propositional attitudes, resulting in a bad representational theory of mind, leading among other things to difficulties with the modeling of non-demonstrative inference, as exemplified by the frame problem. It is therefore not hard to see why Churchland would consider the elimination of folk psychology to be anything but a loss, since folk psychology can be viewed as a profoundly negative influence upon our attempts to understand cognition in cognitive science as well as in epistemology.

If we look at the current perils of orthodox epistemology, Churchland claims, we are bound to conclude that the portrayal of epistemic engines in terms of sets of propositions is, to say the least, unsatisfactory. He notes the problems that orthodox (i.e. propositionally based) epistemology has encountered, among other things, in modeling our pre-analytic judgments of credibility, in explaining learning as the rule-governed updating of a system of propositional attitudes, and in justifying our confirmational practices (1989, p. 154). Furthermore, it is hard for a propositional epistemology to define and measure the role of simplicity as an important factor in determining the credibility of a theory or hypothesis; nor can it explain why simplicity would be relevant to strengthening our belief in the truth of a theory. Finally, orthodox epistemology is incapable of explaining why better theories are closer to the truth, and, indeed, the notion of truth itself is suspect as the supposed aim or product of cognitive activity (1989, pp. 149–150, 157). In all, Churchland holds that little or *none* of human understanding consists of stored sentences, not even the prototypically *scientific* understanding embodied in a practising physicist, chemist, or astronomer. The familiar conception of knowledge as a set of propositional attitudes is itself a central aspect of the framework of folk psychology . . . and it is an aspect that needs badly to be replaced. (1989, p. 112, see also p. 121; 1995, p. 277).

A better view of the nature of information bearing structures in the brain and the processes operating upon them will have radical consequences for our views of what constitutes good cognition. Understanding virtuous intellectual activity and development requires that we go beyond the surface of sentence manipulation and investigate the true nature of our intellectual processes (1979, pp. 141, 127, 137). In the following pages I will concentrate on Churchland's ideas concerning the value of his neuro-computational models for an alternative epistemology as applied to the generation of *good* explanatory hypotheses or, as he prefers to call it, inference to the best explanation. I propose to examine Churchland's claim that his neurocomputationalism can do better than the classical approach, especially with respect to explicating the role of simplicity in the evaluation of hypotheses and theories. Before we can consider Churchland's proposals, we must first explore the consequences of eliminative materialism for epistemology and the nature of the task he confronts.

The necessity of new epistemic virtues

From a neurocomputational perspective, inference to the best explanation can be understood as an appropriate prototype presenting itself in response to certain input patterns (Churchland, 1989, pp. 218–219; 1995, p. 54). We do not, Churchland claims, normally engage in a cumbersome episode of logical reasoning. In fact, inference has got nothing to do with our explanatory understanding. Nor do we generally search for an explanation among a list of many potential ones. There is no time wasted on making choices between numerous alternatives. Irrelevant inferences are automatically precluded by the structure of the activation space:

> a trained network will regularly make an ampliative 'inference' to the best available 'explanation' of the input phenomena. And it will do so in milliseconds. (1992b, p. 40)

At first sight, then, and from a neurocomputational perspective, inference to the best explanation does not involve a comparative evaluation of several potential hypotheses, since the most adequate prototype will present itself automatically. Yet this does not relieve Churchland of the task of indicating how evaluation takes place. After all, even though there is an almost automatic response to incoming information, we should be able to assess the appropriateness of the hypothesis generated, from a general normative point of view as well as from the perspective of the epistemic engine itself. Churchland believes it is possible to show how evaluation can occur in a conceptual scheme that is radically different from the one provided for by folk psychology. This means that the epistemic virtue of a hypothesis will have to be measurable in terms of characteristics of activation vectors.

Here we encounter one of the stronger consequences of Churchland's eliminativism. As stated in Sections 1.2 and 2.2, on the literal interpretation of folk psychology, mental states can be seen as propositional attitudes, specifying the relation of the organism with respect to an abstract truth-valuable entity (which, in the classical account, is represented by a token of a symbolic structure). Simply put, believing a proposition implies that one is likely to proceed (both cognitively and behaviorally) on the basis that the proposition is indeed true, i.e. that the world is as the proposition expresses. A desire can be understood as standing in relation to the proposition such that its symbolic tokening will lead causally to thought and behavior directed at making the proposition true, i.e. by making the world conform to it. If one eliminates folk psychology, one eliminates propositional attitudes. Since Churchland wishes his neurocomputational theory to have consequences for epistemology, he has to refrain from notions such as propositions (and thereby truth) when accounting for the evaluation of explanatory hypotheses. Churchland is quite explicit about this:[18]

> how, on this PDP approach to explanation, are competing modes of under-standing to be evaluated? What makes one explanation better than another? Here we must answer carefully, since we are denied the usual semantic vocabulary of reference, truth, consistency, entailment, and so forth. The cognitive kinematics here being explored does not have sentences or propositions as its basic elements; the basic elements are activation vectors. The various dimensions of epistemic virtue will therefore have to be reconceived in terms that are grounded in this new conception of what cognitive activity consists in. (1989, pp. 220, 16; see also McCauley, 1993, p. 84)

By rejecting truth as a valuable notion of epistemic virtue, Churchland has set himself the formidable task of providing new normative notions, because trying to do entirely without them is no real option. As Putnam (1983, p. 246) has noted, the complete elimination of the normative is 'attempted mental suicide'. Churchland agrees with this verdict, but his aim is not to abolish talk of epistemic virtue but rather to enhance our under-standing of it. By transcending the poverty of the folk psychological (i.e. propositional) conception of rationality we will make, Churchland claims, an enormous advance in our appreciation of real cognitive virtue:

> Eliminative materialism does not imply the end of our normative concerns. It implies only that they will have to be reconstituted at a more revealing level of understanding, the level that a matured neuroscience will provide. (1989, pp. 16–17)

He has tried to steer clear of complete intellectual anarchism by insisting that knowledge is still founded in the causal effects of the surroundings on the organism, and that rational cognitive development is subject to certain formal constraints. It is just that these causal effects and formal constraints are not understandable in terms of propositions, and not correctly statable in sentences (1979, p. 141).

In employing his neurocomputational theory for the development of new notions of epistemic virtue, Churchland is not trying to simplistically base normative or evaluative notions on descriptive models of cognition. Notions like truth and explanation are normative because they are action guiding, approval expressing and therefore interest and context related. But nature itself is neutral, it has no built-in epistemic properties (Putnam, 1983, pp. 290–298). Churchland acknowledges this[19] and his explicit aim is not to straightforwardly derive 'ought' from 'is'. As he says, it is only the *autonomy* of epistemology that must be denied (1989, p. 196, see also pp. 16–19, 50; 1979, p. 150).

In order to replace truth with more deeply penetrating notions based on a neurocomputational understanding of cognition, Churchland resorts to holistic evaluative notions, so-called 'superempirical virtues' such as simplicity, coherence and explanatory power. These global virtues must form the basis for the evaluation of competing explanations, not just as pragmatic devices for evaluation, but as providing the fundamental measures of rational ontology (1989, pp. 146, 151). I would like to investigate the value of Churchland's epistemological work by examining his non-propositional explication of one of the superempirical virtues of theories and explanations, i.e. simplicity. I will concentrate on simplicity because it has been reasonably well worked out by Churchland, and because we have also studied Thagard's analysis of it in Chapter 4.

The neurocomputational understanding of simplicity as an epistemic virtue

The task Churchland faces is twofold: first, how should simplicity be defined or measured, and second, why should simplicity be considered epistemically valuable (1989, p. 179)?

With respect to the first question, Churchland indicates that a 'good' network finds the most general similarity behind the diverse input–output associations it has encountered and processed, on the basis of the feedback it receives. Such a network achieves a maximum economy in representation by partitioning its activation space in the smallest number of category-representing prototype vectors (1989, pp. 179–181, 221–222). So, in neuro-computational terms, one knows an explanation is 'simplest' when the network settles on the most basic partitioning of the activation space possible.

A network can be forced to create an optimal partitioning of the activation space by giving it the adequate amount of computational resources, i.e. an optimum number of hidden units, with respect to the task at hand. If it has too few hidden units, it lacks the resources to represent the relevant dimensions needed for adequately discerning among the input. If it has too many hidden units the network can become 'lazy'. That is, instead of learning the essential aspects of the input, it deals with the information on an *ad hoc* basis, by using whatever partitioning that leads to the proper output, without searching for the most basic one. This will result in bad generalization when new information is encountered. The necessary fine-tuning of the computational resources usually cannot be done by the network itself in the course of action, however. As Churchland notes:

> The needed simplicity must generally be forced from the outside, by a progressive reduction in the number of available hidden units. (1989, p. 181)

I must admit that I find this account of how simplicity can be measured somewhat puzzling. After all, how is it established what constitutes the most basic partitioning of an activation space with respect to a certain domain? Or, to put it the other way around, how does one know that no *ad hoc* hypotheses are relied on by the network to produce the right output? This becomes all the more urgent for a second reason. As Churchland himself indicates, the optimum number of hidden units has to be established from the outside. Forgetting for the moment the question of how 'the optimum number' is established, how can this criterion be applied without external intervention? In order to make his theory at least applicable to human cognition, Churchland should indicate what kinds of mechanisms could perform this function in the human brain. Lacking this, his position is similar to programmers in classical cognitive science models who supply their models with all the necessary information themselves instead of letting the models find it on their own. In this respect, though connectionist networks are generally praised for their self-structuring and learning capacities, one must also observe that many networks are to a substantial degree pre-fetched, in the sense that their exact architecture has been carefully thought out and tested before the actual application to a task is carried out (Christie, 1993, p. 157; Clark, 1990, p. 214).

With respect to the second question (why simplicity would be epistemically valuable), Churchland (1989, p. 195) asserts that a neurocomputational perspective can create a clearer picture of simplicity not only with regard to its nature, but also with regard to its epistemological significance. Churchland starts by indicating what is wrong with the traditional idea that truth is the basic epistemic virtue by which cognitive representations and processes should be judged. Truth is suspect since, from an evolutionary perspective, the fine-tuning of one's behavior, the quality of one's performance, and the survival value of explanatory hypotheses are far more important than pure truth. If we want to describe what an organism is 'aiming' for, then it is not truth it is after, but reproductively advantageous behavior made possible by satisfactory representation of the environment and speedy processing (1989, pp. 150, 298; 1987, pp. 548–549). It can easily be seen why simplicity is important in this respect. Churchland indicates that getting a maximum result with minimum resources is in itself merely a pragmatic advantage. His main point is that a more basic partitioning of an activation space means that more systematic responses to a wider range of phenomena are possible. In short, simplicity leads to superior generalization and this is a genuinely epistemic virtue (1989, pp. 181, 193). Having a simple hypothesis with which to explain the events in your environment is valuable, for it is likely to be useful in future cases as well.

I find this explanation of the epistemological significance of simplicity far less penetrating than Churchland makes it out to be (see also Haselager, 1993a). Merely indicating that greater simplicity is important because it leads to superior generalization is not the same as shedding a new and revealing light on the nature of our normative endeavors. The importance of generalization is well known, and the relation between simplicity and generalization has also been noticed by, for instance, Thagard (Section 4.4). So it is difficult to see where the advantages of a neurocomputational perspective on epistemic virtue really lie.

McCauley (1993, pp. 91–92), for one, is positive about Churchland's 'normative naturalism'. A neurocomputational analysis of the notion of simplicity gives, he says, a 'detailed insight' into the nature of the relation between the unity and simplicity of explanations. The possibility of a neurocomputationally based 'normative naturalism' has become clear. Churchland himself also seems to think that the hardest part is done:

> We can already see how to approach this most vital issue, because we already have in hand the vectorial kinematics and the synaptic weight-space dynamics to which the new evaluative/semantic notions must somehow attach. As our understanding of neural network function increases, we will be better able to define useful notions of representational success and failure, of epistemological virtue and vice. It is not even very difficult. (1992a, p. 422; he explicitly refers to his views in Churchland, 1989, pp. 220–223, which I have discussed above)

However, I think that there are good reasons for tempering this enthusiasm. Even apart from the fact that notions like simplicity and superior generalization are clearly not 'new', Churchland has not shown why a neurocomputational perspective had to be developed in order to see their true nature. Indeed, Churchland's proposals for measuring the super-empirical virtues leaves much to be desired. His suggestions concerning optimally partitioned activation spaces, or the most adequate number of hidden units, are of dubious value for descriptive-psychological purposes and unlikely to be useful when trying to apply the epistemic virtue of simplicity to theories and explanations in realistic settings. Furthermore, it is far from clear that his account of the significance of simplicity is more illuminating than Thagard's observations, which are compatible with orthodox epistemology and with classical cognitive science. So, even though Churchland (1992b, p. 48) claims that 'a new door has opened in normative epistemology', his new empirical theory of thinking has not yet resulted in a genuine improvement in epistemology.

5.4   Conclusion

In this chapter, we considered the possibilities a neurocomputational view of cognition offers for dealing with the frame problem by suggesting new ways to generate, represent and evaluate hypotheses. Interpreting the frame problem along the lines discussed in Chapter 3 (especially Section 3.2), the problem to answer is: how can the relevant knowledge an organism possesses quickly be brought to bear upon the generation of a hypothesis that enables the organism to understand what is going on in its surroundings, to see the relevant consequences of events and react accordingly? Churchland's basic proposal, that this process can be understood as the generation of a prototype vector, has been examined in some detail. I think that his neurocomputational model is well suited, in principle at least, to explain how the relevant knowledge can quickly influence the formation of the prototype. By representing information in a distributed fashion over the set of weights that collectively determine the network's response to incoming information, problems of the fast retrieval and application of relevant information can be evaded in a most graceful way. However, if one examines the representational capacities of connectionist models more closely, one finds that the proposed solution may not be as easily applied to more complex phenomena as Churchland suggests. Representing more complex and especially more structured information is not simply a matter of collecting more units into larger networks. Indeed, at this point it is not at all clear whether connectionism can represent structured information in a way that allows the network to use the structure without thereby becoming an instantiation of the classical architecture. To the extent that something like functional compositionality has been achieved, this turns out to depend in larger part upon the careful design of the architectures of the network and a meticulously arranged training regime. Although I think that Van Gelder's notion of functional compositionality has created the theoretical possibility of an escape from the dilemma of connectionism raised by Fodor, its practical value with respect to realistically complex cases remains doubtful.

I have also examined the strong consequences that eliminating folk psychology can have for our standard views of epistemic virtue and for our evaluative practices. Churchland claims that this only adds to the attractiveness of his theory, since it makes a better understanding of epistemological issues on the basis of an adequate theory of cognition possible. No doubt there are genuine problems with orthodox, propositional epistemology but, if one reviews Churchland's ideas concerning simplicity as an epistemic virtue, it is far from obvious wherein the real progress lies.

All in all, then, although the neurocomputational answer to the frame problem looks promising at first sight, in fact it still leaves much to be desired. Moreover, the promised epistemological gains have yet to be substantiated.

Notes

1 Churchland (1989, p. 208) indicates that for some pathways in the brain up to 100 layers can be distinguished.

2 Another connectionist attempt to model common-sense reasoning can be found in Derthick (1990). However, he concentrates on the advantages of a connectionist implementation of frame-based knowledge representation structures (1990, pp. 111–112), and is therefore of less direct interest for our purposes. Shastri & Ajjanagadde (1993) outline a detailed and ingenious connectionist model of common-sense reasoning. The representational theory that they implement in a connectionist architecture, however, is a rather classical one of (complex) facts, rules and conceptual hierarchies. They explicitly reject the use of distributed representations as being unsuited for representing large amounts of structured knowledge (p. 485). Taking into account their rejection of the use of purely logical rules of inference (p. 420), they provide, in my view, a good example of the classical, scruffy kind of AI as discussed in Chapter 4, even though their model is implemented in a connectionist architecture.

3 CONSYDERR stands for 'Connectionist System with Dual Representation for Evidential Robust Reasoning' (Sun, 1994, p. 246).

4 As in the case of Thagard's ECHO (see Section 4.4) one may question whether the use of the mechanism of parallel constraint satisfaction in itself makes the resulting model a genuine alternative to the classical theory of cognition. I think that the representational format used is far more important in this respect.

5 Rumelhart et al. have also pointed at the promise of connectionist models in this respect, although they put it somewhat more cautiously: 'Existing artificial intelligence programs have great difficulty in rapidly finding the schema that best fits the current situation. Parallel networks offer the potential of *rapidly applying a lot of knowledge* to this best-fit search, but this potential will only be realized when there is a good way of implementing schemas in parallel networks' (1986, p. 109, my emphasis, see also p. 126).

6 Thagard (1992, p. 243) has especially pointed to difficulties involved in representing scientific knowledge by means of distributed representations. Others have ventured similar doubts about the possibilities of distributed representations with respect to capturing the complex internal structure of information. See for instance Holyoak's remark: 'the most serious issues of representational adequacy arise in networks in which concepts that must have a complex internal structure are represented by diffuse, overlapping sets of units' (1991, pp. 315–316).

7 To indicate the representational capacity of such a space, Churchland states that a vector with 10^8 elements can code the contents of an entire book. One space can contain an astronomically high number of these vectors (1989, p. 209). Of course, these 'calculations' are very rough, but they can be accepted as illustrations of Churchland's main point that the brain allows for really high-dimensioned activation spaces.

8 Bever, Fodor, and Garrett (1968) have indicated some principled limitations of purely contiguity-based associationism. However, associationism is a much less simple approach than Fodor makes it out to be. The prominent role that has been regularly granted throughout the history of associationism to the principle of similarity indicates that associationists saw the importance of a structure-sensitive mechanism. Therefore, no matter what one may think of connectionism, associationism itself should not be used as the cliff over which to push it (Jorna & Haselager, 1994; Linschoten, 1957).

9 This point is similar to the one made by Cummins. Since there are no structure-sensitive rules that process the representational elements in a network, even if the representations have syntactic structure, it could not be computationally exploited anyway (1989, p. 6).

10 Two kinds of associationism have to be discerned. The first, 'synchronous' association concerns the combination of representational elements into complex ones. This is to be distinguished from the second, 'diachronic' or 'successive' association of informational states as a way of modeling chains of reasoning.

11 Fodor and Pylyshyn invoke a suggestion of Hume's to illustrate the difficulties encountered by associationism. Hume thought that ideas are like images, and that they have structure. He furthermore assumed an active, structure-sensitive faculty of the mind which he called 'imagination'. In Fodor and Pylyshyn's view, this is 'cheating' because *'qua* associationist Hume had, of course, no right to active mental faculties' (1988, pp. 49–50, n. 29). The lesson, according to them, is that once one accepts structured representations, the temptation to postulate structure-sensitive processes is considerable, thereby adhering to the classical approach to cognition. However, the claim that associationists have no right to postulate structure-sensitive processes is quite unfounded as it rests on an overly impoverished view of associationism. Similarity-based association, especially, is a prime example of the kind of structure-sensitive process that has been assumed by prominent associationists like Locke, Hume and J.S. Mill (see Jorna & Haselager, 1994). The question here, of course, is whether connectionism can provide a satisfactory non-classical mechanism that underlies the associationist principle of similarity. This is why investigations concerning systematicity are also of relevance to long-standing philosophical debates.

12 RAAM is an acronym for 'recursive auto-associative memory'. Basically, it is capable of representing the information inherent in symbolic tree structures of arbitrary depth as distributed activation patterns. It can compress the representations of the terminal nodes into one activation pattern which represents their parent, and then, recursively, compress all parents one layer up into another single pattern, compress these patterns yet again, etc., thus working from the leaves to the root. Similarly it can reconstruct the children from the distributed representation of the root, reconstructing them recursively until the leaves are reached (Pollack, 1990, p. 84).

13 Note that this is not an instantiation of a classical system. This would have been the case if distributed representations were first decomposed into their constituents, then processed, after which the end result would be distributedly represented again. In Chalmers' model things go vice versa, and the processing is performed directly on the distributed representations themselves.

14 It is somewhat confusing, however, that in a later article Chalmers (1993, pp. 312–314) illustrates his earlier work by using correctly formed sentences as examples. This should not be taken to imply that the network is actually able to capture the correct tense and noun–verb agreement after all, since Chalmers in his earlier article (1990, p. 56) quite unequivocally states that no attempt has been made to represent verb tense or subject–verb agreement.

15 It is notable that whereas Chalmers repeatedly and explicitly refers to Van Gelder's work and the notion of functional compositionality, McLaughlin does not discuss or even mention it either in Fodor and McLaughlin (1990) or in McLaughlin (1993).

16 According to Hadley (1994a, pp. 250–251), a network exhibits weak systematicity if it can handle test sentences that contain words that occur only at syntactic positions already occupied by these words in the training set. The training set is then fully representative of the test set. A system exhibits strong systematicity if it can exhibit weak systematicity and moreover can process novel simple and novel embedded sentences containing familiar words in new syntactic positions. Hadley (pp. 252–254) points to much empirical evidence that children exhibit systematicity in this strong sense.

17 A terminological matter needs to be addressed here. Churchland generally uses the phrase 'propositional/sentential states' or 'propositions or sentences' as a means of bypassing discussions surrounding the vague ontological status of propositions. For many logicians and philosophers the ontological existence of these abstract, 'graspable' entities is unacceptable and, for this reason, they prefer to talk of sentences, thus relating logical relations to a specific language (Flew, 1979, p. 291). Unfortunately, conflating propositions with sentences might lead to confusion between the specification of information (in the sense that a proposition specifies the content of a certain belief, for instance) and the representation of information (in the sense that a certain symbolic structure or sentence in the language of thought represents or carries the information). In this section I will try to keep a clear distinction between propositions as informational units, and sentences as representations of information. Put differently, propositions specify informational content, sentential structures represent it.

18 Putnam (1988b, p. 60) seems to think that this elimination of truth is a covert thesis of Churchland (e.g. 'the innocent reader of Churchland's writings is hardly aware that he is also being asked to reject the classical notion of truth'). Yet this accusation of surreptitiousness is somewhat misplaced for, as Churchland (1992a, p. 422) has remarked in reply, he ventured his doubts concerning truth at least as early as 1985 (reprinted in Churchland, 1989, see especially pp. 149–150). Furthermore, he unequivocally stated in his *Scientific realism and the plasticity of mind* that the principles of formal logic can be subject to critical evaluation and rational change (1979, p. 140).

19 So Churchland cannot be accused of falling victim to the 'naturalistic fallacy', as Putnam acknowledges: 'Churchland has made it clear that he does think that there is a normative property which statements can have and fail to have; his suggestion is that we were wrong in thinking that the classical notion of "truth" was the property in question' (Putnam, 1988b, p. 69).

Conclusion

In this conclusion I will review the main points of this book in order to relate them to the issue of the acceptability of the literal interpretation of folk psychology. Folk psychology, I have argued, may profitably be taken literally in its descriptive, explanatory and predictive practices. Interpreting mental states as attitudes with respect to a determinate, propositionally specifiable content, as causal with respect to behavior and other mental states, and as functionally discrete in their operation, is, I have submitted, a straightforward, plausible, and useful way of construing the theory that lies behind our everyday psychological routines. I have also suggested that the elimination of folk psychology has to be properly understood as the replacement of our common-sense conceptual scheme by a radically different one, not as the elimination of mental phenomena as such. Eliminativism in this sense is an entirely reasonable option that cannot be rejected offhand. Although alternative interpretations of folk psychology, as provided by Dennett and Bechtel, are possible, it is not at all clear that these do more justice to the true nature of folk psychology, or are less of a philosophical construction than their literal counterpart. Nor do they preclude the possibility of an eventual displacement of folk psychology.

The tenability of the literal interpretation of folk psychology is, ultimately, an empirical issue. Observations on the indispensability or the radical inadequacy of folk psychology are, by themselves, insufficient to determine the outcome of the debate. The best means we currently have in deciding upon the ontological reality of our beliefs and desires is to see whether they find, in a recognizable form, a place in science. I have suggested that functional discreteness is a valuable characteristic of mental states to focus upon, as it can easily be brought into connection with ongoing empirical research.

Representations play a central role in the scientific study of cognition. I have suggested that the difference between symbolic and distributed representations is a radical and cognitively relevant one, and it can therefore be used for drawing the dividing line between classical cognitive science and connectionism. Furthermore, this difference can be related to the debate about folk psychology.

In the classical view of cognition, folk psychological descriptions and explanations of cognitive behavior, taken literally, turn out to be correct. There are indeed contentful mental states that causally produce behavior and other mental states in a functionally discrete way. Scientifically, these characteristics can be preserved by modeling mental states as computational relations to symbolic structures. The possibility of mechanical rationality is explained on the basis that representations have a syntactic structure utilized by structure-sensitive processes operating upon them. In order to account for another important cognitive phenomenon, systematicity, Fodor urges classical cognitive science to adopt the existence of a constituently structured representational system, called a language of thought.

According to the alternative, neurocomputational model of cognition the basic unit of cognition is not a syntactical structure, but a collection of weights that constitutes the system's knowledge in a distributed way and that determines how the system will react to incoming information. As these weights collectively operate in every cognitive process, there is no neurocomputational equivalent for functional discreteness, which, on the literal reading, is an essential characteristic of our ordinary view of the mental. Therefore, if the neurocomputational theory turns out to provide a better view of cognition, the literal interpretation of folk psychology is in jeopardy, and Churchland's call for elimination gains considerable strength.

As the status of folk psychology has to be decided on empirical grounds, finding a good area in which to compare classical and connectionist models is of considerable importance. I have suggested that the frame problem provides a valuable candidate. The frame problem, I have argued, arises in the context of trying to model the human ability to see the relevant consequences of events in a situation. As such, the frame problem is of importance to the debate about folk psychology for it is intimately related to its area of application: common-sense psychological phenomena as they occur in ordinary reasoning. Furthermore, the frame problem has been portrayed as a difficulty in principle for classical cognitive science, while being almost effortlessly solvable by neurocomputational models. I have related this contrast in the estimation of the severity of the frame problem to the difference between symbolic and distributed representations.

Originally, the frame problem showed up as the problem of having to specify explicit rules indicating what remains the same after an event. I have argued that the interpretation of the frame problem as the issue of non-change is a consequence of pursuing a purely logical (i.e. deductive and semi-deductive) approach to cognition. Such an approach is of limited value to attempts to model the psychological mechanisms that underlie our reasoning capacities.

From a non-deductivist, psychologically oriented, perspective the problem of change can rightfully be seen as the heart of the matter. Being able to see the relevant consequences of an event requires an understanding of the situation. The essential question with respect to the frame problem therefore becomes how cognitive systems can quickly bring relevant information to bear upon the generation and evaluation of explanatory hypotheses which allow them to make sense of events and situations.

At this point, a parting of ways can be observed. The representational approach tries to find a solution by searching for a representational format that, once the right information has been represented, more or less auto-matically results in the generation of good explanatory hypotheses. This has led to discussions about the inadequacies of the symbolic representa-tional scheme, especially since it harbors a distinction (claimed to be unfortunate) between explicitly and implicitly represented information. On the basis of these discussions I have suggested that distributed represen-tations provide a promising candidate for those who favor the representa-tional approach to the frame problem.

The second, inferential approach does not doubt the value of classical symbolic representations, but proposes to engage in a detailed investigation of our actual non-demonstrative inferential practices. A better under-standing of non-demonstrative reasoning should ultimately make a solution to the frame problem possible, while staying within the framework of classical cognitive science. Basically, then, the difference between the rep-resentational and the inferential approach can be related to the question whether distributed or symbolic representations are expected to provide sufficient resources to solve the frame problem.

The form of non-demonstrative inference that is of most interest to the frame problem is hypothetical induction, in which a hypothesis is generated that provides a plausible explanation of the phenomena encountered. On closer examination, two aspects of hypothetical induction can be discerned: the actual generation of hypotheses, and the evaluation of hypotheses in order to select the single most plausible. Paul Thagard has investi-gated these aspects and has devised a model (PI) that implements several of the computational mechanisms that are thought to underlie our non-demonstrative reasoning abilities. I have examined his work as an illus-trative example of mainstream symbolic AI. From this investigation it has become clear that the main mechanism responsible for the selection of relevant information, influencing the generation and evaluation of explanatory hypotheses, consists of the directed spreading of activation. To function adequately, this mechanism depends on the organization of the knowledge of a system. Which hypotheses get generated, and what infor-mation is selected as relevant to their evaluation, is essentially determined by the way the knowledge of a system is structured. Ultimately, then, the course of one's reasoning is strongly influenced by the structure of one's knowledge representation. The value of Thagard's work lies in presenting a clear and careful application of this basic suggestion, in terms of schemata and conceptual hierarchies, to the problem of hypothetical induction. Although I have indicated several points of criticism with respect to Thagard's work, I think that the basic idea underlying it can be seen as of great relevance to the problem of non-demonstrative reasoning, and thereby to the frame problem. Although the inferential strategy has been endorsed by Fodor, he has dismissed proposals of the kind advocated by Thagard as irrelevant and misguided. First of all, I have argued that this makes his position somewhat awkward. The empirical successes of classical cognitive science are an important factor in Fodor's claim that it provides a principled solution to the problem of mechanical rationality and a defense of folk psychology. Yet, if Fodor's diagnosis is correct, not only has classical cognitive science accomplished next to nothing precisely in the area of common-sense rationality, but, worse, it does not even have a clue how to make significant progress in this domain. Although taking such a position is, of course, logically possible, it does lead to suspicions about the trustworthiness of the defense of folk psychology that classical cognitive science is said to offer. Furthermore, it makes the calls for alternative models of cognition that somehow evade these fundamental problems entirely reasonable.

I have endeavored to criticize Fodor's precise characterization of the way the problem of non-demonstrative inference should be looked upon. Details aside, my main point is that Fodor is wrong to dismiss associative links between elements of knowledge as irrelevant to our common-sense reasoning practice. Even though he is right to claim that inference is not, in itself, a matter of association, he is mistaken in not allowing associations to play a role in the *guidance* of our inferences. It is perfectly plausible to investigate common-sense reasoning on the basis of the suggestion that our knowledge about ordinary matters has become so organized in the history of our interaction with our environment that, under normal circumstances, associations between elements of knowledge make rapid and valuable inferences possible. Fodor has, in any case, given insufficient reason for AI not to pursue this line of investigation.

Fodor's main argument is that associative links do not provide a solution to the problem of confirmational holism. The logic of confirmation currently fails to grasp how the holistic characteristics of knowledge help to localize relevant data. The holism of confirmation is a logical problem without visible prospects of a justificationally acceptable solution. However, I have argued that the absence of logically valid rules of non-demonstrative reasoning only constitutes a problem for psychology if the underlying mechanisms of our inferential capacities are assumed to be normatively impeccable. There is a difference between trying to provide a psychologically plausible description of how people reason non-demonstratively and attempting to indicate in a logically satisfactory way how they should so reason. Our psychological inferential mechanisms may be logically imperfect and yet lead to a satisfactory performance under normal circumstances. There is no good reason why associative processes should not be allowed to play a substantial role in psychological models of classical cognitive science.

Fundamentally, I think that in the discussion about the frame problem Fodor has taken the role of logic in cognitive science too far. Though one can use it to get a clear view of the problems involved in non-demonstrative reasoning, one should not expect logic to provide the answers to problems in modeling common-sense rationality. Waiting for progress in the logic of confirmation in order to be able to model central processes is likely to be neither rewarding nor, indeed, necessary. Allowing extra-logical forces into play considerably enhances the prospects of classical cognitive science to adequately deal with non-demonstrative reasoning. From this perspective, the frame problem, though presenting a demanding technical task, does not constitute an abyss for classical cognitive science. It does not provide a principled reason to doubt that folk psychology will turn out to be literally true.

The answer to the frame problem suggested by neurocomputational models of cognition is ironically almost a reversal of the one given by classical AI. Rather than investigating intricate methods of organizing the representation of information, connectionism proposes doing entirely away with any explicit structure. From the neurocomputational perspective, cognition is a matter not of structure-sensitive symbol manipulation but of the resonating of prototypical activation patterns. All the information a system possesses is superposed in the setting of weights. These weights represent the knowledge of a system in a distributed way and determine the system's response to incoming information in a collective and simultaneous way. Thus the swift application of relevant knowledge in order to generate explanatory hypotheses with respect to events in the environment can be accounted for. This view is thought to hold great promise with respect to the frame problem. Optimism has been further encouraged by the potential application of the mechanism of pattern recognition and association to several higher forms of cognition, although a consideration of an actual model of common-sense reasoning indicates that much work remains to be done here. The other side of the coin, however, concerns the representational capacities of distributed representations. It is an especially important issue how structural relations between elements of information can be represented in a way that is of use to the computational system. Increasing the number of dimensions of an activation space is in itself an insufficient method of capturing the structure of information. Suggestions to this effect are an easy prey for the charge of simple associationism. I have considered the more complex proposals of Van Gelder and Chalmers and these indicate that there is at least the possibility that connectionist models can achieve structure-sensitive processing without thereby becoming part of the classical approach to cognition. Yet a careful examination of the model's performance indicates that the modeling results produced so far might well be an artifact of statistical properties of the training and test data used rather than an indication of any genuine ability to utilize the structure implicit in activation patterns. Moreover, serious problems can be raised about the potential of distributed representations to be scaled up to realistically complex tasks. Although the debate continues, one has to conclude that at this moment the price one pays in loss of representational power is too high to accept distributed representations as adequate means for answering the frame problem.

Part of the attractiveness of the neurocomputational perspective lies, Churchland has claimed, in the improved view it provides of human epistemic performance. Once the conception of mental states as propositional attitudes is rejected, a much-needed deeper understanding of epistemic virtue is possible. However, a consideration of Churchland's analysis of simplicity indicates that his suggestions concerning the virtuousness of this notion are far less revolutionary than he has suggested and that the proposed measurement of simplicity is not easily applicable. The neuro-computational solution to the frame problem, though initially appealing, is not unproblematic and the promised gains in epistemology are considerably less substantial than Churchland's optimistic remarks lead one to expect. Ultimately, then, I think Churchland is correct in holding that if the neurocomputational theory of cognition turns out to be empirically prefer-able, folk psychology in its literal interpretation cannot be sustained. However, the neurocomputational approach to the frame problem has, in comparison with the classical approach, no less significant obstacles to overcome.

All in all, then, with respect to the main question of this book, I conclude that whereas Fodor is overly pessimistic about the prospects for classical cognitive science to successfully model central aspects of human cognition, Churchland is excessively optimistic about the potential accomplishments of neurocomputationalism. Severe problems have been indicated for both approaches and the theoretical suggestions as to how to overcome these are empirically far from worked out. At this stage, then, and from the per-spective provided by this book, I see in the frame problem no principled reason to seriously doubt the possibility that the literal interpretation of folk psychology will be vindicated by developments in cognitive science.

The issue does not rest here, of course. I hold the question about the proper place of association in psychological theorizing to be the most prominent of those themes meriting further investigation. As the frame problem clearly indicates, an exclusively logical approach to cognition seems, from a psychological point of view, unsuited to deal with ordinary reasoning phenomena. An exclusive reliance on associative mechanisms is equally unlikely to result in psychologically satisfactory models. So, what role should associative mechanisms be allowed to play in models of common-sense reasoning?

One may observe that cognitive science, in its initial struggle against behaviorism, downplayed the importance of association in comparison with logical processes. Furthermore, the suggestion that a competence theory should function as a guide to the investigation of human inferential per-formance has also led to a relative disregard of associative mechanisms. After all, when one looks at inferential competence one is easily tempted to look at a logical analysis of what constitutes valid reasoning. Simply put, logic investigates ways of justifying the end results of a reasoning process. Association, however, is *a*logical. When pointing at associative mechanisms to explain how a conclusion is arrived at, one provides not reasons but, in effect, a 'just because' answer. From a logical point of view this may be unsatisfactory, but from a psychological point of view things are not so clear-cut. The temptation to conflate logical with psychological issues should be resisted, even in the context of inferential competence. There is no good *a priori* reason why, for instance, our inferential abductive competence, and not just our performance, may not depend on associations to a significant extent. The emergence of connectionism can be taken as an indication that the role of association in cognitive processes should not be neglected. However, the extent to which connectionism can be considered to be an instantiation of associationism is quite unclear. This, I think, is partly a consequence of the fact that the precise content of associationism itself is not easy to determine. Associationism is a complex conceptual structure which has appeared in many different guises throughout history. Using the term as a simplistic label in the debate between classical cognitivists and connectionists is therefore unlikely to be illuminating.

The current situation calls, I think, for a re-evaluation of the precise nature of the advantages and inconveniences of associationism. What, for instance, is exactly the difference between 'simple associationism' and 'associationism with an intelligent face'? How can logical operations and associative mechanisms most plausibly be integrated? Answers to these questions are important not just for connectionism, but for classical cognitive science as well. Whatever the answers may be, whether one supplements logical operations by associative mechanisms or complements associations by logical operations, both components seem to be necessary to an understanding of human reasoning.

In this book I have attempted to relate concrete empirical models to more general theoretical issues that are of importance to the foundations of psychology. The debate about folk psychology touches on some basic elements of psychological theorizing. Are beliefs and desires, as prototypical examples of mental states, the kind of theoretical constructs that are *needed* for psychological research? Can our standard terminology be kept as a useful, if superficial, *manner of speech* in psychology? Or are beliefs and desires altogether misleading inventions that impede psychological progress which should therefore be *eliminated* from psychology? Whatever answer to questions like these may turn out to be the correct one, it is bound to influence the nature of psychological research in many domains.

The discussion about whether mentalistic concepts such as beliefs and desires should play a part in psychological theories has, since the emergence of behaviorism at the beginning of this century, proved to be an important one for psychology. Surprisingly, the rise of cognitive science has not ended but rather intensified this debate. One of the merits of cognitive science, in my view, is that it allows for a well-structured theoretical and empirically detailed investigation of this issue. The (in)adequacy of folk psychology is not a matter to be postulated, and the debate about its value can now be based on the results of precise computational research. Though this does not mean that one may expect to find conclusive results easily, it does make it possible to engage in a systematic investigation of the theoretical and empirical problems at stake. This book is intended as a contribution to such a methodical inquiry, by charting some important topics that have to be dealt with while exploring the domain of common-sense reasoning.

References

Aparicio, M. I., & Levine, D. S. (1994). Why are neural networks relevant to higher cognitive function? In D. S. Levine & M. I. Aparicio (Eds.), *Neural networks for knowledge representation and inference* (pp. 1–26). Hillsdale: Erlbaum.

Baars, J. (1986). *The cognitive revolution in psychology*. New York: Guilford Press.

Baker, L. R. (1995). *Explaining attitudes: a practical approach to the mind*. Cambridge: Cambridge University Press.

Bakker, N. (1995). Implications of Hadley's definition of systematicity. In B. Kappen & S. Gielen (Eds.), *Neural networks: artificial intelligence and industrial applications*. Berlin: Springer Verlag.

Bechtel, W. (1985a). Contemporary connectionism: are the new parallel distributed processing models cognitive or associationist? *Behaviorism, 13*(1), 53–61.

Bechtel, W. (1985b). Realism, instrumentalism, and the intentional stance. *Cognitive Science, 9*, 473–497.

Bechtel, W. (1988a). *Philosophy of mind: an overview for cognitive science*. Hillsdale: Erlbaum.

Bechtel, W. (1988b). *Philosophy of science: an overview for cognitive science*. Hillsdale: Erlbaum.

Bechtel, W. (1993). The case for connectionism. *Philosophical Studies, 71*, 119–154.

Bechtel, W., & Abrahamsen, A. (1991). *Connectionism and the mind*. Oxford: Blackwell.

Bechtel, W., & Abrahamsen, A. (1993). Connectionism and the future of folk psychology. In S. M. Christensen & D. R. Turner (Eds.), *Folk psychology and the philosophy of mind* (pp. 340–367). Hillsdale: Erlbaum.

Bever, T. G., Fodor, J. A., & Garrett, M. (1968). A formal limitation of associationism. In T. R. Dixon & D. L. Horton (Eds.), *Verbal behavior and general behavior theory* (pp. 582–585). Englewood Cliffs: Prentice-Hall.

Boden, M. (1990). *The creative mind*. London: Sphere.

Braaten, J. (1988). Elimination, enlightenment and the normative content of folk psychology. *Journal for the Theory of Social Behaviour, 18*, 251–268.

Buckingham, H. W. (1984). Early development of association theory in psychology as a forerunner of connection theory. *Brain and Cognition, 3*, 19–34.

Butler, K. (1993). Connectionism, classical cognitivism and the relation between cognitive and implementational levels of analysis. *Philosophical Psychology, 6*(3), 321–333.

Callebaut, W. (1993). *Taking the naturalistic turn: or how real philosophy of science is done*. Chicago: Chicago University Press.

Campbell, K. (1986). Can intuitive psychology survive the growth of neuroscience? *Inquiry, 29*, 143–152.

Chalmers, D. J. (1990). Syntactic transformations on distributed representation. *Connection Science, 2*(1 & 2), 53–62.

Chalmers, D. J. (1993). Connectionism and compositionality: why Fodor and Pylyshyn were wrong. *Philosophical Psychology, 6*(3), 305–319.

Chater, N., & Oaksford, M. (1993). Logicism, mental models and everyday reasoning: reply to Garnham. *Mind & Language, 8*(1), 72–89.

Cheng, P. C., & Keane, M. (1989). Explanatory coherence as a psychological theory. *Behavioral and Brain Sciences, 12*(3), 469–470.

Chomsky, N. (1965). *Aspects of the theory of syntax*. Cambridge: MIT Press.

Christiansen, M. H., & Chater, N. (1994). Generalization and connectionist language learning. *Mind & Language, 9*(3), 273–287.

Christie, D. (1993). Comments on Bechtel's 'The case for connectionism'. *Philosophical Studies, 71,* 155–162.

Churchland, P. M. (1979). *Scientific realism and the plasticity of mind.* Cambridge: Cambridge University Press.

Churchland, P. M. (1986). Cognition and conceptual change: a reply to Double. *Journal for the Theory of Social Behavior, 16,* 217–221.

Churchland, P. M. (1988). *Matter and consciousness* (revised ed.). Cambridge: MIT Press.

Churchland, P. M. (1989). *A neurocomputational perspective: the nature of mind and the structure of science.* Cambridge: MIT Press.

Churchland, P. M. (1992a). Activation vectors versus propositional attitudes: how the brain represents reality. *Philosophy and Phenomenological Research, 52,* 419–424.

Churchland, P. M. (1992b). A deeper unity: some Feyerabendian themes in neurocomputational form. In S. Davis (Ed.), *Connectionism: theory and practice* (pp. 30–50). Oxford: Oxford University Press.

Churchland, P. M. (1995), *The engine of reason, the seat of the soul: a philosophical journey into the brain.* Cambridge: MIT Press.

Churchland, P. M., & Churchland, P. S. (1990). Stalking the wild epistemic engine. In W. G. Lycan (Ed.), *Mind and cognition* (pp. 300–311). Oxford: Blackwell.

Churchland, P. M., & Churchland, P. S. (1994). Intertheoretic reduction: a neuroscientist's field guide. In R. Warner & T. Szubka (Eds.), *The mind body problem: a guide to the current debate* (pp. 41–54). Cambridge: Blackwell.

Churchland, P. M., & Churchland, P. S. (1996). McCauley's demand for a co-level competitor. In R. N. McCauley (Ed.) *The Churchlands and their critics.* Cambridge: Blackwell.

Churchland, P. S. (1986). *Neurophilosophy.* Cambridge: MIT Press.

Churchland, P. S. (1987). Epistemology in the age of neuroscience. *Journal of Philosophy, 84,* 544–553.

Churchland, P. S., & Sejnowski, T. J. (1992). *The computational brain.* Cambridge: MIT Press.

Clark, A. (1989). *Microcognition: philosophy, cognitive science and parallel distributed processing.* Cambridge: MIT Press.

Clark, A. (1990). Connectionism, competence, and explanation. *British Journal for the Philosophy of Science, 41,* 195–222.

Clark, A. (1992). The presence of a symbol. *Connection Science, 4*(3 & 4), 193–205.

Cummins, R. (1983). *The nature of psychological explanation.* Cambridge: MIT Press.

Cummins, R. (1989). *Meaning and mental representation.* Cambridge: MIT Press.

Davis, E. (1990). *Representations of common sense knowledge.* San Mateo: Morgan Kaufmann.

De Champeaux, D. (1987). Unframing the frame problem. In F. M. Brown (Ed.), *The frame problem in artificial intelligence: proceedings of the 1987 workshop* (pp. 311–318). Lawrence: Morgan Kaufmann.

Dellarosa, D. (1988). The psychological appeal of connectionism. *Behavioral and Brain Sciences, 11*(1), 28–29.

Dennett, D. C. (1978). *Brainstorms.* Hassocks: Harvester Press.

Dennett, D. C. (1987a). Cognitive wheels: the frame problem of AI. In Z. W. Pylyshyn (Ed.), *The robot's dilemma: the frame problem in artificial intelligence* (pp. 41–64). Norwood: Ablex.

Dennett, D. C. (1987b). *The intentional stance.* Cambridge: MIT Press.

Dennett, D. C. (1991a). Mother nature versus the walking encyclopedia: a western drama. In W. Ramsey, S. Stich, & D. Rumelhart (Eds.), *Philosophy and connectionist theory* (pp. 21–30). Hillsdale: Erlbaum.

Dennett, D. C. (1991b). Real patterns. *Journal of Philosophy, 88,* 27–51.

Dennett, D. C. (1991c). Two contrasts: folk craft versus folk science, and belief versus opinion. In J. D. Greenwood (Ed.), *The future of folk psychology* (pp. 135–148). Cambridge: Cambridge University Press.

Dennett, D. C. (1992). *Consciousness explained.* London: Allen Lane.

Dennett, D. C., & Haugeland, J. (1987). Intentionality. In R. Gregory (Ed.), *The Oxford companion to the mind* (pp. 383–384). Oxford: Oxford University Press.

Derthick, M. (1990). Mundane reasoning by settling on a plausible model. *Artificial Intelligence, 46,* 107–157.

Dietrich, E. (1989). Is Thagard's theory of explanatory coherence the new logical positivism? *Behavioral and Brain Sciences, 12*(3), 473–474.

Dinsmore, J. (1992). Thunder in the gap. In J. Dinsmore (Ed.), *The symbolic and connectionist paradigms: closing the gap* (pp. 1–23). Hillsdale: Erlbaum.

Double, R. (1986). On the very idea of eliminating the intentional. *Journal for the Theory of Social Behavior, 16,* 209–216.

Dreyfus, H. L. (1992). *What computers still can't do: a critique of artificial reason.* Cambridge: MIT Press.

Dreyfus, H. L., & Dreyfus, S. E. (1986). *Mind over machine: the power of human intuition and expertise in the era of the computer.* New York: Free Press.

Dreyfus, H. L., & Dreyfus, S. E. (1987). How to stop worrying about the frame problem even though it is computationally insoluble. In Z. W. Pylyshyn (Ed.), *The robot's dilemma: the frame problem in artificial intelligence* (pp. 95–112). Norwood: Ablex.

Dreyfus, S. E., & Dreyfus, H. L. (1990). Towards a reconciliation of phenomenology and AI. In D. Partridge & Y. Wilks (Eds.), *The foundations of AI* (pp. 396–410). Cambridge: Cambridge University Press.

Dunn, J. M. (1990). The frame problem and relevant predication. In H. E. Kyburg, R. P. Loui, & G. N. Carlson (Eds.), *Knowledge representation and defeasible reasoning* (pp. 89–95). Dordrecht: Kluwer.

Elgot-Drapkin, J., Miller, M., & Perlis, D. (1987). The two frame problems. In F. M. Brown (Ed.), *The frame problem in artificial intelligence: proceedings of the 1987 workshop* (pp. 23–28). Lawrence: Morgan Kaufmann.

Elman, J. L. (1991) Distributed representations, simple recurrent networks and grammatical structure. *Machine Learning, 7,* 195–225.

Etherington, D. W., Forbus, K. D., Ginsberg, M. L., Israel, D., & Lifschitz, V. (1989). Critical issues in nonmonotonic reasoning. In R. J. Brachman, H. J. Levesque, & R. Reiter (Eds.), *First international conference on principles of knowledge representation and reasoning* (pp. 500–504). Toronto: Morgan Kaufmann.

Feldman, J. A. (1989). Neural representation of conceptual knowledge. In L. Nadel, L. A. Cooper, P. Culicover, & R. M. Harnish (Eds.), *Neural connections, mental computation* (pp. 68–103). Cambridge: MIT Press.

Fetzer, J. H. (1991a). Artificial intelligence meets David Hume: a response to Pat Hayes. In K. M. Ford & P. J. Hayes (Eds.), *Reasoning agents in a dynamic world: the frame problem* (pp. 77–85). London: JAI Press.

Fetzer, J. H. (1991b). The frame problem: artificial intelligence meets David Hume. In K. M. Ford & P. J. Hayes (Eds.), *Reasoning agents in a dynamical world: the frame problem* (pp. 55–69). London: JAI Press.

Feyerabend, P. K. (1963/1970). Materialism and the mind–body problem. In C. V. Borst (Ed.), *The mind/brain identity theory* (pp. 142–156). London: Macmillan.

Flanagan, O. (1984). *The science of the mind.* Cambridge: MIT Press.

Flew, A. (1979). *A dictionary of philosophy.* London: Macmillan.

Fodor, J. A. (1968). *Psychological explanation: an introduction to the philosophy of psychology.* New York: Random House.

Fodor, J. A. (1975). *The language of thought.* Cambridge: Harvard University Press.

Fodor, J. A. (1981a). The mind–body problem. *Scientific American, 244*(1), 124–132.

Fodor, J. A. (1981b). *Representations: philosophical essays on the foundations of cognitive science.* Hassocks: Harvester Press.

Fodor, J. A. (1983). *The modularity of mind.* Cambridge: MIT Press.

Fodor, J. A. (1986a). Minds, machines and modules: Een vraaggesprek van C. Brown, P. Hagoort en R. Maessen met J. Fodor. In P. Hagoort & R. Maessen (Eds.), *Geest, computer, kunst* (pp. 90–116). Utrecht: Stichting Grafiet.

Fodor, J. A. (1986b). The modularity of mind: position paper. In Z. Pylyshyn & W. Demopoulos (Eds.), *Theoretical issues in cognitive science* (pp. 3–18). Norwood: Ablex.

Fodor, J. A. (1986c). Why paramecia don't have mental representations. In P. French, J. T. Uehling, & H. Wettstein (Eds.), *Midwest studies in philosophy* (pp. 3–23). Minnesota: University of Minnesota Press.

Fodor, J. A. (1987a). Modules, frames, fridgeons, sleeping dogs, and the music of the spheres. In Z. W. Pylyshyn (Ed.), *The robot's dilemma: the frame problem in artificial intelligence* (pp. 139–149). Norwood: Ablex.

Fodor, J. A. (1987b). *Psychosemantics: the problem of meaning in the philosophy of mind.* ✓ Cambridge: MIT Press.

Fodor, J. A. (1990). *A theory of content and other essays.* Cambridge: MIT Press.

Fodor, J. A. (1991a). Replies. In B. Loewer & G. Rey (Eds.), *Meaning in mind: Fodor and his critics* (pp. 255–321). Cambridge: Blackwell.

Fodor, J. A. (1991b). You can fool some of the people all of the time, everything else being equal; hedged laws and psychological explanations. *Mind, 100,* 19–33.

Fodor, J. A. (1994a). Concepts: a potboiler. *Cognition, 50,* 95–113.

Fodor, J. A. (1994b). *The elm and the expert: mentalese and its semantics.* Cambridge: MIT Press.

Fodor, J. A. (1994c). Fodor, Jerry A. In S. Guttenplan (Ed.), *A companion to the philosophy of mind* (pp. 292–300). Cambridge: Blackwell.

Fodor, J. A., & Lepore, E. (1992). *Holism: a shopper's guide.* Cambridge: Blackwell.

Fodor, J. A., & McLaughlin, B. (1990). Connectionism and the problem of systematicity: why Smolensky's solution does not work. *Cognition, 35,* 183–204.

Fodor, J. A., & Pylyshyn, Z. W. (1988). Connectionism and cognitive architecture. *Cognition, 28,* 3–71.

Gardenfors, P. (1990). Induction, conceptual spaces and AI. *Philosophy of Science, 57,* 78–95.

Gardner, H. (1985). *The mind's new science.* New York: Basic Books.

Garfield, J. L. (Ed.). (1987). *Modularity in knowledge representation and natural language understanding.* Cambridge: MIT Press.

Garnham, A. (1993). Is logicist cognitive science possible? *Mind & Language, 8*(1), 49–71.

Giere, R. N. (1989). What does explanatory coherence explain? *Behavioral and Brain Sciences, 12*(3), 475–476.

Ginsberg, M. L. (1987). Introduction. In M. L. Ginsberg (Ed.), *Readings in nonmonotonic reasoning* (pp. 1–23). Los Altos: Morgan Kaufmann.

Gjertsen, D. (1989). *Science and philosophy: past and present.* London: Penguin.

Goldman, A. I. (1989). Interpretation psychologized. *Mind & Language, 4,* 161–185.

Goldman, A. I. (1992). In defense of the simulation theory. *Mind & Language, 7*(1 & 2), 104–119.

Goodman, N. (1954/1983). *Fact, fiction and forecast* (4th ed.). Cambridge: Harvard University Press.

Gopnik, A. (1993). How we know our minds: the illusion of first-person knowledge of intentionality. *The Behavioral and Brain Sciences, 16,* 1–14.

Gordon, R. M. (1986). Folk psychology as simulation. *Mind & Language, 1,* 158–171.

Gordon, R. M. (1992a). Reply to Stich and Nichols. *Mind & Language, 7*(1 & 2), 87–97.

Gordon, R. M. (1992b). The simulation theory: objections and misconceptions. *Mind & Language, 7*(1 & 2), 11–34.

Greenwood, J. D. (1991a). Introduction: Folk psychology and scientific psychology. In J. D. Greenwood (Ed.), *The future of folk psychology: intentionality and cognitive science* (pp. 1–21). New York: Cambridge University Press.

Greenwood, J. D. (1991b). Reasons to believe. In J. D. Greenwood (Ed.), *The future of folk psychology: intentionality and cognitive science* (pp. 70–92). New York: Cambridge University Press.

Guha, R. V., & Lenat, D. B. (1990). Cyc: a midterm report. *AI Magazine,* 32–59.

Guha, R. V., & Lenat, D. B. (1993). Re: Cycling paper reviews. *Artificial Intelligence* (61), 149–174.

Guha, R. V., & Lenat, D. B. (1994). Enabling agents to work together. *Communications of the ACM*, *37*(7), 127–142.

Hadley, R. F. (1994a). Systematicity in connectionist language learning. *Mind & Language*, *9*(3), 247–272.

Hadley, R. F. (1994b). Systematicity revisited: reply to Christiansen and Chater and Niklassen and van Gelder. *Mind & Language*, *9*(4), 431–444.

Hadley, R. F. (1995). The 'explicit–implicit' distinction. *Minds and Machines*, *5*, 219–242.

Haldane, J. (1988). Understanding folk. *Proceedings of the Aristotelian Society*, *LXII*, 232–254.

Hanks, S., & McDermott, D. (1987). Default reasoning, nonmonotonic reasoning and the frame problem. In M. L. Ginsberg (Ed.), *Readings in nonmonotonic reasoning* (pp. 390–394). Los Altos: Morgan Kaufmann.

Harman, G. H. (1965/1989). The inference to the best explanation. In B. A. Brody & R. E. Grandy (Eds.), *Readings in the philosophy of science* (pp. 323–328). Englewood Cliffs: Prentice-Hall.

Harman, G. H. (1992). Induction: enumerative and hypothetical. In J. Dancy & E. Sosa (Eds.), *A companion to epistemology* (pp. 200–206). Oxford: Blackwell.

Haselager, W. F. G. (1990). *Stratifikatie*. Internal report 90-01, Theoretical Psychology Department, Vrije Universiteit, Amsterdam.

Haselager, W. F. G. (1992). Historical foundations of the computational theory of mind. In H. Carpintero, E. Lafuente, R. Plas, & L. Sprung (Eds.), *Studies in the history of psychology*, vol. 6 (pp. 89–99). Madrid: ECVSA.

Haselager, W. F. G. (1993a). Epistemic virtue and cognitive science. In R. Casati & G. White (Eds.), *Philosophy and the cognitive sciences: the 16th international Wittgenstein symposium* (pp. 207–212). Kirchberg am Wechsel, Austria: Austrian Ludwig Wittgenstein Society.

Haselager, W. F. G. (1993b). Over de legitimatie en eliminatie van meningen en verlangens: de discussie over de 'folk psychology'. *Nederlands Tijdschrift voor de Psychologie*, *48*, 1–15.

Haugeland, J. (1981). Semantic engines: an introduction to mind design. In J. Haugeland (Ed.), *Mind design* (pp. 1–34). Montgomery: Bradford.

Haugeland, J. (1985). *Artificial intelligence: the very idea*. Cambridge: MIT Press.

Haugeland, J. (1987). An overview of the frame problem. In Z. W. Pylyshyn (Ed.), *The robot's dilemma: the frame problem in artificial intelligence* (pp. 77–94). Norwood: Ablex.

Haugeland, J. (1991). Representational genera. In W. Ramsey, S. P. Stich, & D. E. Rumelhart (Eds.), *Philosophy and connectionist theory* (pp. 61–89). Hillsdale: Erlbaum.

Hayes, P. J. (1987). What the frame problem is and isn't. In Z. W. Pylyshyn (Ed.), *The robot's dilemma: the frame problem in artificial intelligence* (pp. 123–136). Norwood: Ablex.

Hayes, P. J. (1991). Commentary on 'The frame problem: artificial intelligence meets David Hume'. In K. M. Ford & P. J. Hayes (Eds.), *Reasoning agents in a dynamic world: the frame problem* (pp. 71–76). London: JAI Press.

Heil, J. (1991). Being indiscrete. In J. D. Greenwood (Ed.), *The future of folk psychology: intentionality and cognitive science* (pp. 120–134). New York: Cambridge University Press.

Hempel, C. G. (1965). *Aspects of scientific explanation*. New York: Free Press.

Hewson, C. (1993). Why the folk psychology debate matters to psychology and cognitive science. In R. Casati & G. White (Eds.), *Philosophy and the cognitive sciences: the 16th international Wittgenstein symposium* (pp. 213–217). Kirchberg am Wechsel, Austria: Austrian Ludwig Wittgenstein Society.

Hinton, G. E. (1990). Preface to the special issue on connectionist symbol processing. *Artificial Intelligence*, *46*, 1–4.

Hirst, G. (1989). Ontological assumptions in knowledge representation. In R. J. Brachman, H. J. Levesque, & R. Reiter (Eds.), *First international conference on principles of knowledge representation and reasoning* (pp. 157–169). Toronto: Morgan Kaufmann.

Hoenkamp, E. (1987). Non-monotonic reasoning in man and machine. In P. R. Asveld & A. Nijholt (Eds.), *Essays on concepts, formalisms, and tools* (pp. 261–278). Amsterdam: CWI.

Holland, J. H., Holyoak, K. J., Nisbett, R. E., & Thagard, P. R. (1986). *Induction.* Cambridge: MIT Press.

Holyoak, K. J. (1991). Symbolic connectionism: toward third-generation theories of expertise. In K. A. Ericsson & J. Smith (Eds.), *Toward a general theory of expertise: prospects and limits* (pp. 301–335). Cambridge: Cambridge University Press.

Horgan, T., & Woodward, J. (1985). Folk psychology is here to stay. *The Philosophical Review, XCIV*(2), 197–226.

Hume, D. (1739/1978). *A treatise of human nature* (2nd Selby-Bigge/Nidditch ed.). Oxford: Oxford University Press.

Hummel, J. E., & Holyoak, K. J. (1993). Distributing structures over time. *Behavioral and Brain Sciences, 16*(3), 464.

Janlert, L. E. (1987). Modelling change – the frame problem. In Z. W. Pylyshyn (Ed.), *The robot's dilemma: the frame problem in artificial intelligence* (pp. 1–40). Norwood: Ablex.

Jepson, C., Krantz, D. H., & Nisbett, R. E. (1993). Inductive reasoning: competence or skill? In R. E. Nisbett (Ed.), *Rules for reasoning* (pp. 70–89). Hillsdale: Erlbaum.

Johnson-Laird, P. N. (1983). *Mental models.* Cambridge: Cambridge University Press.

Jorna, R. J. (1990). *Knowledge representation and symbols in the mind.* Tuebingen: Stauffenburg.

Jorna, R. J., & Haselager, W. F. G. (1994). Associationism: not the cliff over which to push connectionism. *The Journal of Intelligent Systems, 4*(3–4), 279–309.

Kant, I. (1787/1956). *Kritik der reinen Vernunft.* Hamburg: Felix Meiner Verlag.

Katz, J. J. (1974). The relevance of linguistics to philosophy. In G. Harman (Ed.), *On Noam Chomsky: critical essays* (pp. 229–241). New York: Anchor Books.

Kirsh, D. (1990). When is information explicitly represented? In P. Hanson (Ed.), *Information, language, and cognition* (pp. 340–365). Vancouver: University of British Columbia Press.

Kitcher, P. (1990). Kant's dedicated cognitivist system. In J. C. Smith (Ed.), *Historical foundations of cognitive science* (pp. 189–209). Dordrecht: Kluwer.

Koestler, A. (1959). *The sleepwalkers.* London: Penguin.

Krause, P., & Clark, D. (1993). *Representing uncertain knowledge: an artificial intelligence approach.* Dordrecht: Kluwer.

Kyburg, H. E., Loui, R. P., & Carlson, G. N. (1990). Introduction. In H. E. Kyburg, R. P. Loui, & G. N. Carlson (Eds.), *Knowledge representation and defeasible reasoning* (pp. viii–xviii). Dordrecht: Kluwer.

Laird, J. E., Newell, A., & Rosenbloom, P. S. (1988/1993). Soar: an architecture for general intelligence. In J. E. Laird, A. Newell, & P. S. Rosenbloom (Eds.), *The Soar papers: research on integrated intelligence* (pp. 463–523). Cambridge: MIT Press.

Levelt, W. J. M. (1989). De connectionistische mode: symbolische en subsymbolische modellen van menselijk gedrag. In C. Brown, P. Hagoort, & T. Meijering (Eds.), *Vensters op de geest: cognitie op het snijvlak van filosofie en psychologie* (pp. 202–218). Utrecht: Stichting Grafiet.

Lindsay, R. K. (1988a). Can this treatment raise the dead? *Behavioral and Brain Sciences, 11*(1), 41–42.

Lindsay, R. K. (1988b). Images and inference. *Cognition, 29*, 229–250.

Linschoten, J. (1957). *'A gentle force': beschouwingen over het associatiebegrip.* Groningen: J. B. Wolters.

Lipton, P. (1991). *Inference to the best explanation.* London: Routledge.

Loewer, B., & Rey, G. (1991). Introduction. In B. Loewer & G. Rey (Eds.), *Meaning in mind: Fodor and his critics* (pp. xi–xxxvi). Oxford: Blackwell.

Looren de Jong, H. (1992). *Naturalism and psychology, a theoretical study.* Kampen: Uitgeversmaatschappij J. H. Kok.

Lormand, E. (1990). Framing the frame problem. *Synthese, 82*, 353–374.

Luger, G., & Stern, C. (1993). Expert systems and the abductive circle. In R. J. Jorna, B. Van Heusden, & R. Posner (Eds.), *Signs, search and communication: semiotic aspects of artificial intelligence* (pp. 151–171). Berlin: Walter de Gruyter.

Lycan, W. G. (1989). Explanationism, ECHO, and the connectionist paradigm. *Behavioral and Brain Sciences, 12*(3), 480.

MacCorquodale, K., & Meehl, P. E. (1948). On a distinction between hypothetical constructs and intervening variables. *Psychological Review, 55*(2), 95–107.

Margolis, H. (1987). *Patterns, thinking and cognition.* Chicago: University of Chicago Press.

Marostica, A. H. (1993). Abduction: the creative process. In R. J. Jorna, B. Van Heusden, & R. Posner (Eds.), *Signs, search and communication: semiotic aspects of artificial intelligence* (pp. 134–150). Berlin: Walter de Gruyter.

Marr, D. (1982). *Vision.* San Francisco: Freeman.

Masterman, M. (1970). The nature of a paradigm. In I. Lakatos & A. Musgrave (Eds.), *Criticism and the growth of knowledge* (pp. 59–89). Cambridge: Cambridge University Press.

McCarthy, J., & Hayes, P. J. (1969). Some philosophical problems from the standpoint of artificial intelligence. In B. Meltzer & D. Michie (Eds.), *Machine intelligence* (pp. 463–502). Edinburgh: Edinburgh University Press.

McCauley, R. N. (1986). Intertheoretic relations and the future of psychology. *Philosophy of Science, 53,* 179–199.

McCauley, R. N. (1993). Brainwork: a review of Paul Churchland's *A neurocomputational perspective. Philosophical Psychology, 6*(1), 81–96.

McCauley, R. N. (1996). Explanatory pluralism and the co-evolution of theories in science. In R. N. McCauley (Ed.), *The Churchlands and their critics* (pp. 17–47). Cambridge: Blackwell.

McClelland, J. L., Rumelhart, D. E., & the PDP group (Eds.). (1986). *Parallel distributed processing: explorations in the microstructure of cognition. Vol. 2: psychological and biological models.* Cambridge: MIT Press.

McDermott, D. (1987a). AI, logic, and the frame problem. In F. M. Brown (Ed.), *The frame problem in artificial intelligence: proceedings of the 1987 workshop* (pp. 105–118). Lawrence: Morgan Kaufmann.

McDermott, D. (1987b). We've been framed: or, why AI is innocent of the frame problem. In Z. W. Pylyshyn (Ed.), *The robot's dilemma: the frame problem in artificial intelligence* (pp. 113–122). Norwood: Ablex.

McDermott, D. (1989). Optimization and connectionism are two different things. *Behavioral and Brain Sciences, 12*(3), 483–484.

McLaughlin, B. P. (1993). The connectionism/classicism battle to win souls. *Philosophical Studies, 71,* 163–190.

McNamara, P. (1993). Introduction. *Philosophical Studies, 71,* 113–118.

Meijering, T. C. (1993). Neuraal vernuft en gedachteloze kennis: het moderne pleidooi voor een niet-propositioneel kennismodel. *Algemeen Nederlands Tijdschrift voor Wijsbegeerte, 85,* 24–48.

Meijering, T. C. (1994). Fodor's modularity: a new name for an old dilemma. *Philosophical Psychology, 7*(1), 39–62.

Meijsing, M. (1986). *Mens of machine?* Lisse: Swets & Zeitlinger.

Meijsing, M. (1993). Connectionisme, plasticiteit en de hoop op betere tijden. *Algemeen Nederlands Tijdschrift voor Wijsbegeerte, 85,* 49–69.

Mill, J. (1829). *Analysis of the phenomena of the human mind.* London: Baldwin & Cradock.

Minsky, M. (1977). Frame-system theory. In P. N. Johnson-Laird & P. C. Wason (Eds.), *Thinking: readings in cognitive science* (pp. 355–376). Cambridge: Cambridge University Press.

Minsky, M. (1981). A framework for representing knowledge. In J. Haugeland (Ed.), *Mind design* (pp. 67–94). Montgomery: Bradford.

Minsky, M. (1986). *The society of mind.* New York: Simon & Schuster.

Morris, W. E., & Richardson, R. C. (1995). How not to demarcate cognitive science and folk psychology: a response to Pickering and Chater. *Minds & Machines, 5,* 339–355.

Newell, A. (1981). Physical symbol systems. In D. A. Norman (Ed.), *Perspectives on cognitive science* (pp. 37–85). Norwood: Ablex.

Newell, A. (1982). The knowledge level. *Artificial Intelligence, 18,* 87–127.

Newell, A. (1990). *Unified theories of cognition.* Cambridge: Harvard University Press.

Newell, A. (1992). Precis of unified theories of cognition. *Behavioral and Brain Sciences, 15*(3), 425–492.

Newell, A., Rosenbloom, P. S., & Laird, J. E. (1989). Symbolic architectures for cognition. In M. I. Posner (Ed.), *Foundations of cognitive science* (pp. 93–131). Cambridge: MIT Press.

Newell, A., & Simon, H. A. (1972). *Human problem solving*. Englewood Cliffs: Prentice-Hall.

Newell, A., & Simon, H. A. (1981). Computer science as empirical inquiry: symbols and search. In J. Haugeland (Ed.), *Mind design* (pp. 35–66). Montgomery: Bradford.

Niklasson, L. F., & Van Gelder, T. (1994). On being systematically connectionist. *Mind & Language, 9*(3), 288–302.

Oaksford, M., & Chater, N. (1991). Against logicist cognitive science. *Mind & Language, (6)*1, 1–38.

O'Brien, G. J. (1991). Is connectionism commonsense? *Philosophical Psychology, 4*(2), 165–178.

Palmer, S. E. (1978). Fundamental aspects of cognitive representation. In E. Rosch & B. B. Lloyd (Eds.), *Cognition and categorisation* (pp. 259–303). Hillsdale: Erlbaum.

Paul, G. (1993). Approaches to abductive reasoning: an overview. *Artificial Intelligence Review, 7*, 108–153.

Pickering, M., & Chater, N. (1995). Why cognitive science is not formalized folk psychology. *Minds and Machines, 5*, 309–337.

Pollack, J. B. (1990). Recursive distributed representations. *Artificial Intelligence, 46*, 77–105.

Preston, J. M. (1989). Folk psychology as theory or practice? The case for eliminative materialism. *Inquiry, 32*, 277–303.

Putnam, H. (1960/1975). Minds and machines. In H. Putnam (Ed.), *Mind, language and reality: philosophical papers*, vol. 2 (pp. 362–385). Cambridge: Cambridge University Press.

Putnam, H. (1975). *Mind, language and reality: philosophical papers*, vol. 2. Cambridge: Cambridge University Press.

Putnam, H. (1981). *Reason, truth, and history*. Cambridge: Cambridge University Press.

Putnam, H. (1983). *Realism and reason: philosophical papers*, vol. 3. Cambridge: Cambridge University Press.

Putnam, H. (1984). Models and modules. *Cognition, 17*, 253–264.

Putnam, H. (1988a). Much ado about not very much. In S. R. Graubard (Ed.), *The artificial intelligence debate: false starts, real foundations* (pp. 269–282). Cambridge: MIT Press.

Putnam, H. (1988b). *Representation and reality*. Cambridge: MIT Press.

Putnam, H. (1992). *Renewing philosophy*. Cambridge: Harvard University Press.

Pylyshyn, Z. W. (1980). Computation and cognition: issues in the foundations of cognitive science. *Behavioral and Brain Sciences, 3*, 111–169.

Pylyshyn, Z. W. (1984). *Computation and cognition: toward a foundation for cognitive science*. Cambridge: MIT Press.

Pylyshyn, Z. W. (Ed.). (1987). *The robot's dilemma*. Norwood: Ablex.

Pylyshyn, Z. W., & Demopoulos, W. (Eds.). (1986). *Meaning and cognitive structure: theoretical issues in cognitive science*. Norwood: Ablex.

Quine, W. V. O. (1951/1980). Two dogmas of empiricism. In W. V. O. Quine (Ed.), *From a logical point of view* (pp. 20–46). New York: Harper.

Quine, W. V. O. (1960). *Word and object*. Cambridge: MIT Press.

Quine, W. V. O. (1969). Epistemology naturalized. In W. V. O. Quine (Ed.), *Ontological relativity and other essays* (pp. 69–90). New York: Columbia University Press.

Ramsey, W. (1992). Connectionism and the philosophy of mental representation. In S. Davis (Ed.), *Connectionism: theory and practice* (pp. 247–276). Oxford: Oxford University Press.

Ramsey, W., Stich, S., & Garon, J. (1991). Connectionism, eliminativism, and the future of folk psychology. In J. D. Greenwood (Ed.), *The future of folk psychology* (pp. 93–119). Cambridge: Cambridge University Press.

Reichenbach, H. (1947). *Elements of symbolic logic*. New York: Free Press.

Reiter, R. (1992). Twelve years of nonmonotonic reasoning research: where (and what) is the beef? In B. Nebel, C. Rich, & W. Swartout (Eds.), *Principles of knowledge representation and reasoning* (p. 789). Cambridge: Morgan Kaufmann.

Rorty, R. (1982). Comments on Dennett. *Synthese, 53*, 181–187.

Ross, D. (1990). Against positing central systems in the mind. *Philosophy of Science, 57*, 297–312.

Rumelhart, D. E. (1992). Towards a microstructural account of human reasoning. In S. Davis (Ed.), *Connectionism: theory and practice* (pp. 69–83). Oxford: Oxford University Press.

Rumelhart, D. E., McClelland, J. L., & the PDP group (Eds.). (1986). *Parallel distributed processing: explorations in the microstructure of cognition. Vol. 1: foundations.* Cambridge: MIT Press.

Russell, B. (1940). *An inquiry into meaning and truth.* London: George Allen & Unwin.

Ryle, G. (1949). *The concept of mind.* Harmondsworth: Peregrine.

Sanders, C. (1972). *De behavioristische revolutie in de psychologie.* Deventer: Van Loghum Slaterus.

Sanders, C., Eisenga, L. K. A., & van Rappard, J. F. H. (1976). *Inleiding in de grondslagen van de psychologie.* Deventer: Van Loghem Slaterus.

Schank, R. C., & Abelson, R. P. (1977a). *Scripts, plans, goals, and understanding: an inquiry into human knowledge structures.* Hillsdale: Erlbaum.

Schank, R. C., & Abelson, R. P. (1977b). Scripts, plans and knowledge. In P. N. Johnson-Laird & P. C. Wason (Eds.), *Thinking: readings in cognitive science* (pp. 421–432). Cambridge: Cambridge University Press.

Schiffer, S. (1986). The real trouble with propositions. In R. J. Bogdan (Ed.), *Belief* (pp. 83–117). Oxford: Clarendon Press.

Schwartz, J. (1991). Reduction, elimination, and the mental. *Philosophy of Science, 58*, 203–220.

Searle, J. R. (1992). *The rediscovery of the mind.* Cambridge: MIT Press.

Sellars, W. (1963). *Science, perception and reality.* London: Routledge & Kegan Paul.

Shastri, L., & Ajjanagadde, V. (1993). From simple associations to systematic reasoning: a connectionist representation of rules, variables and dynamic bindings using temporal synchrony. *Behavioral and Brain Sciences, 16*(3), 417–494.

Simon, H. A. (1981). Cognitive science: the newest science of the artificial. In D. A. Norman (Ed.), *Perspectives on cognitive science* (pp. 13–25). Norwood: Ablex.

Simon, H. A. (1989). ECHO and STAHL: on the theory of combustion. *Behavioral and Brain Sciences, 12*(3), 487.

Skinner, B. F. (1953). *Science and human behavior.* New York: Free Press.

Skinner, B. F. (1974). *About behaviorism.* New York: Vintage Books.

Skinner, B. F. (1986). Why I am not a cognitive psychologist. In T. J. Knapp & L. C. Robertson (Eds.), *Approaches to cognition: contrasts and controversies* (pp. 79–90). Hillsdale: Erlbaum.

Sleutels, J. (1989). Zakjapanners, superchinezen en hersenschimmen: de hedendaagse filosofie van de cognitiewetenschap. In C. Brown, P. Hagoort, & T. Meijering (Eds.), *Vensters op de geest: cognitie op het snijvlak van filosofie en psychologie* (pp. 252–290). Utrecht: Stichting Grafiet.

Sleutels, J. (1994). *Real knowledge: the problem of content in neural epistemics.* Dissertation, Katholieke Universiteit Nijmegen.

Smolensky, P. (1988). On the proper treatment of connectionism. *Behavioral and Brain Sciences, 11*(1), 1–74.

Smolensky, P. (1989). Connectionism and constituent structure. In R. Pfeiffer, Z. Schreter, F. Fogelman-Soulie, & L. Steels (Eds.), *Connectionism in perspective* (pp. 3–24). Amsterdam: Elsevier.

Smolensky, P. (1991). The constituent structure of connectionist mental states: a reply to Fodor and Pylyshyn. In T. Horgan & J. Tienson (Eds.), *Connectionism and the philosophy of mind* (pp. 281–308). Dordrecht: Kluwer.

Sterelny, K. (1990). *The representational theory of mind.* Oxford: Blackwell.

Stich, S. (1983). *From folk psychology to cognitive science.* Cambridge: MIT Press.

Stich, S. (1990). *The fragmentation of reason.* Cambridge: MIT Press.

Stich, S. (1991). Causal holism and commonsense psychology: a reply to O'Brien. *Philosophical Psychology*, *4*(2), 179–181.

Stich, S. (1992). What is a theory of mental representation? *Mind*, *101*, 243–261.

Stich, S., & Nichols, S. (1992). Folk psychology: simulation or tacit theory? *Mind & Language*, *7*(1 & 2), 35–71.

Stich, S., & Ravenscroft, I. (1994). What is folk psychology? *Cognition*, *50*, 447–468.

Stillings, N. A., Weisler, S. E., Chase, C. H., Feinstein, M. H., Garfield, J. L., & Rissland, E. L. (1995). *Cognitive science: an introduction*. Cambridge: MIT Press.

Stone, T., & Davies, M. (1995). Introduction. In M. Davies & T. Stone (Eds.), *Mental simulation* (pp. 1–18). Oxford: Blackwell.

Sun, R. (1994). Connectionist models of commonsense reasoning. In D. S. Levine & M. I. Aparicio (Eds.), *Neural networks for knowledge representation and inference* (pp. 241–268). Hillsdale: Erlbaum.

Thagard, P. (1988). *Computational philosophy of science*. Cambridge: MIT Press.

Thagard, P. (1989). Explanatory coherence. *Behavioral and Brain Sciences*, *12*, 435–502.

Thagard, P. (1992). *Conceptual revolutions*. Princeton: Princeton University Press.

Tragesser, R. S. (1992). Inference. In J. Dancy & E. Sosa (Eds.), *A companion to epistemology* (pp. 206–207). Oxford: Blackwell.

Van Bendegem, J. P. (1991/1992). Niet-monotone logica's. *Wijsgerig Perspectief*, *32*(2), 34–39.

Van der Lubbe, J. C. A., & Backer, E. (1993). Human-like reasoning under uncertainty in expert systems. In R. J. Jorna, B. Van Heusden, & R. Posner (Eds.), *Signs, search and communication: semiotic aspects of artificial intelligence* (pp. 113–133). Berlin: Walter de Gruyter.

Van Gelder, T. (1990). Compositionality: a connectionist variation on a classical theme. *Cognitive Science*, *14*, 355–384.

Van Gelder, T. (1991a). Classical questions, radical answers: connectionism and the structure of mental representation. In T. Horgan & J. Tienson (Eds.), *Connectionism and the philosophy of mind* (pp. 355–381). Dordrecht: Kluwer.

Van Gelder, T. (1991b). What is the 'D' in 'PDP'? A survey of the concept of distribution. In W. Ramsey, S. P. Stich, & D. E. Rumelhart (Eds.), *Philosophy and connectionist theory* (pp. 33–59). Hillsdale: Erlbaum.

Van Gelder, T. (1992). Defining 'distributed representation'. *Connection Science*, *4*(3 & 4), 175–191.

Warren, H. C. (1921). *History of the association psychology*. New York: Scribner's Sons.

Watkins, J. W. N. (1965). Hume, Carnap and Popper. In I. Lakatos (Ed.), *The problem of inductive logic: proceedings of the international colloquium in the philosophy of science* (pp. 271–282). Amsterdam: North Holland.

Watson, J. B. (1920). Is thinking merely the action of language mechanisms? *The British Journal of Psychology*, *XI*(1), 87–104.

Wilkes, K. V. (1984). Pragmatics in science and theory in common sense. *Inquiry*, *27*, 339–361.

Wilkes, K. V. (1986). Nemo psychologicus nisi physiologus. *Inquiry*, *29*, 169–186.

Wilkes, K. V. (1991a). The long past and the short history. In R. J. Bogdan (Ed.), *Mind and common sense: philosophical essays on commonsense psychology* (pp. 144–160). Cambridge: Cambridge University Press.

Wilkes, K. V. (1991b). The relationship between scientific psychology and common-sense psychology. *Synthese*, *89*, 15–39.

Wilks, Y. (1990). Some comments on Smolensky. In D. Partridge & Y. Wilks (Eds.), *The foundations of AI* (pp. 327–336). Cambridge: Cambridge University Press.

Zytkow, J. M. (1989). Testing ECHO on historical data. *Behavioral and Brain Sciences*, *12*(3), 489–490.

Name Index

Subject Index